Regulatory Innovation

Regulatory Innovation

A Comparative Analysis

Edited by

Julia Black

Law Department, ESRC Centre for Analysis of Risk and Regulation, London School of Economics

Martin Lodge

Department of Government, ESRC Centre for Analysis of Risk and Regulation, London School of Economics

Mark Thatcher

Department of Government, ESRC Centre for Analysis of Risk and Regulation, London School of Economics

Edward Elgar
Cheltenham, UK • Northampton, MA, USA

Published by
Edward Elgar Publishing Limited
Glensanda House
Montpellier Parade
Cheltenham
Glos GL50 1UA
UK

Edward Elgar Publishing, Inc.
136 West Street
Suite 202
Northampton
Massachusetts 01060
USA

A catalogue record for this book
is available from the British Library

ISBN 1 84542 284 8 (cased)

Typeset by Cambrian Typesetters, Camberley, Surrey
Printed and bound in Great Britain by MPG Books Ltd, Bodmin, Cornwall

Contents

Tables

Contributors

Julia Black is a Reader in Law and a member of the ESRC Centre for Analysis of Risk and Regulation at the London School of Economics. She has published widely in the area of regulatory theory, regulatory techniques and in the specific areas of financial services regulation and the regulation of gene technology.

Christopher Hood is Gladstone Professor of Government at All Souls College, Oxford and a member of the ESRC Centre for Analysis of Risk and Regulation at the London School of Economics. He has published widely on changing doctrines in public administration, regulation inside government and on risk regulation.

Robert P. Kaye is a Research Officer at the ESRC Centre for Analysis of Risk and Regulation at the London School of Economics. His main fields of expertise are in the ethics regulation of politics and the regulation of the professions.

Martin Lodge is Lecturer in Political Science and Public Policy in the Department of Government and a member of the ESRC Centre for Analysis of Risk and Regulation at the London School of Economics. He has published on comparative regulatory regimes, in particular railway regulation, and comparative public administration.

Colin Scott is a Reader in Law and a member of the ESRC Centre for Analysis of Risk and Regulation at the London School of Economics. His main fields of expertise are in governance and regulatory theory, regulation of government, communications regulation and consumer protection.

Mark Thatcher is a Reader in Public Administration and Public Policy in the Department of Government and a member of the ESRC Centre for Analysis of Risk and Regulation at the London School of Economics. His research lies in comparative regulation and public policy, particularly telecommunications, utilities and independent regulatory agencies in the UK, France, Germany and Italy and at the EU level.

Preface

Interdisciplinary work is much in demand from policy-makers and research funding bodies alike. Understanding social phenomena is said to require a move by the different sciences beyond their disciplinary silos and some of the most significant breakthroughs in our knowledge and understanding occur at the edges of disciplines. At the same time, individual career incentives usually demand publications in each respective discipline's 'top ten' journals, offering a powerful counterweight to any attempt at working and publishing across disciplines. One way to address these largely incompatible pressures is to seek key concepts that appeal to a diversity of disciplines and attempt to establish a structured environment for conversations and research around them.

Over the past four years, the ESRC Centre for Analysis of Risk and Regulation (CARR) has provided such an environment for a conversation across disciplines on 'regulatory innovation'. As with any innovation, this book has gone through many iterations, with many avenues explored and dismissed. Participants at various conferences and workshops will bear witness to these various attempts to find a framework in which to understand regulatory innovation, for example at the Socio-Legal Studies Association, the Political Studies Association annual meetings in Britain, or seminars in CARR, and we are grateful for the comments received on these various occasions. We are also grateful to Tim Besley, a fellow member of CARR and LSE colleague, for contributing to many of our conversations, and to Bronwen Morgan and Karen Yeung, who generously participated in (endured!) a whole day of our deliberations.

This has been a truly collaborative project, and we have all read and discussed more drafts of each person's case study than we care to remember. Different members of the group have played different roles during its many stages. The idea of exploring regulatory innovation was proposed initially as a joint project by Mark Thatcher and Colin Scott, and was later broadened out to become a collaboration between all the political scientists and lawyers within CARR. Christopher Hood inspired us with his energy and incisive comments throughout. Mark Thatcher worked valiantly in the early stages to document and make sense of our numerous discussions. In the later stages, Julia Black provided the analysis of regulatory innovation and the account of the 'worlds of regulatory innovation' that provide a framing device for our respective explorations. Martin Lodge and Julia Black corralled everyone into line at the end and attempted to draw the many threads together in the conclusion.

This book does not seek to provide the ultimate perspective on something as broad as 'regulatory innovation', but it is an initial and novel attempt at a systematic and comparative exploration of this concept that has much resonance across the disciplines represented in this research group in particular, and CARR more widely. One of the prerequisites for truly interdisciplinary work is a sustained period of conversations and learning across disciplines, and we are grateful to the ESRC and to CARR itself for offering us an infrastructure that allowed for our conversation to sustain itself over the different stages of this research project. Finally, we express our thanks to the staff at Edward Elgar, in particular Luke Adams, for their support in bringing this product to fruition.

Julia Black, Martin Lodge and Mark Thatcher
London School of Economics, August 2005

1. What is regulatory innovation?

Julia Black

INTRODUCTION

Innovation is the cure currently prescribed for the ailing state. It is a key part of the 'reinventing government' debate (Osborne and Gaebler 1993) and occupies a central role in debates on regulatory reform (e.g. OECD 1995; European Commission 2002). Just as companies have long been told to 'innovate or die' (Schumpeter 1976), public agencies are being told that innovation should become one of their 'core activities' (Cabinet Office 2003). 'How to' guides to public policy innovation proliferate (e.g. Osborne and Gaebler 1993; Sparrow 2000; Cabinet Office 2003), government departments, statutory bodies and pressure groups exist to promote public sector innovation (e.g. the New South Wales Innovation Centre, the US Institute for Policy Innovation, the Bertelsmann Stiftung in Germany) and awards for innovation are features of the administrative landscape in many countries including the USA, the UK, Germany, Canada and Australia.

In contrast, for others, innovation is the treatment which causes its own disease. For example, contrary to the 'innovation as success' message of the regulatory reform literature, Michael Moran's thesis is that innovation has been a 'fiasco', with the negative consequences of innovation in turn prompting more innovation in an ever ascending, or descending, spiral. Moran argues that in the UK, the last 30 or so years have been an era of 'hyper-innovation', 'the frenetic selection of new institutional modes, and their equally frenetic replacement by alternatives' (Moran 2003, p. 26). In Moran's argument, hyper-innovation takes the form of new institutional forms of governance, ranging from the regulatory agencies established to regulate privatized utilities, the rise of new institutional and increasingly formalized forms of governance within government, the reformation and re-regulation of Victorian inspectorates of pollution control, schools, and food safety, the reconstruction of regulation in key areas such as financial markets, and the expansion of the state into new social spheres. Hyper-innovation has been accompanied by the rise of 'high-modernism' and the corresponding decline (though not complete removal) of the 'old' style of 'club government'. Hyper-innovation is thus characterized by a greater emphasis on transparency and accountability, an increase in formal controls, an increase in the number and range of institutional actors involved in regulation, greater attempts at systematization and co-ordination through a single regulatory institution; attempts to make explicit and measurable what was previously tacit and judgemental, and a shift in regulatory style from a co-operative and negotiative character towards a more adversarial system (Moran 2003, pp. 133, 159). In short, the most notable and enduring feature of the changes, he argues, is the drive towards 'synoptic legibility':

> installing systems of comprehensive reporting and surveillance over numerous social spheres; the consequential pressure to codify and standardize, and the creation of new institutions, notably the specialized regulatory agency, to help enforce all this. (Moran 2003, p. 154)

Are we, thus, living in an age of hyper-innovation, which we may take more loosely to mean that regulatory regimes are in a permanent state of innovative flux, or is it rather an age in which there is simply a lot of hype about innovation? Academia has also been afflicted with innovation-hype (and indeed, perhaps, hyper-innovation). Innovation and diffusion studies in political science date back to the 1960s, and there has been a recent revival of interest in studying specific examples of policy innovation in the delivery of public services by governmental and voluntary organizations (e.g. Borins 2000, 2001; Doig 1997; Light 1998; Maddock 2002; Osborne 1998a, 1998b; Osborne and Flynn 1997; Schall 1997; Walker and Jeanes 2001). There are university units dedicated to the study of innovation, such as the 'Centre for Innovation in Law and Policy' at the University of Toronto, and indeed a web-based journal devoted to the topic (*The Innovation Journal*). But is the study of 'innovation' so special, or unique in some way, that it requires its own set of interpretations and explanations that are distinct from the broader debates on policy formation, or even, for example, organizational behaviour? Is a concern with policy innovation simply a concern to understand and, for some, to engineer policy changes: the standard fare of policy analysis, but dressed in more eye-catching colours, or is it something more? In other words, do academics themselves fall victim to the 'innovation' rhetoric (and indeed their own institutional pressures to 'innovate'), leading them to seek 'innovative' explanations for innovation when there are already well-established potential explanations out there which would do the job perfectly well?

This book seeks to explore these issues by focusing on three main questions: what is regulatory innovation, how do we account for it, and are we living in an age of hyper-innovation, or simply one in which there is a lot of hype about innovation? The individual chapters explore these questions in the context of a deliberately diverse and eclectic set of policy domains: ethics in legislatures, railways, 3G mobile phone licence auctions, Internet gaming, dangerous dogs, and financial services. Each takes a comparative perspective, exploring whether and how different countries in the respective domains produced 'innovative' responses to similar policy issues. Some of these are high-tech areas: the regulation of Internet gaming; the introduction of auctions for 3G mobile licences; some are low-tech: the regulation of dangerous dogs, or ethics in legislatures. Some are highly fashionable and seen as key aspects of the 'regulatory state': telecoms and, to a somewhat lesser extent, railways, and/or as areas of 'hyper-innovation', such as financial services. In contrast the policy domains of dangerous dogs and legislatures are largely unfashionable, and never feature in these grander meta-theories.

Before exploring each of these three interrelated questions in the individual case studies, some groundwork needs to be done. That is undertaken in this chapter and the next, and together these chapters provide the framework for the detailed case studies. In essence, if we want to explore regulatory innovation we need to be able to identify what regulatory innovation is, and in particular whether and how it can be distinguished from change. Moreover, if we are to be able to say whether or not the innovations have led to 'success' or 'fiasco', we need some criteria against which to assess success or failure. Tackling those issues is all too rarely done, and is the subject of this chapter. The much broader question, how do we understand and explain innovation, is the subject of the next section.

WHAT IS 'REGULATORY INNOVATION'?

There are competing images of regulatory innovation, just as there are competing images of regulation. Probably the most dominant image is that regulatory innovation is a matter of refining the technologies of regulation: the search of better tools of governance, the development of 'smart regulation' (e.g. Osborne and Gaebler 1993; Sparrow 2000; Gunningham and Grabovsky 1998). As such, 'regulatory innovation' is inherently characterized by 'newism' and bias of benevolence. The continual search for refinement is often justified in terms of the need to foster economic growth and to provide better protection for individuals from the excesses of the market (e.g. European Commission 2002; OECD 1995; Cabinet Office 2003), and as such relates to the argument that the search for regulatory effectiveness is part of the endless pursuit of legitimacy by governments in societies where responsibility for economic well-being has been 'privatized' (Teubner 1986, 1987). For others, regulatory innovation is seen as necessary in order to improve strategies for managing risk, manifested, for example, in the rise of 'new public risk management' (e.g. Sparrow 2000; Cabinet Office 2000, 2003; Strategy Unit

2002). In this image, regulation, and thus regulatory innovation, is the pursuit of state legitimacy in the risk society (Beck 1992). More generally, regulation, and regulatory innovation, is seen as the pursuit of a modernist project of rationalization, systematization and ordering (Meyer, 2000), and as such bound to fail (Rhodes 1997; Moran 2003). At a deeper theoretical level, regulatory innovation is seen as an adaptive response by a system or organization to its environment, which acts either strategically (e.g. Hall and Soskice 2001), isomorphically (DiMaggio and Powell 1983), or autopoetically (Teubner 1986, 1987). Finally, in contrast, regulation and regulatory innovation is seen as the outcome of a political contestation of power and interests, mediated, for some, by institutional structures (e.g. Hall, 1986, 1993) and (global) social interactive and communicative processes (Braithwaite and Drahos 2000; Strang and Meyer 1993).

These competing images of regulatory innovation have conflicting normative and cognitive implications, and so far as they offer explanations for why regulatory innovation occurs, they cut across the different 'worlds' of innovation explored in the next chapter. Defining innovation is thus not merely a semantic exercise: 'innovation' has normative overtones that infect the discussion on what 'innovation' is. In an attempt to avoid such infection, a normatively neutral definition of regulatory innovation is deliberately deployed in the case studies throughout this book. Regulatory innovation is understood here to be the use of new solutions to address old problems, or new solutions to address 'new' (or newly constructed) problems, but not old solutions to address old problems. Whether 'novelty' is defined in subjective or objective terms is left open. More specifically, regulatory innovations are second or third-order changes in the performance of regulatory functions, institutional structures and organizational processes which have an impact on the regulatory regime. The impacts and outcomes of innovation may be unintended, and innovations are not always successful.

Each of these elements needs some explaining. Should innovation be assessed objectively or subjectively; how does innovation relate to invention and diffusion, how can or should we distinguish innovation from change in a regulatory regime, and how should we assess success or failure?

Innovation: All in the Eye of the Beholder?

At its core, innovation is the introduction of something new, or the alteration of something established (*New Shorter Oxford English Dictionary*). 'Innovation' thus embraces both novelty and change. Identifying change is relatively simple: it is the move from state of being x to state of being y. However, identifying the threshold of change or novelty which marks out 'innovation' from mere change can be less straightforward. In particular, how can one establish that a particular regulatory policy or instrument has never been used in any domain in any country at any time? It is empirically challenging, if not impossible.

Studies of innovation remain surprisingly undisturbed by this potentially fatal problem. Instead, innovation studies avoid it in one of two ways, although the implications of the choice go largely unremarked. The first technique is to adopt an objective definition of innovation, but define innovation implicitly or explicitly in contextual terms. Novelty is measured in the particular context of, for example, a geographical area (the UK, Ohio, the Baltic states), a policy domain (telecommunications, health and safety, environment), or some other unit of analysis (an organization, individual, nation state), or some combination of the three (health and safety regulation in the UK, equality policies in XYZ plc). Thus in one of the seminal works in innovation and diffusion studies, Walker defines innovation as 'a program or policy which is new to the states adopting it, no matter how old the program may be or how many other states may have adopted it' (Walker 1969, p. 881).

The second technique is to use a subjective definition of innovation. Rogers, for example, author of the seminal text on the diffusion of innovations, defines innovation as 'an idea, practice or object that is perceived as new by an individual or other unit of adoption. What matters is the individual's perception of the innovation: if an idea seems new to the individual, it is an innovation' (Rogers 2003, p. 12). In this definition, it does not matter if anyone else has adopted the innovation; what is important is that the adopter thinks that they have done something new.

The choice of definition has significant analytical and methodological implications. An objective definition such as that deployed by Walker and many similar and subsequent studies of innovation clearly suits some types of methodologies. Walker was engaged in a large-scale empirical study attempting to measure the 'innovativeness' of US states, in which he used the title of legislative enactments as data to measure the relative speed of adoptions of innovations. Walker studied the adoption of 88 policies or programmes in 48 of the US states from the time of the state's formation to 1965 (in most cases a 95-year time span). Such a large-scale, quantitative and positivist study needs an easily measurable dependent variable, and a legislative enactment with a 'new' title provides one. However, this indicator of innovation clearly has limitations. It is not always possible to tell from the title of a statute whether or not the new enactment did in fact introduce a 'new' policy or simply re-labelled an old one, or whether it had any effects on the ground. But objective measures, even if they succeed in using indicators which have a greater degree of granularity, require some method for assessing relative 'newness'. Radical changes in policy direction are obvious: privatization of utilities industries in the 1980s was 'innovative' on most objective measures.

Nonetheless, how to measure innovation is contested and unclear. Moreover, very few studies of innovation adopt the historical dimension which would be necessary to analyse the degree of change satisfactorily (see also Hall 1993). Most look at the state of affairs at t_{+1} and compare it with t_0; they do not consider whether t_{+1} is an 'innovation' which in fact occurred at t_{-1}. This lack of historical perspective risks identifying as 'innovations' changes which are in fact regressive moves back to something that has been tried before, but about which institutional memory may be lost, by 'innovators' and academic observers alike.

A subjective definition of innovation enables the analyst to avoid these murky waters, for the focus here is on the perceptions of those adopting the innovation. It does not matter whether the innovation is 'really' new, just whether the person adopting it thinks it is. Again, the different definition suits different methodologies, and different lines of analytical inquiry. Rogers' work is part of a strong sociological and anthropological tradition of innovation and diffusion studies, where the focus is on individual and social behaviour, and the methodologies employed entail detailed observation and questioning of individual subjects. If the actor being studied perceives the idea, object or practice to be new, then that is what counts, for that is what determines his or her behaviour.

A subjective definition of innovation thus suits detailed empirical studies in which the focus is on individual behaviour, and although the methodology may be either quantitative or qualitative, a subjective definition is clearly more appropriate for interpretive analyses than an objective definition. However, a subjective definition too has limitations, depending on the type of question one is asking. It does not tell us about the degree of 'innovativeness' of an agency, just how it perceives itself. Interpretivists will not be concerned, but those of a more positivist bent may well be frustrated at the inability of a subjective definition to provide an answer.

Given the different methodological and analytical purposes that subjective and objective definitions serve, there is clearly no 'right' way to conceive of innovation, and this book does not impose one. Whilst the methodology used in the case studies is qualitative and inductive, the book does not attempt to argue for a subjective definition over an objective one, or vice versa, and many chapters assess innovation in both subjective and objective terms. Definitions are analytical constructs that serve particular purposes. What is asked is that analysts be clear of the implications and limitations of the definition that they use.

Innovation and Invention

Regulatory innovation, in both subjective and objective terms, is distinguished here, as elsewhere, from policy ideas or policy inventions that have not been implemented (e.g. Rogers 2003, p. 12; Altshuler and Behn 1997; Altshuler and Zegans 1997). The study of regulatory innovation should not simply be the study of ideas. The study of ideas may be an important component of an analysis of regulatory innovation, but it is just a component. In the definition of innovation being adopted here, innovations are enacted ideas; they are those which have made it through the political or organizational decision processes to implementation. Innovation is thus also distinguished from invention: to adopt Mohr's phrase, invention is the bringing of something new into being, innovation is the bringing of something new into use (Mohr 1969, p. 112).

Defining innovation as enacted ideas that are new, or perceived as new, to those adopting them emphasizes that innovation is both a process and an outcome. It is a process in that it involves the formulation, elaboration and ultimately operationalization and implementation of a new idea, and has outcomes which, like any regulatory measure, may be unforeseen and unanticipated. Analysing regulatory innovation should thus involve analysing not just the enactment of ideas, but their impact. Adopting a dynamic approach to the study of regulatory innovation offers the potential to show how assessments of 'innovativeness' may have to be modified over time, as the apparent innovativeness of a policy or programme may be denied by the manner of its subsequent implementation. Thus the introduction of the RPI-X form of price control for utilities was assessed as innovative at the time, on both subjective and objective criteria. However, it is widely argued that the 'price-cap' type of regulation in its actual methodology has reintroduced many of the methodologies underlying rate of return regulation, therefore being far less distinguishable than anticipated.

Innovation and Diffusion

The main literature on innovation is associated with diffusion studies, but although the two are often conflated, diffusion refers more properly to the socially mediated spread of a policy or practice, its communication over time among members of a social system (Rogers 2003, p. 14; Strang and Meyer 1993). In diffusion studies, what researchers are interested in is the speed and pattern of the spread of a new idea or practice. 'Innovativeness' in most of this work is used to describe the degree to which an individual or other unit of adoption is earlier than others in *adopting* an innovation, not the degree to which they are inventive. The biggest impact on the field of diffusion research is attributed to rural sociologists in the 1940s (especially Ryan and Gross 1943). Their studies set the main questions of contemporary diffusion research across all intellectual disciplines: what variables are related to innovativeness, what is the rate of adoption of an innovation over time and what factors explain its speed of adoption, and what are the mechanisms of diffusion; in other words what role do different communication channels play at various stages in the innovation-decision process (Rogers 2003, p. 55)? The more recent communications research on marketing has focused in addition on how the perceived attributes of an innovation affect its rate of purchase, and on the use of new technology as well as its purchase (Rogers 2003, pp. 82–3). The normal pattern of the rate of adoption is an 'S'-shaped curve, with inventors and early adopters at the base, moving to the early majority, the late majority, and the laggards tailing off at the end, with the categorization of adopters taking the shape of a bell-shaped curve (Rogers 2003, p. 281).

Thus diffusion usually connotes innovation for the adopter; however, the converse is not necessarily true: innovation does not necessarily connote diffusion. There are plenty of examples of innovations which are implemented, but which remain specific to a particular firm, individual, regulatory system and so on, and moreover whose non-diffusion is not explicable in terms of the sub-optimality of the innovation. Other innovations flourish, even though better technologies exist. Well-known examples include the dominance of the QWERTY keyboard (e.g. Rogers 2003, pp. 8–10) and the dominance of Microsoft operating systems. Moreover, parallel invention is perfectly possible: an innovation may be simultaneously or sequentially arrived at in two separate areas without diffusion/communication having occurred between the two. As the contributions to this book demonstrate, the comparative study of innovation may entail the study of diffusion, but as some of the case studies in this book illustrate, more often the implementation of similar 'innovative' policies at similar times represents instances of parallel innovation, where the same policy solutions are adopted in the same domains in different countries without any diffusion (learning) occurring at all.

Innovation and Orders of Change

Innovation is thus distinct from invention and diffusion. Nonetheless, is 'regulatory innovation' simply another way of describing 'regulatory change'? Or more particularly, if all innovation is change, is all change innovation? Is there a threshold above which a change in a regulatory regime is an 'innovation'? Trying to distinguish change from innovation is in danger of becoming an exercise in counting angels on the head of a pin: the worst kind of academic hair-splitting. However, if we are to take seriously the various claims as to the absence or prevalence of innovation, or its desirability or failure, we need to have some ability to distinguish 'innovation' from (mere) change.

Innovations are often argued to involve a 'step change', to mark some disjuncture with what has gone before (e.g. Osborne 1998a). They are often divided into two groups: incremental or progressive innovations, consisting of successive improvements on existing products, processes and services, and radical, systemic or transformative innovations, consisting in firms of substantial shifts in product lines, the development of new products or major changes in production processes, or in public policy terms, involving fundamental changes in organizational, social and cultural arrangements (e.g. Hall and Soskice 2001, p. 38; Cabinet Office 2003, paras 2.1–2.5).

The language of 'products' and 'services' may fit well with the activities of profit-making firms, and can arguably be extended with little modification to public service provision by non-profit actors, be they state or non-state institutions; however it does not fit so easily with the activity of regulation, again whether by state or non-state institutions. Moreover, whilst 'radical' innovations are easy to spot, those changes which are not accompanied by complete 're-thinks', but which nonetheless mark a new departure for the regulatory regime in some way, are harder to classify. For example, in an RPI-X formula, an increase in X from 3 to 30 is in some senses a 'step change' – it is a significant increase which is likely to have considerable impact. But is it really 'innovative'? Arguably not. Some further analysis of what 'innovation' consists of is required.

Innovation here is seen as being the application of new solutions to old problems, or new solutions to new (or newly constructed) problems, but not old solutions to old problems. Employing Hall's' typology of policy changes can help to explain what this means. Hall identifies three forms of policy change: first-order changes are changes to the levels or settings of basic instruments (Hall 1993, pp. 278–9). Second-order policy changes are changes in instrument or technique, but not in the overall goals of policy or understandings on which it is based. Third-order changes are changes in the goals of the policy and understandings on which it is based, accompanied by second and first-order changes. In Kuhn's terms third-order changes are 'paradigm shifts', changes in the overarching terms of a policy discourse: the understandings on which it is based and the goals which are pursued (Kuhn 1962).

Playing this into a regulatory context, first-order changes in price regulation, for example, where price regulation is based on RPI-X, is a change in X (as in the example above); a first-order change in pollution abatement based on specification of emissions is a change in the level of emissions permitted. First-order changes are not considered here to be innovations. They are the equivalent of sharpening the scythe. Thus, in contrast to the definition of innovation used in public sector service provision, successive changes in existing techniques or processes of regulation are not considered to be 'innovations'. This is not to say that first-order changes may not be significant in terms of scale or impact: a shift of X from 3 to 30 in an RPI-X price formula is a significant change in the setting of an instrument, and one which is likely to have a major impact on regulated firms. Moreover, the cumulative effect of several first-order changes may over time have radical or transformative effects. However, first-order changes mark nothing new (as opposed to significant) in the regulatory regime; they are a continuation of practices which existed before, albeit that the continuation may have significant and unanticipated effects (for example the requirement to gain the utility licence holders' consent to modifications in the licence, which was a continuation of the negotiated relationship of nationalized industries, and so marked nothing 'new' as such, has had a significant impact on the operation of these regulatory regimes).

In contrast, second-order changes are changes in the techniques or processes being used: the move from the scythe to the combine harvester. For example, in price regulation a second-order change would be a move from RPI-X to rate of return regulation; in pollution control it would be the intro-duction of specification standards to abate pollution (which specify the types of equipment which have to be used, for example) in favour of target stan-dards (e.g. a standard that the level of pollution permitted is the lowest emis-sion as is reasonably practicable). They may take the form of changes in the type of instruments used in a regulatory regime: a shift from 'hard law' to 'soft law', from legal rules to economic incentives, or from 'beauty contests' to auctions as a means of allocating scarce resources (e.g. spectrum use for 3G mobiles). They may also consist of more radical institutional restructur-ings (the creation of new regulatory agencies or independent commissioners, for example) or changes in organizational processes. They may not involve a change in instruments (e.g. legal rules) but nonetheless may be a change in regulatory technique: the introduction of gatekeeper strategies in the regula-tion of Internet gaming, for example, which is achieved through the use of legal rules, but those rules are targeted at non-gaming operators. Innovations may alternatively be realized through radical recombination of existing tech-niques of regulation, or the development and prototyping of new regulatory techniques (to adapt Hood 1986, chapter 5). Because second-order changes occur within existing normative and cognitive paradigms, they may serve to entrench those paradigms, and thus, paradoxically, may be stabilizing in their effects, and may not in practice have the 'reformatory' effects that may have been intended (for examples in environmental regulation, see e.g. Jordan et al. 2003).

Finally, third-order changes are 'paradigm shifts': changes in the cognitive or normative framework of the regulatory regime. Third-order changes are, or may lead to, innovations. A third-order change or innovation is, for example, a move to re-nationalization, or, in environmental regulation, an abandonment of standards in place of tradeable emission permits. In regulatory terms, they are significant transformations in instruments, institutions and organizational structures and processes arising from radically changed cognitive and norma-tive structures, and may be accompanied by first and second-order changes. However, whilst third-order changes or innovations may be towards the radi-cal end of the spectrum in their design, the transformative effects that may be anticipated, and perhaps even observed, when the innovation is introduced may not in practice be forthcoming over time.

WHAT FORMS MIGHT 'REGULATORY INNOVATION' TAKE?

In analyses of organizational innovation, innovation is usually identified as being in the organization's products, services, markets, structures or processes (e.g. European Commission 2002). So innovation by firms consists of, for example, the renewal of products and services, the enlargement of markets, the establishment of new methods of production, supply and distribution, and the introduction of changes in management, work organization, working conditions and skills. This model of innovation is often transposed to voluntary organizations (Osborne 1998b) and to the public sector (e.g. Osborne and Gaebler 1993). Thus the recent Cabinet Office paper on innovation identified innovation in existing services or processes, or in organizational structures (Cabinet Office 2003, paras 2.1–2.5).

Whilst this model of innovation may fit with that side of the state that is involved in service delivery, it needs adjustment to apply to regulation. In particular, whilst innovation in regulatory processes may have a direct parallel with public service provision, innovation in the 'product' or 'service' needs some further elaboration to be applied in the regulatory context. Sparrow has identified a different trilogy of innovation in his study of the winners of the Ford Foundation's Annual Awards in Innovation in American Government. These are innovations in regulatory processes, in risk identification and reduction, and in risk analysis and management (Sparrow 2000, chapter 7). However, this also does not capture all of the dimensions of regulatory regimes, and does not fit easily with most discussions and analyses of regulation.

In this volume, regulation is understood as the sustained and focused attempt to alter the behaviour of others according to standards or goals with the intention of producing a broadly identified outcome or outcomes, which may involve mechanisms of standard-setting, information-gathering and behaviour-modification. This conception of regulation does not assume any particular justifications or explanations for why regulation occurs. Nor does it deny that the outcomes in fact produced may be unforeseen or unanticipated, or that regulation may be ineffective, or that the standards agreed on may not be the product of chance, contingency or 'non-rational' modes of behaviour. It does, however, imply that regulation is a dynamic exercise in collective problem-solving which involves attempts to change the behaviour of others, and that it is not an activity confined to the state (Black 2002).

Regulatory innovation is innovation in any aspect of the regulatory system or regulatory regime. This is a wider conception of regulatory innovation than that of either Sparrow (innovation in modes of risk regulation: Sparrow 2000) or Moran (innovation in institutional arrangements: Moran 2003). A regulatory regime is the set of interrelated units which are engaged in joint problem solving to address a particular goal, its boundaries are defined by the definition of the problem being addressed, and it has some continuity over time (Hood et al. 2001, pp. 9–17). As Hood et al. explain, it is 'the complex of institutional geography, rules, practice and animating ideas' that are associated with the regulation of a particular risk or social or economic activity (Hood et al. 2001, p. 9). The advantage of using the notion of a regulatory system or regime is that it draws attention both to the range of participants in the system and their interrelationship, thus moving away from a single organization-centred approach dominant in the innovation literature. A regime perspective thus expands the potential sites for the study of innovation beyond the rule-making activities of state-based regulators, or a single regulatory body, and it draws attention to the importance of examining the interaction of participants within the regulatory system to understanding its operation, and thus to analysing the processes and impacts of innovation.

Thus regulatory innovation consists of innovation in the performance of regulatory functions, institutional structures and organizational processes in the regulatory regime. Where these are implemented without a change in the cognitive or normative framework of the regulatory regime, they are second-order innovations; where they are accompanied by such changes, they are third-order innovations.

More specifically, innovation in the performance of regulatory functions includes innovation in the modes and identification and specifications of problems to be solved and goals to be achieved (which *pace* Sparrow, may extend beyond risk identification and risk management); innovation in information gathering and assessment; and innovation in the design and implementation of regulatory techniques for changing behaviour, including but extending well beyond modes of enforcement to embrace all forms of regulatory instrument or technique.

Innovation in institutional structures includes the creation of new organizations, and the innovations in the norms, rules and standard operating procedures that characterize the regulatory system, and which may themselves be the product of changes in the cognitive and normative dimensions of the regime. Innovation in organizational processes turns the focus inside the organizations that comprise the regulatory regime, including regulated firms, and includes the introduction, for example, of new management systems (e.g. Barzelay and Campbell 2003), new processes for publicizing enforcement actions to 'name and shame', or new co-operative procedures with other organizations (e.g. Bardach 1998).

These dimensions of regulation are clearly interrelated, and there is fluidity between them. The classification of, for example, a new mode of issuing 3G mobile licences in telecommuncations could be seen either as a new instrument of regulation, or a new organizational process. The exact classification is less important, however, than the clear emphasis and delineation of the wide range of areas in which regulatory innovation may occur.

INNOVATION: 'SUCCESS' OR 'FIASCO'?

The dominant assumption in many of the debates on innovation is that innovation is always and everywhere 'a good thing'. In Mohr's influential definition, innovation is defined as the 'successful introduction into an applied situation of means or ends that are new to that situation' (e.g. Mohr 1969, p. 112). The implication that innovation is always successful is critical to its current advocacy in public policy circles. As noted above, public management documents use 'innovation' synonymously with 'reform' and 'progress' (e.g. New Zealand Institute of Economic Research 2002). 'Innovation' is defined by the UK Cabinet Office as 'new ideas that work', and more precisely as 'the creation and implementation of new processes, products, services and methods of delivery which result in significant improvement in outcomes, efficiency, effectiveness or quality' (Cabinet Office 2003, para 2.1). In the 'reinventing government' agenda set out by Osborne and Gaebler (1993), innovation is seen as critical to creating effective government. Public policymakers are being told that innovation should be 'a core activity of the public sector': it helps public services improve performance, increase public value, enhance efficiency and respond and adapt to the expectations and needs of users (Cabinet Office 2003, para 3.1). Moreover, regulatory innovation is a significant part of the 'regulatory reform' agenda (e.g. OECD 1995; European Commission 2002), and regulatory innovation is frequently seen as essential to facilitating and enhancing the capacity of firms to innovate, and thus as vital for economic growth and competitiveness. Thus regulatory innovation is seen as improving the effectiveness of regulation whilst reducing costs of compliance, and providing flexibility for firms to develop their own innovations and effective competitive strategies.

The identification of innovation with success and progress is a direct importation of the idea of innovation in the economic sphere into the world of public management, and is essential to the reform agenda. Following the Schumpeterian dictate, 'innovate or die', innovation is seen as critical to competitive success, and management literature offers reams of advice and models for what makes an innovative firm (e.g. Christensen 2001; Christensen and Raynor 2003; Christensen et al. 2001; Drucker 1985; Peters and Waterman 1982).

In contrast, Moran argues that Britain's state of 'hyper-innovation' has encouraged a 'fiasco' (Moran 2003); Osborne also identifies a series of less high-profile innovation 'failures' in the voluntary sector (Osborne 1998a), while Paul Light explores difficulties in sustaining innovative charity organizations (Light 1998). Innovation, quite clearly, need not be successful, and moreover being in a constant state of innovation can itself be counterproductive: initiatives are not given the time to be properly implemented; costs are imposed through the constant need to change systems and processes to implement new policies, and no policy is around for long enough for its success or failure to be properly assessed. So whilst some innovation of the right sort may be a good thing, too much innovation, or innovations of the wrong type, may be quite the opposite.

However, how, and when, 'success' or 'failure' is measured, and from whose perspective, are all moot points (see e.g. Moran 2003, p. 172; Bovens and t'Hart 1996, and see the debate between Dunleavy 1995 and Gray 1996). Attempts at measuring 'innovation' and the outcomes of innovation have been made, but there is no clear consensus on what an adequate measure either of innovativeness or of the actual outcomes of innovation (see e.g. Coombes et al. 1996; Osborne 1998a; Walker et al. 2002), nor indeed of when the 'success' or 'failure' of an innovation should be measured: immediately after its introduction; a year later, five years later? Moreover, attempts to measure the outcomes of innovation are in danger of ignoring the fact that innovations within a regulatory regime may be enacted for reasons which are not to do with the attempt to solve collective social or economic problems, but simply to move an issue off the political agenda, or to appease a dominant interest group. If they succeed in these, less socially justifiable aims, they may be judged successful by those who introduced them even if they have no impact on behaviour or on improving collective social or economic welfare. Furthermore, assessments of success or failure often depend on where you stand: innovations, like any regulatory action, will have winners and losers, and the formers' assessment will inevitably be more favourable than the latters'. So, as the subsequent case studies explore, not only are innovations not necessarily either successes or failures, who judges what is 'good', at what point in the innovation's 'life cycle', and against what criteria, inevitably remain critically open questions.

CONCLUSIONS

The aim of this chapter has been to provide some of the groundwork necessary before any exploration of regulatory innovation can occur, and in particular the groundwork necessary for answering two of the key questions of this book: what is regulatory innovation, and how much of it is there about: are we living in an age of 'hyper-innovation', or is it rather an age in which there is a lot of hype about innovation? In exploring regulatory innovation, innovation needs to be clearly distinguished from invention, diffusion and change; the various forms that it can take need to be identified; and the difficulties and contestability of assessing outcomes have to be raised. Regulatory innovation is understood to be the use of new solutions to address old problems, or new solutions to address 'new' (or newly constructed) problems, but not old solutions to address old problems. More specifically, regulatory innovations are second or third-order changes in the performance of regulatory functions, institutional structures and organizational processes which have an impact on the regulatory regime. However assessing that impact is a complex and contentious exercise. Regulatory innovations should not be assumed to be successful: the definitions of innovation which equate innovation with success, which dominate the regulatory reform literature, are thus deeply flawed, and assessments of either 'success' or 'fiasco' often need to be accompanied with more detailed exposure of the criteria and methodologies used for making them.

We may now have a clearer idea what it is that we are looking for when seeking to analyse regulatory innovation, but how can regulatory innovation be accounted for? Why does it arise, and what influences the form that it takes? The groundwork for answering this, the third key question of the book, is set out in the next chapter.

2. Tomorrow's worlds: frameworks for understanding regulatory innovation

Julia Black

INTRODUCTION

The first chapter explored what 'regulatory innovation' consists of; the more difficult questions are how and why does it occur. This is clearly not the first time these questions have been asked, and the explanations and theories range from the particular personality characteristics of individual innovators to the macro-economic measures and political structures of states, from communication networks to models of rationality and actorhood, from institutional structures to ideational properties.

The different sets of explanations tend, however, to occupy different 'worlds', and intellectual travel between them is often limited. These 'worlds' are, of course, analytical and often disciplinary constructs. They are delineated here to be used in part as heuristic devices to map a path through conflicting and yet often overlapping debates on innovation. They are not mutually exclusive, nor are they necessarily internally coherent, rather the boundaries between them are fluid and as the chapters in this volume will suggest, explanations for regulatory innovation may resonate with one or more aspects of different 'worlds', and competing images of regulatory innovation cut across them. Nonetheless, a 'world' is a site of analysis, each focusing on different actors, mechanisms, levels of analysis and methodologies, combining to produce somewhat differing answers to the questions of how and why innovations are introduced. The outline given of each world is not intended to be a complete account of the theories of innovation that may potentially exist or be grouped within those worlds, not least because the literature which specifically refers to innovation is itself quite narrow, and does not always seek to engage with wider questions relating to policy change. Such an exercise would be a book in itself. Rather they are thumbnail sketches of some of the more significant aspects of the arguments relating to innovation, intended to provide a broad framework in which to situate more specific analyses, or indeed be refuted by them. All too often accounts of innovation remain situated in one or two worlds, or aspects of worlds, and rarely look above their own disciplinary horizons. The worlds are thus intended to encourage, and facilitate, intellectual travel.

The 'worlds' identified are fivefold: the world of the individual, the organization, the state, the global polity and the innovation. Each has its own site of analysis, or 'gravitational pull', around which different explanations for innovation in that world have traditionally revolved. In the world of the individual it is the individual as both the site and agent of innovation. The organizational world focuses on innovations within organizations, traditionally profit-making organizations, but increasingly non-profit public and private sector organizations. The site of analysis in the state world is the public policy-making processes of the state. The global polity world focuses on policy-making by global polity bodies and networks. Finally, the world of the innovation revolves around the idea or innovation itself. Each world often remains distinct in accounts of innovation; one of the aims of this book is to see whether or not explorations to more than one of them can provide richer understandings of regulatory innovation, and journeys to which, if any, are more relevant in particular cases than others.

THE INDIVIDUAL WORLD OF INNOVATION

The individual world of innovation focuses on the individual as both the site and agent of innovation, for example as the person taking a personal decision to plant a new type of seed, or to buy a particular mobile phone, or as the policy entrepreneur or person 'championing' the innovation through a collective decision process within an organization or political system.

Historically, research on innovation could more accurately be described as research on the diffusion of innovations throughout a society through the multiplication of individual decisions. The site of analysis was the individual and the society, or subset of society, in which the individual was located. Most of the work has focused on innovations in farming practices, medical and health care practices, educational techniques and the adoption of new technologies (Rogers 2003, ch. 2). The earliest work, done by anthropologists in the 1920s and 1930s, used small-scale qualitative studies based on participant observation to study the diffusion of practices between different cultures, and the interrelationship of culture and innovation in the rate, patterns and consequences of adoption. Subsequently sociologists were concerned with understanding the processes of social change, and traced the diffusion of a single innovation over a particular geographical area using large-scale, quantitive models. Later, communication scholars focused on the diffusion of news events using 'fire house' research methods (quick-response data gathering), and the diffusion of technological ideas, particularly on the marketing of commercial innovations (e.g. mobile phones, the Internet) and of public policy messages, e.g. on safe driving, drug use, smoking or alcohol consumption ('social marketing') (Rogers 2003, pp. 74–90). The subjective definition of innovation was critical for these studies: the focus was on understanding why individuals adopted something which they perceived to be new. It was the influence of that very perception of newness on behaviour which analysts sought to explain.

The world of the individual expanded beyond a focus on personal decisions to innovate and has been highly influential in explaining innovations in collective or authoritative decision-making structures, i.e. those of political systems and organizations. In explanations of innovation in organizations or in public policy, early adopters of innovations are often seen as critical, acting as 'champions', 'policy entrepreneurs', 'model mercenaries' or 'model mongers', forcing the innovation onto the agenda and pushing it through to adoption (Baumgartner and Jones 1993; Kingdon 1984; Polsby 1984; Mintrom 1997; Mintrom and Vergari 1996).

Policy entrepreneurs, or model mongers and model mercenaries (Braithwaite and Drahos 2000), seek to initiate dynamic policy change through attempting to win support for ideas for policy innovation. The strategies used vary and include identifying problems, networking in policy circles, shaping debates and building coalitions. This emphasis on individual champions is echoed in much of the work in public sector innovation, and there is a large swathe of literature which studies the characteristics of public policy entrepreneurs and their role in introducing innovations in public service delivery and organizational processes, although much of this remains unconnected to the original sociological and anthropological work on innovation and diffusion (e.g. Borins 2000; Moon 1999; Morris and Jones 1999; Osborne 1998a; Bartlett and Dibben 2002).

The role of the 'champion', a charismatic individual who backs the innovation, is also emphasized in studies of innovation within firms. In the organizational context, the characteristics of organizational 'champions' echo those of individual innovators: they are risk-preferring, open to new ideas, persuasive, empathetic and occupy key strategic positions within organizations. Indeed, the innovation that an individual may champion may vary with the position that they occupy within the organization. Thus middle managers have been found to be effective champions of first or second-order innovations, and those in more senior positions of more radical innovations (Day 1994; Rogers 2003).

Indeed individual innovators, whether they are operating outside or within organizations or political structures, are found to share key personality and socio-economic characteristics (Rogers 2003, ch. 7). Generally speaking, individual innovators are well educated and, in particular, have an ability to understand complex ideas or technical information; they have a high social status and a high degree of opinion-leadership; they have sufficient financial resources to absorb losses from unprofitable innovations; and they are well connected in extensive communication networks which extend beyond local peers (although early adopters are a more integrated part of the local social system than innovators, and are opinion leaders within that local system: once that person has adopted, others are likely to follow) (Mohr 1969; Rogers 2003, pp. 282–92). In terms of personality characteristics, innovators can cope with a high degree of uncertainty, have an ability to deal with abstractions, are more intelligent and more 'rational' (in the sense of using the most effective means to achieve a given end) than later adopters, are less fatalistic, have higher aspirations, are less dogmatic, more empathetic, have a favourable attitude towards change and are risk-preferring. They are also said to share many of these personality characteristics with social deviants (Mohr 1969).

Identifying the characteristics of innovators and adopters is clearly only one aspect of how and why innovation occurs and is diffused, but mechanisms by which this happens are clearly critical and left unexplained by the character portraits (although in some cases these are assumed by a discussion of characteristics). For individual-optional decisions the mechanism is the individual's decision process. The core elements of the individual decision process are gaining knowledge about an innovation, forming an opinion about it, making a choice to adopt or reject it often through trialling, prototyping or piloting, implementing the innovation, and seeking confirmation of the decision made. The process thus has cognitive and affective aspects: the cognitive dimension is the acquisition of knowledge about an innovation and how it works; the affective dimension is the development of an attitude towards it, including what information about it the individual regards as credible and how that information is processed. For policy or organizational decisions, where adoption involves the mobilization of others, the decision process to adopt an innovation, and indeed the process of invention itself, is clearly more complex, and the individual world arguably needs to overlap with one of the other worlds if it is to have much purchase.

In essence, therefore, in the world of the individual, innovation is explained by the presence and actions and influence of one, or sometimes two, key individuals, who share particular certain personality and socioeconomic characteristics, and who, in organizational or policy innovations, occupy a strategic position with respect to the decision-making process such that they are able to push their preformed innovation through critical decision junctures or 'policy windows'. Whilst other factors may play a role, in the world of the individual, if such 'champions' were not present, innovation would simply not happen.

THE ORGANIZATIONAL WORLD OF INNOVATION

Early studies of innovation within organizations tended to be dominated by the world of the individual. They focused primarily on the role of individuals within the organization, either ignoring their organizational situation (e.g. research on the adoption of teaching methods by individual teachers) or reducing the organization to one individual, the chief executive (Rogers 2003, p. 407). These studies simply transferred the models and methodology used to investigate individual innovativeness to organizations, focused on innovation as a product (the adoption of a new technology or process), and sought to determine the variables that characterized innovative or non-innovative organizations. Subsequent work has recognized that given the different nature of individual and organizational decision processes, a simple transposition from one to the other cannot be made, and so work has focused on the process of innovation within an organization; in other words on innovation as a process, not innovation as a product (Zaltman et al. 1973; Rogers 2003, pp. 408–9).

The characteristics of inventiveness (creation) and innovativeness (rate of adoption) in organizations are equivalent in many respects to the characteristics of individuals, although organizations have features that clearly have no counterpart in individuals. It is these features which lead to a stronger divide between the characteristics of inventiveness in organizations and those of innovativeness. On the whole, innovation is usually seen to be a complex mix of individuals, organizational culture, organizational structure and organizational environment.

The invention, or the initiation of innovation, is to a degree associated with organizations in which the leader or leaders have a positive attitude towards change, which have low centralization, which have members who have a relatively high degree of knowledge and expertise, in which procedures are not highly formalized, in which there is a high degree of interpersonal connections between the organization's members, and a high degree of organizational slack, for example, the degree to which uncommitted resources are available to an organization, with the biggest factor being size: large organizations are more innovative than smaller (Rogers 2003, pp. 409–11; Mahler and Rogers 1999). The breadth of organizational goals and the absence of domination by one professional ideology have also been noted as significant predictors of innovation and adoption (Mohr 1969, p. 112) as have the existence of cultures which are risk-taking and which can tolerate mistakes and failures.

However the research thus far has not shown a strong correlation between many of the variables relating to organizational structure (other than those relating to size) and innovation; moreover it appears that the conditions which are necessary for innovation are those which impede implementation (Rogers 2003, 407–13; Zaltman et al. 1973). In particular adopters of innovation are characterized by centralization and formalization, whereas initiators of innovation are marked by decentralization and flexibility. Moreover, where the two sets of organizational characteristics collide within an organization (e.g. where the research and development units, or 'skunkworks' meet corporate hierarchy), the cultural distance between the two may be such that the innovation fails to be adopted by the organization as a whole (Smith and Alexander 1988).

Nevertheless, the public management literature is littered with suggestions for the optimal organizational design that bureaucracies should adopt to facilitate innovation in public service provision. Osborne and Gaebler, for example, argue that innovation is fostered by decentralized organizations, improved communication flows within organizations, incentives for officials to innovate, 'champions' who will push through innovations which originate at the lower levels of the organization, and acceptance of the fact that mistakes may be made, as well as by competition and public demand for public services (Osborne and Gaebler 1993). Recent Cabinet Office publications make similar suggestions (Cabinet Office 2003).

Given the ambiguity of the data on the relationships of organizational characteristics and innovation, attention has moved in academic studies to the study of the process of innovation itself within an organization, in which five main stages are usually identified (Zaltman et al. 1973; Rogers 2003; p. 417 et seq.; van de Ven et al. 1999). The first two are stages in the initiation of innovation: agenda setting, where an organizational problem which creates a perceived need for the organization is defined, and the identification of a performance gap, that is a discrepancy between an organization's expectations and its actual performance. Stages three to five relate to implementation of the innovation. Stage three is matching a problem to an innovation. The fourth stage is that of redefining or restructuring both the innovation and the organization so as to accommodate the perceived needs of both. Organizational restructuring may consist of a radical restructuring, or be more modest, for example the creation of a unit dedicated to the development and/or implementation of the innovation. The final stage consists of clarifying and routinizing the innovation: putting it into widespread use in the organization and ultimately incorporating it into the regular activities of the organization such that it loses its uniqueness or 'innovative' character.

Stripped of its nuances, this process model of organizational innovation is in danger of underplaying the role of conflict in innovation and of the potentially destabilizing effects of uncertainty and risk that necessarily accompany any decision to adopt an innovation. Innovations are likely to be opposed, and it is the ability of the innovator or champion to overcome this opposition which will be essential for its implementation (Mohr 1969, p. 114). Organizational scholars who emphasize the role of, for example, power, chance or chaos in decision making would further criticize the process model as excessively rational, denying a role for power and institutional structures in decision making, and neglecting the role of the organizational environment (e.g. March and Olsen 1984; Cohen et al. 1972; Hardy and Clegg 1999; Clegg 1998).

For some theorists, it is this latter factor, the organizational environment, which is critical for understanding organizational behaviour in general, and innovation in particular. There is some consensus that more innovative organizations operate in external environments which are more dynamic and more complex with more sophisticated interactive networks of relationships than those of less innovative organizations (Mohr 1969; Osborne 1998a); however beyond this the theories diverge fundamentally on the theories of behaviour that they assume give rise to these responses.

In Dusenberry's oft-quoted quip: 'economics is about how individuals make choices, sociology is all about how they don't have any choices to make' (Dusenberry, 1960, p. 223; Granovetter 1985), and explanations for organizational responses to their environment may be situated on the spectrum of theories of behaviour which runs through social science: from the pure model of economic rationality through models of bounded rationality (e.g. Simon 1947), structuration (Giddens 1984) and embeddedness (Granovetter 1985) to the pure models of structural determinism. At the rational end of the spectrum, contingency theory holds that organizations, through their management, rationally adapt their structures in order to maintain fit with changing contingency factors in their immediate task environments, such as size, technology and strategy, in order to attain high performance (Chandler 1962; Blau 1972; Donaldson 1995). Contingency theory has clear links with the 'how to' guides to management, and indeed to innovation, and research on organizational structures has been historically geared to providing managers with guides to optimizing their performance based on the assumption that strategic and optimal adaptation was possible and was a goal that would (and could) be pursued by management (Donaldson 1995).

Differentiation between organizations is explained in contingency theory by differentiation in the organization's task environment. More recent work in rational choice institutionalism takes a wider perspective and explores the interaction of the firm, its own task-environment, and its broader environment in the strategies, including innovation strategies, of profit-making firms. The 'varieties of capitalism' literature argues that the reasons why innovations take different forms in different varieties of capitalist economies is that they involve the deployment of different technologies (Kitschelt 1991), which in turn are differently supported by the institutions of the political economic environment in which the firm is situated (Hollingsworth and Boyer 1997; Soskice 1999; Hall and Soskice 2001). Radical innovation is supported by the institutional structure of liberal market economies (LMEs) and is particularly important in rapidly changing technology sectors which call for innovative design and rapid product development based on research, such as bio-technology or software development, and in the provision of complex systems, such as telecommunications or defence systems and comparable areas in the service sector: airlines, advertising, corporate finance, where success requires a capacity for taking risks and the rapid implementation (and withdrawal) of innovations. Incremental innovation is supported by the institutional structure of coordinated market economies (CMEs) and is particularly important for the production of capital goods, such as machine tools, factory equipment, consumer durables, or specialized transport equipment (Hall and Soskice 2001, p. 39). However the very characteristics that foster radical innovation in LMEs inhibit incremental innovation, and vice versa.

The 'varieties of capitalism' literature assumes a boundedly rational model of actorhood. In contrast, population ecology and sociological institutionalism assume a far less autonomous and reflective model of behaviour. Population ecology focuses on selection rather than adaptation to explain organizational change (McKinley and Mone 2003, p. 358). Those organizations which have features which match the external environment have a competitive advantage and are therefore selected for survival; those that do not die out. 'Matches' are not necessarily the result of intentional design, however, but usually occur as a result of random variation or organizational inertia (see also Hannan and Freeman 1977, 1984). 'Selection' is measured by numbers of organizational births and deaths, but the exact causes of 'death' in any particular organization are not examined, leading to the criticism that the empirical work conducted in population ecology studies is fatally separated from the theoretical models it is supposed to be testing (Zucker 1989; Young 1988; Donaldson 1995; McKinley and Mone 2003, p. 359).

Sociological institutionalism also seeks to explain organizational behaviour as being constrained and enabled by interactions with its environment (Scott and Meyer 1983; Granovetter 1985; Meyer and Rowan 1977; DiMaggio and Powell 1991; Meyer et al. 1994). Institutions are cognitive schemas, they are macro-level abstractions, typifications, rationalized and impersonal prescriptions that are independent of any entity (such as an organization) to which moral allegiance may be owed (Meyer and Rowan 1977; DiMaggio and Powell 1991, p. 15). They provide shared conceptions of reality, meaning systems and collective understandings that guide decision making and which individuals take for granted. Actors articulate and define their policy problems and solutions by using institutionalized scripts, cues and routines that constitute their cognitive frameworks and empower them to act, but on which they do not reflect (DiMaggio and Powell 1991; Meyer et al. 1994; Scott 1995). Decisions are made to pursue goals, but often the reaffirmation of processes and rituals and the communication of symbols and legitimacy is equally, if not more important (Meyer and Rowan 1977).

Conflicts and variety are de-emphasized; what is stressed instead is homogeneity, as the society-wide rules and structure that comprise an organization's field or environment penetrate the organization, affecting its world view. Organizations become similar to one another through institutional isomorphism (DiMaggio and Powell, 1983). DiMaggio and Powell identified three main isomorphic pressures: coercive pressures to conform, exacerbated for example, through resource dependence; mimetic processes, in which organizations respond to uncertainty, such as technological uncertainty or goal ambiguity, by imitating others; and normative processes, in which isomorphism originates in the development of professions and associated professional networks. This strand of analysis has been enormously influential. However given the vagueness and ambiguity of concepts such as 'environment' and 'isomorphism', the theory has been criticized by many as empirically impossible to verify (e.g. McKinley and Mone 1988).

Thus the explanations of innovation that are provided in the 'organizational world' differ depending on whether the analyst is focusing on the micro-level perspective of how an organization responds to challenges which arise in its own task-environment, or the macro-level perspective of populations of organizations or multi-organizational fields (on macro and micro explanations in organizational theory see McKinley and Mone 2003), and on the theory of behaviour that is employed. At the micro-level, innovation is explained through organizational culture, structure and decision-making processes. Thus it is argued that innovation is fostered by organizational structures which are decentralized, flexible, and which facilitate a high degree of interpersonal relationships, by a culture which is open and tolerant of mistakes, and by the capacity both to dedicate resources to innovations and to cope with their potential failure. These prescriptions are clearly amenable to transposition into 'how to' guides to innovate, and this is just what has occurred in the public sector (e.g. Cabinet Office 2003; Osbourne and Gaebler 1993). At the macro level, both the 'varieties of capitalism' and sociological institutionalism literatures argue that innovations are explained by organizations' responses to their environment, but the former explains this as a boundedly rational response, whereas the latter explains it as a structured response to the forces of institutional isomorphism and in which the pursuit of goals, or the solving of societal 'puzzles' may not be so important as the communication of symbols and legitimacy. Innovations which fit with cognitive schemas or understandings of reality, and with the individual's own constructed understanding of themselves, will be adopted. The latter in particular is a much more difficult set of arguments both to test, and to transpose into management guidelines; and these arguments tend to be correspondingly absent in such discussions.

THE STATE WORLD OF INNOVATION

The site of analysis in the 'state' world of innovation is 'government', either taken as an aggregate, or occasionally a particular unit of government (a local authority, or NHS trust, or more rarely, a regulatory agency). The work on innovation within government comes primarily, as one would expect, from political science. This world is potentially vast. Indeed, if the question 'how and why does innovation in public policy occur' is rephrased as 'how and why does policy change occur' or 'how and why does policy learning occur', then immediately almost any theory of public policy formation would have an answer. Public choice theory would argue that innovations are simply political goods which are sold to the highest bidder or coalition of bidders, and will vary depending on the distribution of costs and benefits on particular groups. Pluralism would argue that they are the result of an interplay of interest group pressures. Public opinion response theory would argue they are the result of public pressure, mediated by the media. Advocacy coalition theory would argue that innovations are the result of the pressure of a particular constellation of interests that coalesced around an issue or set of arguments and thus managed to outweigh opposing interests. Rational theories of bureaucratic behaviour would argue they are the result of self-interested bureaucratic decision making. The list is almost endless.

In contrast, the literature which is most directly associated with 'innovation' is in fact quite narrow, and in the depth of its causal explanations is rather a poor cousin to other more flourishing aspects of public policy analysis. There are two main sets of literature which focus specifically on innovation and diffusion: the self-styled innovation and diffusion literature, and the more recent work on policy learning. However, the institutionalist literature, a far broader set of arguments, also has focused to an extent on innovations, and provides a much richer seam of analysis.

Innovation and Diffusion in Political Science

The self-styled 'innovation' literature in political science seeks to explore innovation and diffusion specifically along the lines of the research traditions in the first two 'worlds: that of individuals and that of organizations. This literature consists mainly of large-scale quantitive studies which seek to identify the key variables associated with innovativeness, and/or the mechanisms of diffusion (Walker 1969; Berry and Berry 1990; Gray 1994; Berry and Berry 1999). Much of this literature seeks to develop models to explain the relative speed of the adoption of a 'new' policy or policies. Some studies have been cross-national (e.g. Heclo 1974; Kraemer et al. 1992; True and Mintrom 2001), but the majority have focused on the adoption of policies by US states.

Some studies focus on only one policy or group of policies, for example state lotteries (Berry and Berry 1990), living wills (Glick and Hays 1991), gender mainstreaming (True and Mintrom 2001), or tax policy (Berry and Berry 1992, 1994); others focus on a wide range of policies (e.g. Walker 1969). The models focus on the timing of legislative enactments, and most seek to model only when a policy was adopted, although some do seek to explore whether later adopters modified the policy in any way (Glick and Hays 1991; Mooney and Lee 1995). Most models accept that influences both external and internal to the jurisdiction play a role, but until the 1990s the models developed focused almost exclusively on either one or other set of influences (Berry and Berry 1999).

Those models, or aspects of models, that focus on influences internal to the state assume that the factors that cause a state to adopt a new programme or policy are the political, economic and social characteristics of the state; in other words some states, or organizations, are more likely to be innovative than others (Berry and Berry 1999, pp. 178–83). The models drew initially on literature on innovation at the individual and organizational level (Mohr 1969). The perspective has subsequently widened to include some of the dynamics of the broader political process, notably the role of policy entrepreneurs (Mintrom 1997).

These models hypothesized that whether an innovation would be adopted by a state at all and/or where the state would be positioned in the leader–laggard spectrum would be determined by the political, social and economic structures of the state, though in a parallel to the criticisms above that the work on the general characteristics of innovators is too totalizing in its assumptions, debate in this area continues as to whether or not one can meaningfully measure a general proclivity of a state for a particular rate of adoption, as opposed to a specific proclivity in a specific policy area (Walker 1969, 1973; Gray 1973). Essentially, it is generally argued in this literature that the motivation to innovate stems from the desire by politicians to win elections, and that whether they will adopt popular or unpopular innovations depends on their degree of electoral security, and in turn on the proximity to elections (Walker 1969; Berry and Berry 1990, 1992; Mintrom 1997). By direct analogy from the work on organizations and individuals, whether a state is an innovator is also argued to relate to its economic development (per capita income, gross domestic product and level of urbanization), though not necessarily overall levels of educational attainment in the population at large (Walker 1969). Walker further argued that the capacity of legislators (resources for offices, research staff) and legislative apportionment (the number of legislators representing urban communities) was directly related to a propensity to adopt innovations.

In contrast, models which focus on influences external to the state focus on the motivation for innovation, the process by which the decision to adopt an innovation is made, and on how information about the innovation is diffused, though the large scale of these studies often precludes any detailed analysis of how these processes operated in any one case. The usual hypothesis is that states emulate each other's policies for one or more of three reasons: reasoning by analogy, competition, and public pressure (Berry and Berry 1999). The first two were set out in Walker's seminal study of the adoption of 88 different policies across the US states (Walker 1969). Drawing on the work of Cyert, March, Lindblom and Simon (Simon 1947; Cyert and March 1963; Lindblom 1965), he argued that innovation is a form of incremental decision making, only in the case of innovation, the decisions which are built on are those taken in other states. Individuals satisfice, and in order to manage the wealth and complexity of the information and state of affairs that surround them they construct simplified world-models which contain only a few variables. In so doing, they adopt certain decision rules which are stable over time and which set the criteria of what information or advice to consider and what not. He argued that when faced with a new need (or one could argue newly perceived need) the dominant decision rule for officials is to reason by analogy. In other words officials ask what has happened elsewhere, and is it analogous to what we need here (Walker 1969; pp. 888–90).

The model of decision process that Walker posits could be interpreted as essentially a rational one, albeit one in which actors are boundedly rational. However, there is still an ordered process which mirrors the process of organizational innovation set out above: other jurisdictions are scanned for information on how they address a particular problem, examples selected, studies done to understand the operation of those policies, an assessment made of the adopters' own situation and problem, a 'matching' process of problem and potential solution, decision to adopt, trialling or prototyping, and implementation, clarifying and routinization.

Walker also argued that the main motivations for innovation were competition and emulation. A policy was more likely to be adopted if it had already been adopted elsewhere, and once a critical mass of states had adopted a policy, it became a badge of legitimacy or credibility to have one (Walker 1969, p. 890). However, as each state would benchmark itself against only a particular set of states, attention should be focused on which jurisdictions were relevant reference points for officials (Walker 1969, pp. 890–2). In other words, if policy innovation is a matter of 'keeping up with the Joneses', one has to know who the 'Joneses' are for any one state. Subsequent studies have emphasized the importance of emulation in the cross-national diffusion of policy models: policies are adopted not because they might work, or even because they are needed to solve a particular problem, but because it is a mark of legitimacy to have one (e.g. Braithwaite and Drahos 2000).

Walker argued that the peer group against which adopters rate themselves is determined by geographical location and, critically, by positions in communication networks. The significance of geographical location has dominated many of the US studies, with studies dividing on whether the states have to be contiguous, or whether there are regional blocs, or identifications of paths of diffusion from a 'core' to a 'periphery' and so on. Others have focused on the significance of horizontal networks of relationships in the diffusion process. Through networks of officials, voluntary organizations, interest groups, academics, think tanks, and so on, new norms or standards of administration are set and pioneering states linked with the more parochial. This has a direct parallel in organizational and individual diffusion studies, and others have argued subsequently that communication networks are the main factor associated with political innovation (True and Mintrom 2001).

The highly positivist, model-based literature on policy diffusion suffers from a number of difficulties, however. The early models which focus either on external environment or internal determinants have been shown to be fundamentally flawed, persistently showing false positives, that is, each found the influence of 'their' factor where it did not in fact exist (Berry 1994). As a result, models have now attempted to combine internal and external influences using new methodologies, notably event history analysis (Berry and Berry 1999; Mintrom 1997; True and Mintrom 2001). Nonetheless, as Berry and Berry point out, these still tend to oversimplify reality in a number of ways, including failing to distinguish between superficial and deep adoption (whether a policy is adopted in name only, or whether changes in policies and practices really do occur). In order to refine the models, they argue, more attention should be given to smaller, more detailed case studies (Berry and Berry 1999).

Perhaps a more fundamental criticism of the literature is that, in common with many large-scale positivist analyses, it conflates correlation with causation (see Yee 1996 for review). It offers no broader theory of policy-making, nor does it systematically draw on one. 'Diffusion' encompasses a number of different processes based on various assumptions about the behaviour and autonomy of policy-makers (Bennett 1997). Various bits of theory are drawn on models of individual action and organizational decision making, with various 'ad hoc' elements sometimes thrown in from the broader literature on policy processes, for example the role of policy entrepreneurs. However, as Schlager comments, the outcomes of these models do not feed into a larger theoretical story. Theory is not developed in the light of the models, and the models are not developed in the light of theory (Schlager 1999). Finally, the broader the research on innovation casts its net in seeking to explain the how and why of innovation, the more it merges with more general policy analysis, yet it fails to explain why it considers only some theories of policy processes rather than others.

Policy Learning

Diffusion studies, even those that focus on the diffusion of only one or two policies, are usually more interested in the mechanisms of diffusion than in what is actually being diffused. Diffusion has been criticized for being a descriptive not explanatory concept, concerned with processes not substance of policy, and the need to look for an equivalence in the policy-dependent variable necessitates a comparison within units of the most similar systems (Dolowitz and Marsh 1996, p. 344). Policy learning, in contrast, argues that the policy itself needs to be taken seriously.

This literature shares the view that evidence about policies and programmes may be used by domestic policy-makers for a number of reasons: to push an issue onto a policy agenda; to mollify group pressure; to search for an optimum policy solution; to legitimate conclusions already reached (Rose 1993; Bennett 1991, 1997; Bennett and Howlett 1992; Dolowitz and Marsh 1996, 2000). This literature seeks to identify more closely the causes and motivations of policy transfer; the mechanisms of transfer, particularly the role of policy communities (Bennett 1997); the types of transfer that may occur (of the goals, content or instruments of policies or programmes); the degrees of transfer (copying, emulation, mixtures and inspiration); which types of actors are involved (for example, politicians, bureaucrats, consultants); what levels of government transfers occur between; and the outcomes of policy transfers (Dolowitz and Marsh 1996, 2000; but see James and Lodge 2003).

The policy learning literature argues that diffusion may be voluntary or coercive to varying degrees, and is likely to be motivated by a product of exogenous factors including global economic or institutional pressures, facilitated by improved mechanisms of communication, and to be a product of analogical reasoning processes marked by bounded rationality (Rose 1993; Dolowitz and Marsh 1996, 2000; Bennett 1991, 1997; Bennett and Howlett 1992; Wolman 1992). Evidence about policies and programmes may be used by domestic policy-makers for a number of reasons: to push an issue onto a policy agenda; to mollify group pressure; to search for an optimum policy solution; or to legitimate conclusions already reached (Bennett 1991, 1997). In particular, policy communities are seen as key agents in the process of cross-national learning – they take relevant evidence about a policy from experience of other jurisdictions and adapt it to their own ends and circumstances; information is then filtered through decision-making channels to the political and administrative elites (Bennett 1997, p. 225). The policy learning literature thus focuses in detail on the substance of the policy decisions, and is not concerned with one of the main questions of diffusion research, which is the rate of adoption; how quickly a particular state adopted an innovation, or whether they were a leader or a laggard, and why; nor is it concerned to analyse whether the policy being 'learnt' is 'innovative' in any sense. Rather it focuses on the degree of, and mechanisms for, knowledge-transfer in the policy-making process.

Thus, as in the world of the individual and the organization, the two main sets of explanatory variables are features which are internal to the unit of analysis, and those which are external. Explanations for innovation within the positivist 'continent' of the state world differ depending on the methodology they use, which entails the selection of different variables, on the emphasis which they place on either internal or external factors, and the mechanisms they identify for the connection of the internal and the external (True and Mintrom 2001). Despite these differences in focus and emphasis, both the positivist and the policy learning continents in the state world literature would nonetheless agree that innovation is in some part the outcome of the analogical and 'learning' decision processes of a more or less autonomous state, in which the position of policy-makers in policy communities and policy networks plays a crucial role.

Broadening the Horizons

Innovation, as noted in the previous chapter, entails change, although not all change is innovation. Nonetheless, the 'continents' of policy innovation and policy learning, discussed above, have to an extent cut themselves off from the broader literature on policy change. That latter literature includes well-known theories of public choice, advocacy coalitions, policy communities, and so on. There is one set of explanations for policy change in particular, however, which because of the extent to which it addresses the issue of policy innovation, needs to be included in the 'state' world, and that is new institutionalism.

'New institutionalism' is an internally disparate set of understandings and explanations of social and political behaviour. Although it is sometimes regarded as a potential bridge across the divergent disciplines of economics, political science and sociology (North 1990), each discipline has its own variant of new institutionalism, reflecting its own concerns, sites of analysis, disciplinary boundaries and cognitive frameworks. The core notion is that 'institutions matter' to individual and social action and interaction because they provide the structure in which the action and interaction occurs. A minimalist definition of institutions is that institutions comprise cognitive and moral structures, rules, norms, conventions or operating procedures which are regarded as socially or legally binding but which are not self-enforcing (Ikenberry 1988; Jepperson 1991; Scott 1995; DiMaggio and Powell 1991). For political scientists, institutions also comprise the key political structures: legislature, executive, voting system, legal system, and bureaucracy. For economists, they also comprise markets, firms and other institutions which facilitate and constrain economic interactions.

Institutions have four key dimensions, which receive differing degrees of emphasis in the various strands of institutionalism: a behavioural dimension (providing the norms of action which are externally enforced), a cognitive dimension (beliefs and understandings of cause and effect relations), a moral dimension (providing norms of appropriateness and legitimacy), and a resource dimension (distributing resources and regulating access and agendas of decision making) (March and Olsen 1984; Hall and Soskice 2001, pp. 1–5). They have both stabilizing and facilitating effects: in particular they explain why, in a situation of multiple Pareto-optimal equilibria, one policy option is chosen over another; how collective action problems are overcome; and the stability of political decision making.

There are two dominant, and competing, theories of institutionalism which are prevalent in the 'state' world. First, rational choice institutionalism (RCI), which is built on the twin foundations of a theory of transaction costs and a theory of behaviour (Williamson 1975, 1985, 1996; North 1990). Institutions reduce uncertainty by establishing a stable structure for interaction. They enable collective action and limit the scope for opportunistic action by reducing transaction costs: providing mechanisms for gathering information, monitoring and enforcement, and some would add, deliberation (Hall and Soskice 2001). Institutions and individuals exist in a reciprocal relationship in which each affects the other (North 1990). However individuals are rational actors in the sense that their preferences are exogenously formed and revealed in their actions and decisions. Actions are taken to maximize preferences and outcomes are the aggregate of individual preferences and actions. The model of behaviour is one of bounded rationality: individuals' ability to seek out information and foresee consequences is limited, and information is filtered and alternatives considered in accordance with the individual's decision frame (Simon 1947). Whilst institutions affect action, the emphasis is still on individual agency.

Thus rational choice institutionalism would argue that regulatory innovations are the product of policy processes and that those which will be successfully implemented and adopted are those for which prior experience and learning is possible from elsewhere (reducing research and thus transaction costs), and which 'fit' with the interests of those most able to dominate the political institutional structures. The 'varieties of capitalism' also has a 'state' world dimension, and argues that different political institutional arrangements support different political economic institutional structures, or at least there is an interrelationship between the two (Wood 2001). As a consequence, Hall and Soskice argue, public policy-making should, and does, support the institutional structure of the political economy (Hall and Soskice 2001). As a consequence, public policy-making, for example with respect to social security benefits or labour laws, has to be 'incentive compatible' with the institutional structures of the economy in which it operates, or in more sector-specific arguments, the economic sector which it is regulating.

Historical institutionalism (HI), in contrast, is a response to behavioural-ism: the theories of pluralism and corporatism, itself a response to the old institutionalism's focus on political structures (for comparative analysis see Hall and Taylor 1996; Black 1997; Campbell 1998). The main thrust of HI is that political institutions of the state are not simply the mirror of social forces, but have the capacity for autonomous action and are themselves significant players in the policy process (Hall 1986, 1989, 1993; Skocpol 1985). The institutional structure of government shapes the interests of actors by estab-lishing their institutional responsibilities and relationships with others, and structures their interactions in pursuing those interests by affecting the distri-bution of access, power and resources. For example, the different structure of gatekeepers in controlling access to decision processes, i.e. the distribution of access and so-called veto points, is argued to affect the propensity to innova-tion within a state (e.g. Bleich 1998; Tseblis 2003). Moreover, individuals within the state do not simply pursue their own self-interests, but act in accor-dance with norms of appropriateness and legitimacy (March and Olsen 1984). In Heclo's terms, governments 'puzzle as well as power' (Heclo 1974). They identify social problems and consider how best to address them.

In particular, historical institutionalism would argue that different orders of change discussed in the previous chapter have different explanations. First and second-order changes, relating to settings and instrument choices, are explic-able through the normal explanations of policy learning in which the state acts autonomously from social actors or interests. The most direct influences are previous policies and key experts who are either working within the state or advising from a privileged position outside it. In the first- and second-order changes, states act autonomously from public pressure (Hall 1993; Weir and Skocpol 1985; Heclo 1974). Third-order changes, which involve paradigm shifts in understandings, occur where anomalies have arisen which are inex-plicable under the current paradigm, where the locus of authority over policy decision shifts, and where the debate spills over into society at large. However, without a change in the underlying normative structures of society, only those changes which fit with those structures will be adopted (Hall 1993).

Thus the institutionalist 'continent' in the world of the state would argue that innovation is explained by the impact of institutional structures on deci-sion making by political actors, including bureaucrats and those in regulatory agencies. Differential responses by regulatory regimes to the same policy issues, and indeed differential construction by regulatory regimes of policy problems, is explained by variety in institutional structures, and thus the form that regulatory innovations may take in different regulatory regimes will be contingent on the extent to which they 'fit' with the surrounding institutional environment. Generalizable solutions to policy problems, and indeed generalizable 'how to' guides to regulatory innovation, are thus not possible, as their 'solutions' will always fall prey to variation in institutional structures.

THE WORLD OF THE GLOBAL POLITY

The site of analysis in the world of the global polity is policy-making by international bodies and networks. The 'global polity world' is distinct from the 'state world' in that it is not concerned with the decision at the level of the state to adopt a policy, and indeed many of the policies may not need state-level action for them to become operative in that state. Rather, the policy is implemented through its adoption by professional bodies (e.g. accountancy standards), economic actors (e.g. technical standards implemented by manufacturers, management standards implemented by firms), or others. As successive studies have shown, states have been relatively passive or bypassed in many areas of policy development which are nonetheless regulatory in character and which fundamentally affect social and economic life. Either they are willing to be instructed by international organizations or epistemic communities as to what action to take (Haas 1992a, 1992b, 1993; Finnemore 1993), or they in effect are bypassed by transnational organizations which set technical or professional standards (Boli and Thomas 1997).

Innovation in the global polity world is explained primarily by transnational networks of communication. A good exponent of these arguments, although not concerned particularly with innovation, is Haas, who shows how international co-operation is achieved through the transnationally organized networks of epistemic communities (Haas 1992a, 1992b, 1993). These are networks of knowledge-based communities with an authoritative claim to policy-relevant knowledge within their domain of expertise. They are characterized by shared values or principled beliefs as to the normative rationales for social action, shared understandings of the nature of a problem and of causal linkages between possible policy actions and desired outcomes, intersubjective and internally defined criteria for validating knowledge; and a common policy enterprise. They influence policy-making by disseminating ideas and influencing the positions of a wide range of state and non-state policy actors, and they exert direct policy-making influence by acquiring bureaucratic power. When this power is somehow consolidated, the influence of the epistemic community is institutionalized. The causal effects of ideas thus become displaced onto the political effects of experts (Yee 1996, p. 86).

In highlighting the role of epistemic communities, Haas demonstrates how ideas may be a motivating source of interest, and how institutional learning mechanisms can influence the policy process. He argues their role is particularly significant in situations of uncertainty, and where state interests are undefined. Under such circumstances, information is at a premium, and leaders look to those with knowledge to suggest ways to address that uncertainty. Epistemic communities can thus be influential in defining the dimensions of a problem, in helping actors to define and recognize their interests, and be privileged in identifying solutions. Nonetheless, his notion of epistemic communities has been criticized for downplaying the conflicts that frequently exist between epistemic communities on the same policy issue (Levy 1994; Jacobsen 1995), and for assuming that the ideas promoted by a community will win purely by force of the better argument (Goldstein 1993). Conversely, he has been criticized for failing to take ideas seriously enough, for although the argument appears to be that ideas have a force of their own (Hall 1993), ultimately they prevail through the institutional position of their advocates (Yee 1996).

Braithwaite and Drahos's study of the global diffusion of regulatory principles in contrast concludes that communication networks are not sufficient (Braithwaite and Drahos 2000). Rather there are six principal mechanisms of diffusion: military coercion, economic coercion, systems of reward, modelling, reciprocal adjustment, non-reciprocal coordination and capacity building. Of these, they argue that modelling is the most important across all the domains they studied, though it was usually interconnected with one or more of the other processes in a 'web of influences' (Braithwaite and Drahos 2000, pp. 532–49).

Modelling is 'observational learning with a symbolic content' (Braithwaite and Drahos 2000, p. 580). It is distinguished from imitation, that is, an actor matching the actions of another actor, usually close in time. Imitation is studied by policy diffusion models; modelling is qualitatively different. Braithwaite and Drahos explore the modelling process in some detail. The process may begin as a proactive sequence, in which individual policy entrepreneurs enrol the organizational power of other actors, or it may begin as a reactive sequence as governments seek to respond to public pressure generated by a disaster or scandal, and seek around for a policy to adopt (Braithwaite and Drahos 2000, pp. 561–2). In each case, modelling has five stages (Braithwaite and Drahos 2000, pp. 578–601). Model missionaries 'invent' the regulatory model or policy. The models are then picked up by model mercenaries (who seek to make money from the adoption of the policy, for example through consultancies, training etc.) and/or model mongers (non-profit organizations), who tout the models around various international and national regulatory fora. The models are adopted either by bureaucrats or states acting with a range of motivations, and who may be acting proactively, or reacting to a political crises or perceived need. Model misers adopt them because they provide a relatively cheap and easy way to address a particular problem: they 'satisfice by rummaging through a rubbish bin full of models that have been known to have been applied to similar problems elsewhere' (Braithwaite and Drahos 2000, p. 590, drawing on Simon 1947 and Cohen et al. 1972), though they may also improve and enhance the model. Alternatively, or in addition, model modernizers adopt them because adoption appeals to desired identities, for example of being successful, modern, civilized, or advanced (following Meyer and Rowan 1977).

Braithwaite and Drahos share similar observations with the various strands of the policy diffusion literature. Each observes the direction of diffusion to be from the core to the periphery. Each emphasizes the role of transnational networks of actors in communicating policies, or in Braithwaite and Drahos's terms, 'webs of dialogue', though the latter make a far greater attempt to theorize the role of dialogue in the processes of policy formation and diffusion. Braithwaite and Drahos also adopt the same understanding of bureaucratic behaviour as Walker: bureaucratic decision making, they argue, should be seen not so much as a process of muddling through than as 'modelling through' (Braithwaite and Drahos 2000, p. 591). Further, although they do not refer to the literature on policy entrepreneurs and policy windows, Braithwaite and Drahos strongly emphasize the role of individual entrepreneurs in shaping global business regulation, and the role played by policy windows, or in their terms opportunities taken by model mongers who have models on the 'back burners' and who wait for the opportunity to market them (Braithwaite and Drahos 2000, pp. 559–63).

Braithwaite and Drahos's theory is, to an extent, a commingling of three different 'worlds' of innovation and their transposition to the global level: that is the world of the individual, of the organization and of the state. However, there is also a strand of literature which is not so subsumable and which has the potential to render the 'world of the global polity' distinct from the other worlds. Within the globalization literature, there is a developing theory of the emergence of a 'world polity' (Meyer 1980, 2000; Watson 1992; Strang and Meyer 1993, Boli and Thomas 1997). The world polity approach is an extension of sociological institutional theories, and emphasizes the institutional character of transnational development. It argues that in numerous ways, the world polity is not reducible to states, transnational corporations or national forces and interest groups. Rather, global structures and processes operate at a distinct level of social reality, and are marked by a distinctive 'world instrumental culture': a set of fundamental principles and models, mainly ontological and cognitive in character, defining the nature and purpose of social action (Boli and Thomas 1997, p. 172). In common with other sociological institutionalist analyses, they argue that culture (institutions) orientates action and shape actors. Worldwide constructs provide social identities, selves and roles by which individuals or collectivities pursue their endogenously defined interests. They define actors as individuals who have certain 'natural' needs, affectations and capacities (Boli and Thomas 1997, p. 173). As a result, they explain the empirically observed homology in a wide range of areas (education, women's rights, constitutional arrangements, environmental policy) as resulting from an overarching world culture in which definitions, principles and purposes are cognitively constructed in similar ways throughout the world (see also Meyer 2000; DiMaggio and Powell 1983).

The shared identities and rules are supplied by world culture of modernism (Meyer 2000). Meyer argues that modernism places significant premium on a model of rational actorhood; social life is seen to be its product and, as a result, social life is reorganized around its claims (e.g. principles of human rights, assumptions about the feasibility of instrumental control). Individual actors are culturally constructed as having the capacity to innovate and reform, and to control and govern (Meyer 2000; Meyer and Jepperson 2000). As a result, when faced with uncertainty, actors are culturally constructed with the expectations that they should address it and stabilize it, which they seek to do through the production of rules. The drive to the creation of common globalized models of instrumental culture is produced by a world culture that has actorhood as its core principle (Meyer 2000, p. 237).

These instrumental models are supplied by vast arrays of individuals (consultants, analysts, academics, epistemic communities) who value modernism: who argue that uncertainties can be stabilized, problems resolved, and that they have the answers. Such actors have proliferated in the last century, as work marking the rise of international non-governmental organizations, of scientific and professional organizations and of consultancy firms attests (Boli and Thomas 1997; Schofer 1999). Problems are seen to have universal characteristics, and thus be suited to universal solutions. However, whilst these are key suppliers of instrumental models (regulatory policies), the main transmission mechanism is not actors per se, but the model of actorhood (Meyer 2000, p. 243).

The key aspect to emphasize is that this theory is not concerned with normative conceptions of justice, rightness, or even epistemological questions of truth. It is not a quasi-Habermasian theory in which deliberation in conditions of the ideal speech situation will both lead to and be based on an acceptance of universal moral principles. Rather, and this is its relevance for studies of regulation, it is concerned with cognitive and ontological questions: understandings of cause–effect relations, of the way the world works. Its argument is that there is a global instrumental culture, not that there is a global moral culture. Conflict and contestation are not denied, however it is argued that in so far as these conflicts relate to instrumentalism, they are essentially about variations of modernity; they rarely seek fundamentally to challenge it (Boli and Thomas 1997; Meyer 2000). Contemporary social actors, including nation-states, have the same relatively scientific conceptions of basic resources, very similar definitions of human nature, and very similar definitions and understandings of collective authority and social control. As a result, there is an unexpected isomorphism in instrumental policies, featuring a high degree of structuring (complex organizational structures, for example), and local decoupling (adoption of solutions that do not work), which in turn leads to reform, stimulating the local and global expansion of modernity. The dramatization of the local is confined to expressive aspects of a culture: dress, food, ceremonial traditions and so on that do not have a direct, rational relation to instrumental actorhood (Meyer 2000, p. 245).

Thus the distinctive explanations for innovation in the global polity world are that innovation is the result of the operation of transnational communication networks, such as epistemic communities, processes of isomorphism in which diffusion of innovations is a socially structured response to the global polity environment, and for some, a rational model of actorhood. What is critical is that the individual characteristics of the state, and even the detail of the micro-level policy processes, are not significant determinants of innovation. In particular, one of the implications of the 'world polity' theory for understanding regulatory innovation is that the more these innovations conform to the principles of modernism, the more rapidly they will be diffused. Theories which propose technologies of governance which are rooted in these rationalistic conceptions of actorhood are therefore likely to diffuse rapidly. However, given that regulation is itself a modernist project, all innovations should be equally likely to be diffused. What the theory does not explain is why one particular theory or regulatory solution rather than another might be diffused, and why variation might arise in instrumental cultures as well as expressive cultures (nor what will happen where the two meet: where instrumental cultures seek to regulate expressive cultures).

THE WORLD OF THE INNOVATION

The world of the innovation focuses on the innovation or idea itself, and the role it plays in explaining its own adoption. Here again a parallel can be drawn between work on innovation in public policy and innovation in other areas. There are three main sets of theories in this world. The first argues that it is the shape of the innovation itself which matters. Rogers, for example, notes that it is the perceived relative advantage of the innovation, its compatability, simplicity, trialability and observability which facilitates its diffusion (Rogers 2003).

The second set of theories is that ideas themselves are important for explaining innovation. Here the 'ideational' turn in new institutionalism is particularly relevant, although ideas play different roles in the different strands of institutionalist analysis (Hall 1989; Goldstein and Keohane 1995a; Blyth 1997; Jacobsen 1995; Yee 1996; Campbell 1998).

Within rational choice institutionalism, ideas play a functional or instrumental role: they reduce transaction costs by reducing research costs, providing information and acting as road maps for policy-makers, and they facilitate collective action by providing focal points around which a divergent set of interests can converge (or 'hooks' on which interests can be hung), signalling one particular Pareto-optimal equilibrium over another (Goldstein and Keohane 1995a). Ideas are not seen as defining or shaping the interests of individuals: these preferences are ontologically prior to ideas. Instead they are functional devices, which are borne by policy-makers, which have no existence independent of interests and which are not independent causal variables in the policy process. Once adopted and implemented they are then encased institutions, rendering ideas and institutions indistinct.

In historical institutionalism, in contrast, ideas are critical as they form the bases of inter-subjective understandings that shape and alter the terms of political discourse, and which provide a link between state and society (Hall 1993). Ideas provide ways of presenting policies and rationalizing them to the public to mobilize popular support, motivate implementation and provide a semblance of consistency, and actions are inevitably based on particular understandings of the world. The terms of the discourse, in which that sphere and the policies appropriate to it are discussed, constrain and enable in often highly specific ways (Hall 1993, p. 291). Discourses set boundaries, define problems and set the limits on what is considered an acceptable set of solutions. Individuals' interests are defined endogenously by the institutional structure and the current dominant discourse, although individuals are seen to have some capacity for self-reflection and strategic action in that they will seek to change a discourse as well as operate within it. Ideas may be appropriated to advance interests, but they have an impact which is independent of them (Hansen and King 2001). Ideas, when linked with institutions, are used to explain change. When there is a change in the political discourse, that is the ideas and standards that identify the goals to be followed, the nature of the problem being addressed and the means to address it, in Hall's terms, in the policy paradigm, then policies will undergo radical, or third-order change. However, only those ideas which 'fit' with the underlying normative structures in a society will be accepted (Hall 1993; Sikkink 1991).

An attempt to synthesize the role of ideas and their differential effect on policy change, and thus innovation, has been made by Campbell (1998). He argues, drawing on organizational and historical new institutionalism, that ideas may be divided into four types, depending on whether they are cognitive or normative, and whether they operate in the foreground or background of the policy debate: progammes, paradigms, frames and public sentiments. Cognitive, foregrounded ideas are programmes: ideas as elite policy prescriptions that help policy-makers to chart a clear and specific course of policy action. Programmatic ideas are technical and professional ideas that specify cause and effect relationships and prescribe a precise course of policy action. They help actors devise concrete solutions to their policy problems. Cognitive ideas which operate in the background are paradigms: elite assumptions that constrain the cognitive range of useful solutions available to policy-makers. Paradigms are underlying theoretical and ontological assumptions about the way the world works, and constitute the broad cognitive constraints on the range of solutions actors perceive and deem useful for solving problems. Normative ideas which operate in the foreground are frames, symbols and concepts that help policy-makers to legitimize policy solutions to the public. Frames provide actors with symbols and concepts with which to frame solutions to policy problems in normatively acceptable terms. Normative ideas which operate in the background are public assumptions that constrain the normative range of solutions available to policy-makers. These constrain the normative range of solutions that are considered politically acceptable, are often conflicting, and are communicated to policy-makers through focus groups, the media and so on, and which they may manipulate for their own ends. Thus whilst it might be necessary for programmatic ideas to provide clear and simple solutions to instrumental problems, it is not sufficient. The proposed innovation has also to conform to existing paradigms, and be capable of being framed in such a way so as to fit with public sentiment.

Strang and Meyer take the role of ideas one stage further in explaining innovation, or more particularly diffusion of innovations and ideas. Building on the notion of a world instrumental culture, they argue that diffusion is facilitated by ideas which take a particular form: theorization of social practices. In other words the 'development and specification of abstract categories and the formulation of patterned relationships, such as chains of cause and effect' (Strang and Meyer 1993, p. 492). Theories, by their nature, are based on abstract generalizations. They have a diffusion generating power as they emphasize homogeneity and thus facilitate the perception that the theory is relevant. They can theorize actors as being equivalent, thus business organizations are theorized as the same despite the cultural, political and economic context in which they sit, with points of difference treated as variable, unnecessary or derivative (Strang and Meyer 1993, pp. 496–8); the same may be said increasingly of regulatory organizations.

Once institutionalized and built into standard schemas which are regarded as authoritative, a theory's diffusion potential increases. Theorization thus

plays a role in the social construction both of the practice in question and of
the adopter. It is also itself a diffusion mechanism: in other words theories can
diffuse in the absence of strong interrelational contacts or interdependencies.
Theorization is a substitute for detailed knowledge of the experiences of
others, and moreover can turn diffusion into an exercise of rational choice in
helping the actor to simplify and abstract from the complexities of others' situations and experiences (Strang and Meyer 1993, 499–500). Finally, theories
which construct and legitimate social entities as rational, purposive actors who
can contribute to social progress will 'fit' with the dominant cultural frame of
modernity, and will thus be more rapidly diffused than models which do not.

In the 'world of the innovation', therefore, whether or not an idea is likely
to be adopted and enacted is dependent not on the characteristics of the state,
or political processes, or on the organizational structures of its bureaucracies,
or on the presence or absence of individual policy entrepreneurs, or on the
presence or absence of communication networks. It will depend primarily on
the shape and form of the innovation itself, and for some, on the degree of 'fit'
that the idea has with prevailing cognitive and/or normative frameworks. The
more the innovation is simply expressed, trialable and observable, the more it
is expressed as a general theory, and the more it fits, or can be represented as
fitting, with dominant cognitive and normative schemas, the more likely it is
the idea or innovation will be adopted.

EXPLORING THE 'WORLDS'

As explained at the outset of this chapter, each of the 'worlds' is an analytical
construct, a heuristic device introduced with the aim of delineating broad
groups of explanations of how and why innovation occurs. They are clearly
not hermetically sealed units, they are not mutually exclusive, and they do not
exhaust the range of possible explanations that may exist. Many studies of
innovation contain elements of more than one world: thus the world of the
individual and the state is combined in theories of policy entrepreneurs; that
of the organization and the individual in work on 'innovation champions' in
both public and private sector organizations. Further, in drawing attention to
the need to maintain a normative coherence between an idea and normative
frames and assumptions, new institutionalism tempers the influence of both
the 'world of the innovation', in which the shape of the innovation, and in
some cases its analytical correctness will cause it to prevail, and the relatively
closed model of analogical reasoning by bureaucratic elites which characterizes that part of the state world inhabited by the diffusion models of, for example, Walker (1969) and the policy learning literature, and that part of the global
polity world inhabited by Braithwaite and Drahos (2001), each of which tends

to assume a process of model selection and matching in which the state is autonomous from external forces. Autonomy might characterize first and second-order change, but fails to understand the processes of third-order innovation (Hall 1993).

There are obvious theoretical limits to the extent to which the worlds, or elements of the different worlds, can be combined in explaining regulatory innovation. In particular, the same fractures of the relative roles of agency versus structure in explaining behaviour cut through explanations of innovation in all five worlds. Explanations of regulatory innovation cannot, without further elaboration, combine elements of the state world which emphasize rational action with elements of the organizational world which emphasize the role of institutional isomorphism, for example. But that word of warning aside, regulatory innovation in any particular case may well draw on explanations derived from the different worlds, and indeed one of the main arguments of this book is that explorations of innovation should visit all the worlds to consider whether aspects of them are relevant for the journey. In undertaking such an exercise, one is inevitably prey to the criticism that what is offered is simply a bewildering variety of perspectives or explanations with no clear direction as to which course one should take. That is an inevitable, but not, it is argued, fatal criticism. Innovation studies have to a large extent been characterized by perspectives which are overly narrow, or worse, which see 'innovation' as something 'special', which can be explained without recourse to broader explanations for organizational or policy processes. The aim of this chapter has been to provide an analytical framework for much richer explorations; it is the role of the subsequent chapters to see which, if any, are needed on voyage, and which, if any, survive the journey home.

THE JOURNEYS UNDERTAKEN

Robert Kaye examines regulatory change within the apex of governance, the regulation of legislators themselves, in Chapter 3. At this apex, the various world views tend to converge: the interests of the legislators as individuals, as regulators, as legislators are distinct but not necessarily distinguishable. Legislators are not only members of a collective legislature, they are individual members of the regulated group. Even at the organizational level the distinction between the legislature as regulated and as regulatee collapses. Concentrating on the House of Commons and the US Congress since the 1970s, two paradigm shifts are identified: a shift in focus from corruption to conflict of interest, and a shift in the position of transparency from a tool to a value in itself. But these shifts in value and purpose do not align perfectly with institutional reform. In the 'world of the individual' we find not entrepreneurships and leadership, but

'cranks' with leverage. In the 'world of the state' and the 'world of the organization' we find very little cross-national or cross-institutional learning. And
at the 'world of the global polity', there is little supra-national steering what-
soever. Instead, the debate – precisely because the issue is seen as an 'internal'
matter – has been little informed by the outside world(s). At the same time,
however, the very absence of factors such as policy entrepreneurship may not
mean that such factors are unimportant; rather that their absence explains the
limited scope of parliamentary reform. Finally, the analysis suggests that innovations thrive because of environmental suitability rather than regulatory
appropriateness: in particular, because reform in parliament has been sought to
address the *perception* of misconduct, high-visibility solutions have been
adopted. Adoption, however, is not the same as success; indeed the very
factors that make adoption likely may curtail or hinder the effectiveness of
reforms in practice. The result has been a pattern of 'moral panic' followed by
cosmetic reform, and a misalignment of tools and objectives.

In Chapter 4, Martin Lodge charts regulatory innovation in the railways
domain in two countries, Britain and Germany, across three specific critical
junctures. It assesses regulatory innovation in the two states in the 1990s and
then considers whether these supposedly innovative forms of regulation were
indeed innovative when considered in the light of the experience in the inter-
war years and the period immediately after the Second World War. The chapter emphasizes the contested nature of regulatory innovation. It is interested in
the ways in which the different causal mechanisms that underlie three worlds
of regulatory innovation (the 'global polity', the 'organizational' and the
'state' worlds) offer persuasive accounts of the way in which regulatory innovation in the two countries across the three time periods occurred, especially
in the way in which particular policy templates were rejected and endorsed.
The chapter argues that far from being deterministic, regulatory innovation
appears as a product of strategic actors within particular institutional constellations.

In Chapter 5, Mark Thatcher explores the reasons why third-generation
mobile phone licences were allocated through auctions or 'beauty contests' in
Britain, France, Germany and Italy, rather than being given away or sold for
nominal sums to 'national champion' operators in a closed licensing process,
as had been the practice previously. The chapter examines three issues relating to worlds of innovation regarding the state and entrepreneurs. It shows
how new technology offers new opportunities for actors to alter long-standing
policies, instruments and relationships. It argues that regulatory innovation
can lead to reactions that run counter to forms of regulation expected by interest group theories that predict state regulation favouring large, concentrated
supplier interests. It provides a rare clear-cut case for cross-national policy
comparison of regulatory innovation, and shows how some form of cross-

national learning counteracted inherited institutional differences and the extent to which policy-makers followed similar innovations despite operating in diverse national institutional contexts. Finally, it argues that the role of individual entrepreneurs, especially economists, was more limited than has been claimed, as innovation was largely the product of agreement rather than heroic individuals breaking through inertia and resistance.

Colin Scott examines innovation in the context of the regulation of Internet gaming in Chapter 6. The chapter contrasts the regulatory response to Internet gaming of three jurisdictions, New York State, Australia and the UK. It explores how different conceptualizations of the problem of Internet gaming have led to varying regulatory responses, each with its own limitations. The chapter examines these regulatory responses in the historical context of regulation within these domains, illustrating how the worlds of the state, the entrepreneur and the organization coalesce in different ways to produce divergent regulatory innovations in response to similar problems.

In Chapter 7, Christopher Hood and Martin Lodge explore regulatory innovation in dealing with dangerous dogs. Across the world, the 1990s and early 2000s witnessed the emergence of breed-based approaches towards the control of dogs associated with particular heightened levels of aggressiveness. The chapter explores the case of regulatory innovation with a particular emphasis on Britain and Germany and argues that the case represents an example of 'Pavlovian regulatory innovation' that represents a distinctive conjuncture of three of the worlds of regulatory innovation. In the world of Pavlovian regulatory innovation, policy entrepreneurship, state institutions and organizational constellations play out in peculiar ways that are not ordinarily highlighted in the innovation literature. In assessing this 'model' of regulatory innovation, the chapter concludes by exploring how far it reflects a paradoxical rationality – by 'economizing on rationality'.

Chapter 8 moves 'inside' the regulatory agency to examine the development of risk-based frameworks for regulatory decision making, focusing on three financial services regulators in the UK, Australia and Canada. Julia Black argues that the development and diffusion of risk-based frameworks show the importance of the 'organizational world' and the 'innovation world' in understanding regulatory innovation. The chapter first explores the varying degrees of opportunity for, and organizational openness to, policy learning, and the processes by which innovation developed, in which the 'inner logics' of the organization far outweighed the play of external interests in determining the shape of the innovation. Second, the chapter suggests that the uncertainty that accompanies any innovation may stultify normal political pressures as the very novelty of the innovation may make it hard for 'winners' and 'losers' to identify themselves. Finally, it is argued that the shape of the innovation itself is an important factor in its diffusion. Risk-based regulatory frameworks offer a tempting formula for rationalizing and systematizing the regulatory task, enhancing internal control mechanisms and managing political expectations; they provide an apparent solution to regulatory problems that many are likely to find hard to resist.

Finally, in Chapter 9, Julia Black and Martin Lodge return to the three questions posed at the outset: what is regulatory innovation, how can we account for it, and are we living in an age of hyper-innovation, or one in which there is simply a lot of hype about innovation? In drawing out the arguments from the case studies, they argue with respect to the first question, 'what is regulatory innovation', that both subjective and objective definitions of innovation can be useful, and that innovations can be distinguished from mere change in a regulatory regime. But, in contrast to the dominant trend in studies of regulatory and policy innovation, innovations should not be presumed to be successful by definition – learning from failures can be as valuable as learning from successes.

As for the second question, how to account for regulatory innovation, the conclusion argues that the five worlds of innovation emphasize the nature and extent of the differences between accounts of innovation, accounts which sometimes compete and sometimes are complementary, and the danger of confining explanations or accounts of innovation to one world alone. It argues that in the analyses given in the individual case studies, the worlds of the state and the organization dominate, in contrast to the world of the individual, which did not provide a particularly powerful account of innovation in the case studies presented here. In addition, it notes that a 'new world' of innovation, Pavlovian innovation has been identified. With respect to the third question, whether we are living in an age of 'hyper-innovation', the conclusion argues that although there is considerable hype about innovation, across the different domains studied there is not evidence of substantial hyper-innovation as Moran describes it, and indeed that Britain is not particularly innovative in comparison to other countries studied here, although it should be emphasized that further work needs to be done to test Moran's hypothesis fully. Finally, the conclusion argues that the 'worlds' of innovation can contribute to the debate on 'how to do' innovation, and offers suggestions for further research.

3. Reluctant innovators: regulating conflict of interest within Washington and Westminster

Robert P. Kaye

INTRODUCTION

This chapter deals with an age-old low-technology risk: the danger that private interests will subvert the official actions of elected legislators. There is nothing new about this issue: the English Parliament grappled with cases of conflict of interest over a century before the founding of the United States, with both a Lord Chancellor and a Speaker of the House of Commons expelled for corruption in the seventeenth century.

Moreover, this chapter concerns two institutions – the British House of Commons and the United States Congress – that might be thought by outsiders to be insular, self-serving and conservative to the point of reactionary. The term 'regulatory innovation' can convey notions of newness, modernity, radicalism and originality. Regulatory *change* in Congress and in Parliament has frequently been characterized by the very opposite characteristics. Yet, occasionally, there has been genuine innovation. From an international perspective, ethics regulation in Washington and at Westminster is relatively advanced compared with other national legislatures. Prolixity, reluctance and back-sliding, it would appear, are endemic to legislatures.

Moreover, while second-order change – the application of new technology to the problem – is the most common manifestation of innovation, there can also be third-order change where the underlying rationale for regulation changes, with or without change in formal regulatory structure. Where this is sufficient to amount to a revolution in conceptual world view, we can talk of a paradigm shift (Kuhn 1962). Although the prime mischief at which conflict of interest regulation has been directed has not changed over the 30 years examined below, not only has the 'solution' to it changed over time, but the normative framework in which that takes place has shifted.

When we try to apply conventional explanations of regulatory innovation to regulation *inside* politics, however, we encounter a fundamental problem: the distinction between a world of the organization and the world of the state collapses. Explanations, such as Moran's (2003) thesis of hyper-innovation in the British regulatory state, are posited on a clash of interests between politicians and the regulated sector. But when looking at politicians as a regulated sector, this becomes meaningless. Equally, however, what innovation we do find does not seem to suit explanations either of entrepreneurial individualism, or of cross-institution or cross-border transfer. Those pushing change have not been policy leaders, but somewhat obsessive and generally obscure members of the legislature. There has been virtually no learning, and little awareness, of overseas regulation, and still less evidence that it has informed domestic policy. The question should not be cast in terms of a positive push for certain ideas, but in terms of a minority of solutions taking hold despite general hostility to reform. Much can be explained by looking at how attractive an idea would be to members of the legislature that would enact it, rather than how suitable it would be for the problem posed. This might in turn explain why reform has frequently been unsuccessful, given the selection of cosmetic rather than substantive solutions.

ETHICS REGULATION IN WASHINGTON AND WESTMINSTER

The history of ethics regulation in Congress and the House of Commons, in which most of the action takes place in the past 40 years, involves two phases of second-order change. In the first phase, both states move from a minimalist system of ethics, to a corporate system of regulation, based on the disclosure of conflicts of interest. In the second, however, while both seek to address conflict of interest by reducing the potential for conflict, the choices of strategy are diametrically opposed: the United States sought to transform politics into a single career, with the extra-curricular activities of legislators curtailed in order to ensure the primacy of their legislative duties. By contrast the House of Commons sought to prevent conflict of interest while maintaining the amateur status of MPs, who, although it would curtail their parliamentary freedom somewhat, remained free to pursue any interests outside the House that they saw fit.

At least two paradigm shifts are exhibited over the period in question: a move from the punishment of corruption to the regulation of conflict of interest; and the emergence of 'transparency' as an absolute value in the late-1980s and early-1990s, itself the result of a more open, egalitarian and participatory view of politics. A move from self-regulation to a measure of outside scrutiny might be seen as second-order change if it is merely a new

Table 3.1 Development of ethical regulation in Congress and the House of Commons

	USA: House	USA: Senate	UK: House of Commons
Ethics Committee introduced (Move from honour to self-regulation)	1968: Select Committee on Standards of Official Conduct	1964: Select Committee on Standards and Conduct 1977: Select Committee on Ethics	1974–76: Members' Interests Committee/1996: Standards and Privileges Committee
Registration and disclosure of interests introduced	1968 (of gifts and honoraria) 1977	1968	1974
Measures to prevent conflict of interest	1976: Obey Commission: caps on outside earnings	1977: Limit on gifts; 1989: Restrictions on outside earnings	1995: Advocacy ban
	1989: Pay for ethics, honoraria ban	1991: Pay for ethics; honoraria ban	

way of pursuing existing policy goals; but it can become a third-order change if it reflects a paradigm shift in values, from self-regulation as a good-in-itself to transparency as a good-in-itself. The pursuit of openness has been recognized as a trend across policy domains (Hood and Rothstein 2001). Arguably this explains much of the pressure for openness in relation to conflict of interest, even though openness alone does little or nothing to prevent such interests from influencing the official actions of legislators. Table 3.1 provides an overview of developments in ethical regulation in Congress and the House of Commons.

Phase 1: From Corruption to Conflict of Interest; from Individual Conduct to Collective Ethics

Virtually all progressive[1] moves on legislative ethics have been prompted by political scandals, and in particular by a confluence of individual political scandals that point to a systemic problem. (Retrogressive change by contrast is often justified by the absence of political scandal, even though the lack of misconduct might actually be indicative of functioning ethics rules.) Prior to 1964, the US Senate relied on unwritten norms of conduct, and where an inquiry was necessary an *ad hoc* investigative committee was formed (for instance, to investigate allegations against Senator Joseph McCarthy in 1954). The Senate set up its Select Committee on Standards and Conduct in 1964 after the resignation in 1963 of Lyndon Johnson's protégé Senator Bobby Baker, over links to organized crime. A subsequent Joint Committee of Congress in 1965 recommended that both Houses adopt Codes of Conduct, but the House did not follow suit until 1967 after the fraught expulsion of Adam Clayton Powell for misuse of expenses (Allen et al. 1991). The Codes for both chambers included provision for reporting gifts and financial interests. The reforms in Congress were doubly innovative. First, they represented a shift from individual to corporate ethics, most vividly illustrated in the introduction of a Code of Conduct (the vertical imposition of collective values onto individual Congressmen). Second, while the proximate causes involved actual corruption, the new rules aimed at a less tangible conflict of interest.

In the UK, political scandal in the 1960s was dominated by sexual misconduct, frequently with a link to Soviet espionage (see Allen et al. 1991). Despite a handful of cases in the mid-1940s, conflict of interest remained off the political radar. There was no dedicated institutional mechanism for handling conflicts of interest among MPs until 1976, and the House depended on a handful of *ad hoc* resolutions passed over the years in response to specific cases of misconduct. With a few exceptions, relating exclusively to *private* legislation (as opposed to public policy) these rules were aimed at actual, not potential, corruption. The norm was for backbench MPs to have outside careers or income, while Labour MPs were frequently sponsored as official representatives of trade unions.

An indication of emerging concern can be taken from the response to the revelation in 1969 that a Labour MP had been paid as a 'parliamentary consultant' to the Greek military government. A parliamentary committee was formed to inquire into MP interests – suggesting that the question was now cast in terms of conflict of interest rather than corruption. Its explicit rejection of a register of interests can itself be taken to indicate that the issue had at least risen onto the policy agenda. However, its inherently conservative and explicitly anti-innovative reasoning can be seen most vividly in its rejection of a register on the grounds that this would expose 'much more information than is declared under the House's present custom' (1969/70: HC 57, para. 74). Using such reasoning, first-order change would seem to be on the agenda, but out of the question.

If concern was emerging by the late 1960s, what crystallized it was the resignation in 1972 of the Home Secretary, Reginald Maudling, over his considerable financial links with the corrupt architect John Poulson (see Allen et al. 1991, pp. 241–4; Doig 1979). Poulson was shown to be at the centre of a web of local government corruption, and was jailed in 1974. Yet, even when the incoming Labour Prime Minister Harold Wilson appointed a Royal Commission on Standards in Public Life, Members of Parliament were omitted from its terms of reference (Williams 1985, p. 63; Salmon Commission 1976). It was only when a Labour MP threatened to substantiate earlier comments that a number of Labour MPs could be bought that Wilson agreed to support a register of MPs' interests. In a series of highly partisan votes, the proposals were approved by MPs in May 1974 (Williams 1985, pp. 163–5; HC Debs, 22/5/1974, vol. 743, cols 533–44). The register was to be overseen by a permanent Select Committee on Members' Interests, a self-regulating body composed exclusively of MPs. Effectively the Commons had gone through the same process of change as Congress. But as the House of Commons was dragged reluctantly into tackling conflict of interest, Congress was already entering Phase 2.

Phase 2: Preventing Conflicts of Interest; and the Rise of Regulation

Registering and declaring conflicts of interest does not solve them. Indeed, by making such conflicts known it may serve only to heighten concern. Concern over political ethics in the USA was undoubtedly strengthened by the impeachment proceedings against President Nixon in 1974, but a string of scandals in the 1970s suggested that misconduct was not limited to the executive branch. In 1976, two Representatives were penalized for failing to disclose stockholdings and for keeping a mistress on the House payroll respectively, while a number of Congressmen (including both House and Senate Ethics Committee chairmen!) were found to have received undisclosed hunting trips from defence contractors (Williams 1985, pp. 118–19). One Representative was convicted of bribery and embezzlement (Thompson 1987, p. 187) and, in the 'Koreagate' scandal, a lobbyist for the South Korean government admitted making gifts and campaign contributions to 30 Congressmen. Three Congressmen were later censured, and one jailed, for their behaviour (Allen et al. 1991, p. 422). At this point, Congress moved beyond disclosure to adopt actual limits on non-legislative activity, a further second-order change. In 1977 both chambers adopted new Codes of Conduct restricting outside earnings, including honoraria –

payments for speeches. The provisions were recognized in a wider Ethics in Government Act, but this Act, although subject to the jurisdiction of the courts, left implementation of most of the rules on ethical conduct in the hands of the congressional ethics committees.

At a superficial level this might be seen as a consequence of the separation of powers, which requires at least a degree of mutual non-intervention. However, separation of *powers* is something of a misnomer: what one really finds is three overlapping jurisdictions. One consequence of this is that the US system provides a role for other branches of government in legislative ethics: 'Congress has been obliged to share responsibility for the conduct of its members' (Atkinson and Mancuso 1991).

Perhaps the starkest example of this was the role played by President George Bush Sr. in the 'pay for ethics' manoeuvre of 1989. Under this compromise, the House, although not initially the Senate, agreed to accept an outright ban on honoraria. New rules would prevent Representatives from acting as lawyers, would prevent them transferring campaign contributions to their personal use, and would introduce 'future employment' restrictions. In return, legislators received a 25 per cent increase in salary. A key facet of the US case is that the President had 'leverage' – he was able to target Congressional ethics because of his role in setting federal salaries.[2] At the same time, the process was marked by strident bipartisanship. Bush won, narrowly, because he had to reach out beyond his own party and form a coalition across the House, including making concessions and cutting deals with party leaders. The House and Senate Majority and Minority leaders agreed to defend members of the other party should their vote for the pay rise be attacked during the 1990 election campaign.

By contrast, in the UK ethics reform has been characterized by high degrees of partisanship, and in particular by the opposition to greater disclosure of MPs' interests by Conservative members (who generally had more to disclose than Labour MPs). The election of a Conservative government in 1979 did much to diminish the effectiveness of the new regime. The measures introduced by the House of Commons in 1974 were, overall, a failure. For the first 11 years, the principle of registering interests was thwarted by the House's failure to take any action against a single member who refused to comply. In 1989, however, the first MP was punished under the new regime, and for a brief period the Register of Members' Interests seemed to be taken seriously.

From 1992, political misconduct came to be a significant party-political issue and 'sleaze' became a catch-all smear against the Conservative government. At the same time, much of the informal inter-party co-operation on which the House depends broke down. As the House's disciplinary committees came to adjudicate in a series of contentious cases, partisan tensions ripped them apart. In 1994 the Members' Interests Committee broke up when the Conservative majority refused to investigate allegations that the Trade Minister Neil Hamilton had accepted cash payments for tabling (i.e. asking) parliamentary questions (Leigh and Vulliamy 1997; HC 34i–iv: 1997/98).

Hamilton represented a crisis point. On 25 October 1994, the day that Hamilton was forced to resign, John Major set up an independent inquiry into Standards in Public Life under Lord Nolan. This was doubly innovative. Previously such bodies had been excluded from considering the ethics regime *within* Parliament, and such issues had been left to the House's own committees. Even more significantly, the Committee on Standards in Public Life was set up as a standing body, becoming a permanent part of the country's ethics infrastructure (Hennessy 1996). Although it has only an advisory role and does not investigate individual allegations, it is an important part of the regulatory regime, involving standard setting, and monitoring of the ethics infrastructure. Crucially, its continued existence should act as a brake on any tendency to water down or sideline its recommendations.

Nolan's remit was deliberately wide-ranging, but its first report was directed at the most contentious areas – MPs, ministers, civil servants, quangos, and NHS trusts.

Nolan's main recommendations for MPs included:

- A code of conduct for Members of Parliament, incorporating seven universal principles of public life (selflessness, integrity, objectivity, accountability, openness, honesty and leadership);
- A strengthened Privileges Committee to oversee the code (this merged with the existing Members' Interests Committee);
- An independent Parliamentary Commissioner for Standards (PCS) to provide advice and investigate allegations of non-compliance with the code (although the extent to which the PCS should investigate was ambiguous);
- Full disclosure by MPs of agreements *and remuneration* relating to the provision of Parliamentary services;
- A ban on MPs providing services to consultancy firms.

Although the Prime Minister immediately accepted its 'broad thrust' (Seldon 1997, p. 556; *The Times*, 12 May 1995), in an attempt to stave off a potential rebellion by backbench MPs, a special Commons committee was formed. Although the committee's task was to implement, not to review Nolan's recommendations (Hennessey 1996, p. 193), a number of Conservative members sought, successfully, to reject these recommendations. The Tory majority did not accept the point on multi-client consultancies (Oliver 1997). Nor did they, in truth, accept disclosure of remuneration for activities deriving from membership of the House. Instead they recommended a different strategy, a ban on 'paid advocacy': MPs would be prevented from initiating parliamentary activity whenever they had a pecuniary interest in the matter concerned, and from participating in activity that related specifically to that interest.

This was truly innovative. The only previous rule which acted as a constraint on MPs' freedom of action – a Speaker's ruling of 1811 – related to private bills alone. Across the Anglo-Saxon world – which realistically was the cognitive limit for the Nolan reforms – 'public business', 'state policy' or 'government measures' had been exempt from provisions designed to extinguish conflict of interest. Preventing compromised MPs from participating in parliamentary proceedings was a second-order change. But its radicalism is explained in part by the antagonism to the alternative, especially to the disclosure of income, albeit that these involved only first-order change.

The proposals then passed to the House of Commons. Conservative members were informally told to reject Nolan's recommendations on full disclosure and support the advocacy ban instead. Despite Labour's previous, principled objections to the possibility of restrictions on parliamentary activity (Nolan 1995-I, p. 28), they could not attack the alternative moral high ground that the Tories had erected. No amendment was tabled to the advocacy ban, and Labour members were formally required to support it.

If this was a Conservative strategy to forestall full disclosure, however, it failed: a number of Conservatives either rebelled or abstained and 'full disclosure' was passed not as an alternative but in addition to the advocacy ban. The narrowness of the government's majority was a key reason for the success of the reforming motions. Thus while there were general trends which provided necessary conditions for reform – decline of public trust, political scandal – the actual process of reform contained high levels of contingency. One perverse effect of this contingency was that the House adopted both strategies – far in excess of what anyone wanted. (As a postscript, the advocacy ban was unworkable, and in 2002 the ban was relaxed: MPs would only be prevented from seeking *to confer a benefit* on a person or body outside Parliament from whom they had received a benefit.)

A Parliamentary Innovation: the Parliamentary Commissioner for Standards

Arguably the most innovative recommendation in the Nolan Report was for a new officer, the Parliamentary Commissioner for Standards, to take responsibility for ethical matters in the House of Commons. The key importance of this recommendation was the extent to which it marked a move away from internal self-regulation. The constitutional and administrative lawyer Sir William Wade was able to say – during the hearings – 'the House has been jealous of its privilege of self-regulation, but some members have now proposed that there should be an independent element'. But it is notable that this desire did not manifest itself as a desire to dilute, say, the Privileges Committee, with outside members.

Notwithstanding this, the PCS has antecedents in British governance arrangements. For Nolan (recognizing that there is a good deal of ambiguity) the PCS was to be modelled on the Comptroller and Auditor General (the C&AG) and the Parliamentary Commissioner for Administration (the Ombudsman). Like these, he was to be an officer of Parliament, although in practice he would not enjoy the protection that the C&AG has. Whereas the C&AG is appointed by the Sovereign, has life tenure and is only removable by a resolution of both Houses of Parliament, the PCS was appointed by the House (whose members he was to investigate), put on a three-year contract and could be removed by simple resolution of the Commons (whose members he was to investigate). This does not seem to have been an act of deliberate creative adjustment. The PCS did not have the statutory powers of the C&AG because it was believed that the statutory process would be both cumbersome and unnecessary. In practice, without the statutory powers available to these office-holders, the formal position of the PCS was somewhat more like a House of Commons clerk – indeed, bizarrely, Nolan does not seem to have left a significant role for the Commissioner in a tough case where facts are disputed. Where the Commissioner found a prima facie case, but the Member disputed the facts, the case would go before a subcommittee of the Privileges Committee. This would mean the Commissioner became effectively a legal advisor to the subcommittee; a role for which the Commissioner's abilities to 'find a case proved' and to publish his 'findings' would be redundant. Yet these were precisely the cases where a strong independent investigator would be necessary; and a committee, or subcommittee of politicians, entirely inadequate.

The mismatch between public expectations of the Commissioner as a powerful 'sleazebuster', and the detail in the Nolan reforms, were not initially addressed by the House of Commons. Although the House made provision for the Commissioner to report, as Nolan intended, to a subcommittee of what then became the Standards and Privileges Committee, in practice, the Commissioner was asked (by the Standards and Privileges Committee) not only to try to reach an agreement with the Member, but also to reach conclusions. This strengthening of the Commissioner's role was based on a number of factors: the creation of a subcommittee was seen as unworkable and none was ever formed, not least since any appeal from its findings would be to the full committee (less those of its members who had been on the subcommittee), meaning that the less-involved and less-informed MPs would have the final say; the scale of the early investigations was thought to make investigation by a committee composed of busy MPs impractical. Most fundamentally, however, there was a problem of credibility. Neither a committee, nor a subcommittee, composed exclusively of MPs was likely to bring credibility, even if acting only as an appellate body. If the committee or subcommittee upheld the Commissioner's findings, it would be seen as superfluous. If it rejected those findings, those of the independent Commissioner would have more credibility and legitimacy and the parliamentary side of the process would be seen as either a self-protecting whitewash, or a politically motivated witch-hunt. So in practice the Commissioner became a one-man tribunal of inquiry (Woodhouse 1998, p. 58), and the full Standards and Privileges Committee his appellate body. When the Committee on Standards in Public Life subsequently returned to the issue in its sixth and eight reports (2000 and 2002 respectively) the question was how to shoehorn protection for MPs under investigation into the new structure, and its preferred solution was to replace the full Standards Committee as an appellate body. Any initial ambiguity was resolved in favour of the Commissioner who became, and is, investigator and magistrate.

This was a constitutional innovation. Single-person regulators were the norm in the 1980s and 1990s (albeit heading substantial quasi-departments). Single-person ombudsmen are ubiquitous. On occasion they involve themselves in quasi-criminal investigations (an example would be the Pensions Ombudsman, whose findings occasionally involve fraud and misappropriation). But findings against individuals by such officials are largely ancillary to investigations of corporate or administrative failure. Investigations into individual misconduct, especially where that involves criminal or quasi-criminal behaviour, tend to be conducted by a panel or, if it must be a single person, a judge or, at least, a lawyer. In the case of the PCS investigations of misconduct by individuals would be the bulk of the Commissioner's work. There is no extra-judicial precedent for a lay individual with such a job. That this development should occur within Parliament is doubly surprising.

If innovation was present in the institution of the PCS it was all the more evident in the PCS's work. Although the basic technology of control remained – oversight, specifically adjudication – there *has* been innovation, in particular the incorporation of unconventional techniques into the investigatory process. Previous inquiries had been modelled on a combination of select committee hearing and tribunal of inquiry: a complaint was made, accounts were taken, documents submitted, evidence tested orally and a judgment made. The first two Parliamentary Commissioners could make use of new techniques which would not have been used by a committee of MPs, including audit, forensic testing, and even simple investigative techniques such as making searches of the land register or Directory Enquiries.[3]

EXPLAINING CHANGE: A VIEW FROM THE WORLDS

The fact that change can be identified, which qualifies both quantitatively and qualitatively as innovation, needs to be put into context: change remains the exception not the norm. However, this is not necessarily a barrier to understanding the process and drivers of change. Whichever 'world' one is observing, each period of reform can be analysed, but crucially so too can the long periods of stasis. One is not only trying to explain innovation: in order to understand what makes innovation possible it is necessary to understand the circumstances in which it is not.

The World of the Individual

In the USA, pressure for ethics reform has been applied more or less consistently over the past 30 years by groups such as Common Cause and the League of Women Voters of America (Wyatt 2002). Likewise in the USA much of the movement towards transparency has been under pressure of groups like Common Cause and the ACLU who see transparency not as a simple solution to political problems but as a prerequisite to other solutions. In the UK, groups such as the Campaign for Freedom of Information, Charter 88, and Transparency International have been pivotal in pushing transparency and openness as a value in itself – but for the first two at least, political ethics has been seen as a subset of a wider problem.[4] What the 'transparency movement' does seem to have achieved is a shift in the underlying assumptions of citizens and legislators. In pushing transparency as a value, they have increased the intellectual and emotional appeal of policies based on openness and accountability. That is to say, they have created a more propitious environment for particular innovations – those based on a 'right to know' – to flourish.

While organizations might conceivably play the role of policy entrepreneur, in reality they have been far more important in setting the political agenda. They are attractive as possible entrepreneurs because of their tendency to associate themselves explicitly with reforms. But it is not clear that there is any neat causal relationship.

Turning to individuals, the literature on policy entrepreneurs generally stresses the role of practitioners and policy-makers. If we are to consider the innovation of Parliamentary Commissioner for Standards, some degree of responsibility must lie with the first Commissioner, Sir Gordon Downey. His extensive second inquiry was fundamental in moving towards a rigorous forensic role for the Commissioner, while his 'take it or leave it' attitude to the Standards Committee showed that he regarded his role as involving coming to conclusions that were, to an extent, determinative. However, Sir Gordon was doing no more than the public expected of the PCS. His use of

forensic techniques including Electrostatic Discharge Analysis (ESDA) testing, handwriting analysis and audit might have been surprising had he been
presiding over adversarial hearings. For a one-man investigator, however, it
would have been surprising if he had not used at least some innovative tools
of inquiry.

Indeed, if Nolan was ambiguous over the Commissioner's role, it is
unlikely that his proposals would have garnered support if they had not at least
left open the possibility of a powerful Commissioner. So was Nolan the innovator? Nolan recommended not one but two independent commissioners in his
first Report alone, the other to oversee public appointments. Alternatives such
as self-regulation or a new quango with a wider remit were not pursued
(indeed given that quangos were one of the public concerns that prompted the
creation of the Nolan inquiry, it is hardly surprising that he did not suggest
another one). By contrast, under Nolan's successor Lord Neill, there seems to
have been a preference for committees – his institutional innovations were the
Electoral Commission and the (local government) Standards Board for
England. This does not mean, however, that the choice was a case of simple
personal preference (Nolan v. Neill); it could equally have been temporal
(mid-1990s v. late 1990s), or, more likely, related to the environment and
context within which Nolan was operating. Indeed, the idea that a single-
person regulator would be appropriate appears to have seemed obvious to
members of the Nolan Committee from the outset. The 'Commissioner idea'
succeeded because the sort of institutions – specifically the Ombudsman –
which it resembled were viewed as effective at the time that the decision was
taken. The Ombudsman model seems to have been at a peak in the mid-1990s
(Bennett 1997), as can be seen in Roy Gregory's simultaneous description of
the Ombudsman in 1997 as both a 'successful institution' and a 'burnt-out
star' (Gregory 1997; Gregory and Giddings 1997). That is to say, the institution of the Ombudsman was reaching a situation approaching saturation – but
a point at which it was simultaneously vulnerable to new challenges. The
likely next development was for the principles behind ombudsmanship (an
independent, single person, investigator) to take hold in new institutional
settings. It was a case of 'right idea, right time, right place, right people'.

If Nolan merely caught a passing burnt-out star we can look further back in
the proceedings to identify who proposed a commissioner. The idea of a
parliamentary ethics advisor was raised in the first day's evidence-taking by
the former deputy leader of the Labour party, Roy Hattersley. But a better
candidate would Labour MP, Dale Campbell-Savours, who after years of
workmanlike failure to promote change as member of the Commons'
Members' Interests Committee, presented Nolan with a list of 21 fully-formu-
lated recommendations. Of the nine relating to Members of Parliament, five
were adopted by Nolan, and the other four were subsequently implemented by

the House. And the idea of a powerful commissioner was one of Campbell-Savours's proposals. A similar tale can be told for the reforms of the 1970s when the Labour back-bencher Joe Ashton, having been dragged somewhat unwittingly into the ethics debate (he had tried to play down the number of Labour MPs who 'could be bought, and was instead exhorted to 'name the guilty men') used his leverage (he threatened to substantiate his claims publicly) to force an unwilling Prime Minister to support reform. Both Ashton and Campbell-Savours seem to employ the technique of the policy entrepreneur, pouncing when a 'window' is available for them to introduce a policy that they already wanted to see in place. At the same time these two obscure backbenchers make somewhat implausible entrepreneurs. Rather they would seem better to fit the description of policy cranks. Such a description not only conveys a sense of eccentricity, but also implications of hard work – possibly futile[5] – and leverage. Crucially, however, they exploited a temporary position of influence rather than a permanent office or position of power.

Taking the process as a whole, it is impossible to identify a single person, or group, or even a loose alliance of individuals driving the reform agenda. Viewed through the lens of the individual, the PCS is a puzzle, an innovation without an innovator. Contrary to entrepreneurial hypotheses, the innovation of the Parliamentary Commissioner for Standards succeeded despite there being no real entrepreneur pushing it.

The World of the Innovation

An argument from the world of the innovation is made by Hood (1995) who examines the rational basis for adopting different ethics strategies. 'Pay for ethics', he argues, is an attractive strategy: it provides high material reward for legislators. But it is a difficult strategy because it relies on a high degree of collective action, and a risky strategy because if the public does not believe that behaviour is any different then the public face of pay for ethics is simply more pay. Indeed, for a rational legislator pay for ethics is no more rewarding, harder to achieve and just as risky than a strategy of covert corruption.

There is a simplistic appeal to banning paid advocacy. It obviates any possibility of conflict of interest. The difficulty is that it is such a potentially powerful weapon that it must in practice be circumscribed. The result is that limits are placed on both the types of interest (generally private, financial, and often above some *de minimis* level) and the types of legislative action (in the UK now, only interventions which seek to benefit the MPs' interest specifically). But such nuancing strikes at the heart of its simplicity, for it allows legislators to pursue a variety of self-advancing acts that fall outside the ban. And it allows legislators to portray the new rules as complex, confusing, contradictory, and riddled with qualifications.

By contrast, disclosing interests does little to prevent those interests from influencing public officials; indeed it may even exacerbate the problem. But it is a low-cost solution for the legislators concerned: the only 'costs' are a diminution in privacy and the inconvenience of having to complete disclosure forms. Crucially, however, the legislator is not obliged to shed his interest. More importantly, however, it is a high-visibility solution. The 'politician's syllogism' – 'We must do something; this is something; therefore we must do this' – suggests a knee-jerk reaction to political issues, but does not explain why one policy option is to be preferred over another. But if the syllogism holds, what really matters most is *to be seen* to be doing something. Disclosing interests involves a continuing performance of ethical behaviour. Likewise, compulsory disclosure of remuneration may, as some MPs have it, be motivated by jealousy and prurience. But this may also help explain the appeal and success of such a strategy. By tapping into the public's desire for possibly prurient detail it does at least satisfy the need for reassurance without forcing legislators to forgo certain benefits. Indeed, if the public really does want prurience and salaciousness, then we should opt for a system that produces misconduct but exposes it, rather than one which prevents it completely.

Insofar as all this is true, however, it is useful to ask whether the world of the innovation provides answers based on universal norms (for instance, that simple innovations are more likely to be adopted) or, more persuasively, based on particular circumstances. The latter may mean nothing more than that particular circumstances encourage certain types of innovative response. But it also means that finding an innovative solution is insufficient; what is important is to find an innovative solution that will be adopted.

The World of the Organization and the World of the State

When considering how legislatures innovate for their own regulation, and how they way they regulate themselves responds to developments outside the legislature, the distinction between the world of the organization and the world of the state becomes blurred, and may eventually collapse. The legislature, along with the core executive, is at the heart of a nation's policy style; but it is also an organization. The structure of the legislature *qua* organization in turn structures how the legislature makes policy – an interrelationship which becomes even more introverted when we consider how it regulates itself.

There is a further facet of the structure of legislatures which sets them apart from most other organizations: by virtue of being elected, they are open, not just cognitively but actually, to penetration by the world outside. It is not the simple fact of election which matters – after all, most self-regulatory organizations and professional bodies elect their ruling councils – but the fact that elections are theoretically open to all-comers, even if in practice there are substantial barriers to participation. Consequently, no one world-view is hard-wired into the institutions' collective psyche (with the possible exception of a commitment to democratic norms).

But if legislatures are open, how does this relate to their capacity to innovate? At one extreme, the purest case of innovation, invention, presupposes that innovators are not simply implementing strategies adopted elsewhere, but are autonomous. Policy adoption, whether by borrowing, transfer, imposition or copying, might amount to innovation, but it guarantees that the innovation is not so radical as to be an invention. Likewise, policy diffusion can be diametrically opposed to policy learning where the adoption of policies in a new jurisdiction is unquestioning and uncritical – what Dolowitz and Marsh (2000, p. 17) describe as 'uninformed transfer'. The point is that both capacity to invent and capacity to adopt seem to be encouraged by cognitive openness. That is, not only is the organization which is receptive to outside ideas more likely to accept diffusion, but such openness is likely to encourage innovation (Sparrow 1998).

Cases of policy transfer towards Congress or the House of Commons are hard to identify. But we can identify transfer from them. An obvious example of this would be the case of Australia, whose MPs were required to register their interests from 1984. The remit of the Australian Members' Interests Committee is lifted almost wholesale from that of its British counterpart (it differs by a mere three words). This points at the existence of an epistemic community of parliamentary officials and scholars enabling policy to be diffused between states. Australia has long been recognized as a social, cultural and political laboratory, but here we find it adopting a reform from elsewhere – some evidence pointing at Sparrow's argument.

Despite a tendency to concentrate on the 'copying', 'emulation' and 'borrowing' of policies, policy learning can be both positive and negative. A positive example would be the visit in 1989 by the British Members' Interests Committee to the USA and Canada on a fact-finding exercise. They came back impressed with the Canadian system for registering lobbyists and recommended that it be copied in Westminster, where prior and subsequent committees had and have concluded that it would not be possible to identify 'lobbying organizations' – a conclusion invariably reached in the isolation of a panelled room in central London (uninformed non-transfer). This stands in sharp contrast to a more pronounced culture of negative learning found in Westminster where there is a tendency to use the regulatory systems of the USA as a model to be avoided as a shining example of restrictive measures, excessive legalism, petty bureaucracy and undue formalism – a criticism supported by a burgeoning literature on the supposed 'ethics explosion' (Mackenzie 2002; Stark 2001).

Learning can also be inappropriate (Dolowitz and Marsh 2000, p. 17), and the adoption of disclosure requirements is possibly the clearest example of this. In both the UK and the USA there was a long-standing tradition of declaring relevant interests, considered a matter of personal etiquette, but in part inspired by the use of disclosure of interests by professionals such as lawyers in their dealings with clients. The use of disclosure in situations where an advisor has a conflict of interest allows clients to substitute their own judgements, even though this is problematic because it is not clear to what extent clients should 'discount' the advice given when the professional makes a declaration; and disclosure seems to give 'moral licence' to the discloser to no longer give impartial advice (Cain et al. 2005). As an instrument for ensuring legislative propriety, however, disclosure of conflicts of interests fails. The legislator is not proffering advice, but is taking action. There is an outside chance that disclosure will sharpen the MP's senses, making him or her alert to any distinction between their private interest and the public interest: in that sense, what matters is that the MP is disclosing their interest *to themselves*. But that alone will not make them resolve conflicts in favour of the latter. Possibly the MP will fear that by disclosing an interest they will open themselves to a public charge of being improperly motivated, but disclosure contains its own defence: if the legislator was doing anything wrong, he or she wouldn't have drawn attention to it, so by drawing attention to their interest, they show that they were not influenced by it. The corrupt but shameless or astute legislator can also avail themselves of this defence. The only people who might properly behave differently because a legislator discloses a conflict of interest are other legislators, but even here it is not clear how colleagues should and do respond to disclosures.[6] If the lesson taken from the professions is that disclosure of interests is a check on improper influence, then that lesson is (1) overstated, and (2) not relevant when principals (electors or the public) lack a means of control. In that respect, the learning is inappropriate.

We can explain why legislators should choose disclosure, even though it may not address the problem of conflict of interest, for the reasons adduced in the world of the innovation. What learning – whether positive or negative, appropriate or inappropriate – might explain is how such policies make it onto the agenda.

Turning to the enforcement mechanisms chosen, it is puzzling that it is the British House of Commons which moved away from a mainly internal system of regulation, to one using an independent regulator, while the USA, whose system already permits multiple points of entry, vested the main responsibility for regulating ethics in the chambers themselves. The answer to this puzzle is probably not to be found in the degree to which each branch in the USA needs to maintain its autonomy in defence of the separation of powers. The argument from the UK is not that powers have passed to the government – although a pro-Government bias is certainly a criticism that can be made of ethics regulation in the UK (Kaye 2003). Rather it is that the House of Commons – unlike Congress – has been willing to cede power to an independent agency in return for credibility: the classic explanation for independent regulatory agencies (Majone 1994).

Britain has long been characterized as the 'last bastion of self-regulation' (Baggot 1989, p. 435) resting on consensual styles of government (Vogel 1986). Was this development proof of Moran's thesis that traditional forms of club government (Moran 2003; Marquand 1988; Bogdanor 1997) were breaking down? It is difficult to apply Moran's thesis to regulation inside politics. For Moran, the 'grand systemic crisis' of club government of the 1970s provided an opportunity for elected politicians to intervene in previously self-regulating arenas. The parliamentary ethics reforms of the 1970s did indeed see politicians move into an area that had previously been left to individuals; but in doing so *within* the political establishment, club government was reinforced, not diminished. A stronger case can be made for the reforms of the 1990s, but even there the reforms were aimed at retaining self-regulation, a mode of regulation for which the Committee on Standards in Public Life has continually expressed a preference. Indeed the composition of the first Committee on Standards in Public Life, including a judge, three parliamentarians, one Professor, a former diplomat turned head of a Cambridge college, a former director of the Bank of England, and a former Clerk of the House of Commons – three knights, two Lords and a Dame – represented, in some respects, Club Britain.

In the case of the House of Commons, 'club government' never functioned effectively and the use of Select Committees as ethics bodies was particularly inappropriate.[7] First, Select Committees are appointed reflecting the party political composition of the House. Given the quasi-judicial nature of an ethics committee's work, there is no reason why party affiliation should be a relevant factor (although in practice it is a strong indicator of an individual member's behaviour: Kaye 2002). British politics has typically been marked by more strident partisanship than American politics, where the weakness of political parties, the importance of a local base, and parties that are internally more heterogeneous and comparatively more homogenous than the two main British parties, has enabled a bipartisan approach to ethics. Third, appointments to the Committee, although nominally made by the House itself, are gifts of the Whips, and there is good reason to believe that both main parties have abused this in order to secure a compliant committee (Kaye 2003). While the more multi-party composition of the House of Commons would have made it impossible and inappropriate simply to import the American model there were no real moves towards bipartisanship made until the late 1990s; these moves have included selecting the Chair from the opposition, and removing the Government's majority on the Committee. By the time that the system came under Nolan's scrutiny, the self-regulatory system was discredited – merely tinkering with composition along US lines would probably have been insufficient to command public support. Instead, Nolan, and Parliament, took a quantum leap in moving to what is substantially not a self-regulatory regime.

In contrast, the role of outsiders in the Congressional system is much more restricted. There is counsel to the Committee, and to the majority and minority leaders, and on occasion the House has appointed a Special Counsel to investigate complaints.[8] But this 'prosecutorial' model is very different to charging an outsider with acting as an ongoing regulator. The apparent juridification of the US process is quite in line with a 'national style of regulation' that stresses adherence to legal principles as opposed to a British preference for 'government by consent' (Vogel 1986, pp. 269–80). But in spite of this, the US Congress remains self-regulating; the House of Commons does not. The role of counsel in Washington is very much circumscribed – they aid the Committee, they do not substitute for it. A political process that allows multiple access points (Vogel 1986, p. 276) seems to have allowed the two houses of Congress to retain a large degree of control over their own affairs.

A further curiosity that arises is that the presence of institutional innovation in the UK confounds supply-side expectations based on the absence of institutional variety, specifically, that we should find more innovation in federal systems than unitary systems. Certainly it is true – if almost axiomatic – to say that we find more variety at the subnational level, and presumably this manifests in more innovation. For instance, Australian states have innovated considerably in the creation of specialized Commissions against Corruption (whose remits have included state legislators). But just as it is claimed that open, diverse organizations create opportunities for innovation (Sparrow 1998), federal systems should allow states to function as a policy laboratory (Volden 2003; cf. Sparer 1997). There is certainly variety to be found in Australia and Canada. We find some variety among the states of the USA. To that extent there is experimentation. But experimentation also requires that this variety is used to provide meaningful comparisons, and that lessons percolate up to inform wider policy. There is no evidence of this. Even the various Australian state corruption commissions have not percolated upwards. Variety does not seem to lead the national level to emulate, to learn from best practice, or to refine its systems.

By contrast, until recently there was no subnational level of government in the UK, and there is still no real regional government in England. There is, of course, local government, but this has been treated very much as an agency of national government. Conflict of interest provisions have been driven from the centre. Indeed, recent evidence suggests that where local initiatives do occur, they are vulnerable to the homogenizing tendencies of the centre. For instance, proposals from the Committee on Standards in Public Life to reinvigorate local government standards, with a measure of self-regulation were neutered, with councils required to include a Government-craft Model Code of Conduct, which could not be augmented, while central prescription about the composition of standards committees meant that councils had to drop experiments with purely lay bodies (Doig and Skelcher 2001).

Yet the UK House of Commons, without prompting from below, has shown an ability to innovate. The introduction of devolution in the UK has led to the aping of the Commons system by the devolved legislatures rather than vice versa. For instance, all now have some sort of ethics Commissioner reporting to the legislature, albeit tailored to take account of local circumstances.[9] Innovation, when it comes to regulating legislators, seems to be an endogenous process, uninformed by outside events or developments.

CONCLUSIONS

Where the regulation of legislators is concerned, innovation has not been led from the centre, nor from the top. Nor does there seem to have been very much learning from below. And in neither the UK nor the USA has there been very much learning from abroad. This almost seems to support the idea of ideas – including innovative ideas – as independent actors, which latch on to passing politicians, rather than being created by political agents. Given a suitable anti-innovative environment, innovation will be difficult. In an environment which is open to innovation, innovative ideas are more likely to prosper. The danger for legislative ethics is the extent to which existing players – who are both regulator and regulatee – have a vested interest in the *status quo*. What this means for the political process is that points of entry to a political system are less important than veto points: a political system which admits many veto-points is likely to be anti-innovation, one in which veto-players are limited and weak should have greater capacity for innovation. The patches of innovation identified in the American and British histories should be seen in the context of almost 40 years when ideas about how to regulate legislators tended to fail to take hold: sometimes they did not capture the media's imagination; other times they were rejected by legislative committees; still other times they foundered for want of government support. Innovation did occur, but it was the exception, not the norm.

Such an explanation would also help to explain the process of domestication which seems to occur when ideas are transplanted. So in the UK, the idea of an independent person to oversee standards was filtered through the existing models of the Comptroller and Auditor General (and finally squeezed into the straightjacket of a House of Commons clerk). Such a manoeuvre seems to have made the original idea more suitable for its environment. At the same time it has to be recognized that for this one innovation to succeed depended on a huge amount of contingency: a suitably high number of scandals, successful one-person ombudsmen, the discrediting of self-regulation and quangos, close parliamentary competition, a weak Prime Minister, a small parliamentary rebellion, a fatal miscalculation by the governing party. Events could easily have gone very differently.

If the success of ideas depends on them inhabiting a propitious environment, then innovative ideas are at an inherent disadvantage. Put simply, unless the environment changes then existing structures are advantaged. Even if the environment does change, then a successful innovation needs not only to be a suitable answer to the new *problem* but also needs to be capable of surviving a potentially hostile political process. In one respect, however, there is reason to be optimistic about the capacity of legislatures to innovate. Although legislatures might appear relatively closed cognitively, they are open to external penetration; that is, new people are elected to the legislature. This in turn means that there is a constantly changing environment and an idea which fails to take hold in one legislature might take hold in a later incarnation.

NOTES

1. 'Progressive' is meant here to indicate conformity with underlying historical trends, and specifically to exclude situations where moving from t_0 to t_1 involves a return to a state of affairs at t_{-1}
2. This, however, is now constrained. In 1992 Michigan passed what became the 27th Amendment to the US Constitution, which had languished mid-ratification since 1789 (Bernstein 1992). This amendment democratized Congressional pay by requiring that a Congressional election take place before any pay rise, or cut, could take place. This might perversely limit the scope for 'pay for ethics' type reforms, because it makes the first part, pay, so much harder to implement. Congressional pay increases were forgone in the first five years after the Amendment passed, and only reinstated when House leaders adopted a deliberate 'low-key' strategy of 'hiding' pay increases in Appropriations Bills. (http://www.washingtonpost.com/wp-srv/politics/special/pay/stories/co091497.htm)
3. See the Commissioner's Report into Keith Vaz (2001/02: HC 605, Appendix).
4. In this respect Nolan's definition of 'sleaze' as a 'pervasive atmosphere . . . in which sexual, financial, and governmental misconduct were indifferently linked' (Nolan 1995-I, p. 106) seems apposite.
5. 'Turning the crank' was a punishment in Victorian prisons in which prisoners sentenced to hard labour could be made to undertake physically exhausting but utterly pointless work turning a handle under pressure.
6. The evidence from one MP that MPs pay more attention to colleagues with private interests because they 'know what they are talking about' lends support to Cain et al.'s findings.
7. Select Committees composed of MPs, or joint committees of MPs and peers, can be traced back at least to the fifteenth century AD. The Privileges Committee (which later became merged into the Standards and Privileges Committee was the oldest, its function being to protect the House's privileges from outside interference (predominantly by the Crown, but also by the courts and later from improper influence by the media or trades unions). This Committee was also able to act where it appeared that the behaviour of MPs brought the House into disrepute, although ad hoc select committees were also occasionally formed to

investigate particular matters. In 1979 permanent Select Committees were set up to oversee each government department (Drewry 1985).

8. This was first done after Newt Gingrich argued that a conventional inquiry into the then Speaker Jim Wright required 'a higher standard of public accountability and integrity'. It was also done when Gingrich himself, a later Speaker, was investigated seven years later.

9. One example would be the Northern Ireland Ombudsman, who works part-time as the Standards Commissioner for the Northern Ireland Legislative Assembly.

4. Back to the future? Regulatory innovation and the railways in Britain and Germany

Martin Lodge

INTRODUCTION

Regulatory innovation is said to emerge from interaction with, and the influence of, often contradictory internal and environmental pressures (see Julia Black's introductory chapter; also D'Aunno et al. 1991; Thelen 1999; Thelen 2003, p. 211). Why are some pressures more important than others when it comes to the selection of policy templates as part of regulatory innovation? What type of standard operating procedures shape the way in which policy templates are selected, and how? Does the selection of policy templates point to a 'back to the future' effect in that there are noticeable continuities and proposals that continuously reappear or is there a linear progression of policy adjustment (see Abrahamson 1991)?

The diverse worlds of regulatory innovation have addressed these questions in a number of ways. This chapter draws on core arguments from three worlds of regulatory innovation and explores these claims by charting regulatory innovation in terms of institutional design in railways in two countries, Britain and Germany, at three distinctly critical historical junctures in the twentieth century: the age of the first attempts at nationalization in the post-First World War period, the age of the 'positive state' after the Second World War and the supposed age of the 'regulatory state' in the 1990s.

Railways are the 3G equivalent of the nineteenth century. They have been at the forefront of regulatory developments since the early-to-mid nineteenth century and have shaped wider economic policy as well as natural monopoly regulation (McLean and Foster 1992). Throughout the twentieth century, the railways were in relative decline, given competition from other modes of transport, thus requiring tricky political trade-offs between dealing with the railways' financial and economic difficulties and facing electoral demands for the continued high-level provision of railway services, very often regardless of actual usage. Regulatory innovation at these critical junctures (which are characterized by their 'openness' and supposedly rapid innovation when contrasted with longer periods of institutional reproduction (Thelen 2003, p. 209) was one of the key battlegrounds in disputes about how the two respective states were to relate to their national economies.

The literatures on the different worlds of regulatory innovation, as illustrated in Chapter 2, are likely to agree that policy domains are surrounded by competing policy environments that offer different, often contradictory, policy templates; they disagree when it comes to the processes that lead to the selection of certain templates instead of others. Without seeking to be exhaustive or mutually exclusive, this chapter explores three distinctive claims drawn from different worlds of regulatory innovation, namely those that concentrate on the worlds of 'the innovation', the 'organizational' and the 'state'.

One of the central claims of the 'world of the innovation' is that so-called 'paradigms' matter, i.e. particular ideas about certain cause–effect relationships as to how the economy is to be treated by governments (Hall 1993). The emergence of these 'paradigms', often a result of disappointment with previous assumptions about policy, is said to provoke bandwagon effects, leading to international policy diffusion across sectors and therefore growing policy similarity. This chapter investigates three time periods when such trends were said to be particularly strong. In the 1920s, the international trend was said to favour a 'convergence' across national railway systems, with 'private' railway systems moving towards closer state control, if not ownership, while 'state' railway systems were said to be moving towards more decentralized organizational forms (Witte 1932). In the post-Second World War world, the trend was said to encourage 'public corporations' (Robson 1962) and in the 1990s, an international trend was said to facilitate 'privatization' and the move away from a 'positive' to a 'regulatory state' (Majone 1997).

Among the core arguments in the 'organizational' world of regulatory innovation, successful innovation occurs when particular templates 'fit' with the logic of appropriateness or 'meaning system' of that organizational field (see Dobbin 1994, pp. 12–19). Relational networks are said to play a central role in diffusing collectively defined cultural understandings. Widely held beliefs and rules within a policy domain are claimed to influence organizational structures, regardless of resource dependency relationships or technologies. Accordingly, particular forms of regulatory innovation are likely to experience resistance (and failure) because they are seen as 'inappropriate' and alien to the inherent nature or 'taken for granted' policies of the railway domain (see Jensen 2003, pp. 524–5). Railways are often proclaimed to be 'special', particularly regarding their technical complexity. For example, in the 1990s and early 2000s many claimed that vertical separation (i.e. the separation of the service from the infrastructure provision) and private ownership of infrastructure were inherently inappropriate for the running of the railways while since the early 1990s regulatory innovation across Europe, not only in railways, increasingly moved towards a separation of these functions, with EC Directive 91/440 requiring the separation of these tasks at least in accounting terms.

One core claim of the 'state' world of regulatory innovation is that particular structures shape interaction patterns between state and societal actors, thereby influencing the type and direction of regulatory innovation. In a rational choice and functional perspective, Levy and Spiller (1996) suggest that diversity in political and economic institutions requires different institutional devices in order to allow for 'commitment', i.e. the safeguarding of private investment from expropriation by the state (see also Levy and Spiller 1994). More broadly, accounts drawing on the 'national innovation systems' literature (Freeman 1987, 1982; see also Kitschelt 1991; Hall and Soskice 2001; Nelson 1993; Werle 2003) in relation to technology as well as the 'national policy style' literature (Richardson 1982) have pointed to the mixture of formal and informal institutional effects in constraining and empowering particular actors, thereby leading to particular types of regulatory innovation.[1] A comparison of Britain and Germany contrasts two very different political and economic systems, the former being defined as a unitary and majoritarian political system and a liberal market economy state, the other as a cooperative federalist and coalition government with a coordinated market economy. At the same time, an investigation of time periods following two world wars should present a particularly tough case – given that Germany in both cases lacked formal sovereignty. For example, in the case of the 1920s, regulatory innovation emerged in the context of international reparation negotiations.

To explore these three worlds of regulatory innovation in more detail, this chapter first briefly examines regulatory innovation in the British and German railway systems at three critical junctures. During all three episodes, debates about how to innovate regulation in railways was linked to wider contemporary debates regarding the appropriate relationship between state and the national economy. The final section returns to the three worlds of regulatory innovation and considers to what extent they can account for the observed pattern in regulatory design across the two states and the three time periods.

THREE AGES OF REGULATORY INNOVATION IN RAILWAYS[2]

It is not difficult to find someone suggesting that regulatory innovation in the British railways in the 1990s hit the buffers. Authors outdo each other in proclaiming regulatory innovation in the railways in the last decade of the twentieth century as a 'fiasco', resulting from an ideology of high modernism (a policy approach that, according to Michael Moran, places a premium on pushing through radical policy measures with a minimum of preparation) that produced in the particular case of the British railways a 'great leap forward' type of policy-making which ended in the proverbial buffers (Moran 2003, pp. 177–8). Terry similarly enquired why policy had 'gone so wrong so disastrously' (Terry 2001, p. 4). In Germany, railway privatization also occurred in the early to mid-1990s, but privatization occurred only in legal form, did not establish an economic regulator and kept the incumbent as one entity. And while the British government introduced legislation to establish a new regulatory approach to the railways in late 2004, the German railways was engaged in an ongoing conflict with its owner, the federal government, umbrella business associations and federal parliamentarians about its preparations for the flotation of the operator on the stock exchange. Any flotation was, in late 2004, postponed by the federal government until 2009 (*Die Welt*, 26 November 2004).

In order to assess what type of design ideas were accepted and rejected, and to establish whether there was any genuine 'innovation', in the sense of there not being any recurring or specifically periodic reform themes or distinctly national innovation patterns, the following section briefly sets out the chronology of the three eras of regulatory innovation. Table 4.1 provides an overview of the chosen institutional arrangements. In line with the title of this chapter, this section begins with regulatory innovation in the 1990s and then considers the episodes of the 1920s and the 1940s.

Regulatory Innovation and the Age of Privatization

In Britain, interest in regulatory innovation in the railways domain emerged relatively late in comparison to other network industries. To some extent, this reflected political reluctance to deal with railway unions and, to some extent, it reflected the complexity of the industry, in particular the regulation of an industry that required continued financial subsidy for particular services that were politically too sensitive to be axed. Nevertheless, the 1993 Railway Act and, more importantly, subsequent developments leading to the transfer of the last passenger franchise just prior to the 1997 general election, represented arguably the culmination of regulatory reform experience in the British context and therefore justify classifying it as a truly regulatory innovation.

Political interest in a railway privatization emerged fully only after John Major had become prime minister. Different proposals were floated, ranging from British Rail's official preference, privatization as a single entity (although parts of British Rail were not averse to a privatization along 'business sector' lines, a reform that had been initiated within British Rail in the late 1980s (Gourvish 1990), the preference by the Department of Transport for a privatization of vertically integrated, commercially viable business sectors,

Table 4.1 *Regulatory innovation and regulatory institutions in the railways*

	1990s		Post-First World War years		Post-Second World War years	
	Britain	*Germany*	*Britain*	*Germany*	*Britain*	*Germany*
Basic conflict	Type of industry reorganization	Extent of organizational fragmentation and ownership status	Railways as an essential part of post-war reconstruction	Maintenance of domestic autonomy over rate-setting	Design of public corporation to ensure economic efficiency	Federal ministerial control over railway operator
Organizational structure	Fragmentation of the industry, split between private infrastructure provider, passenger service franchises, freight services and rolling stock companies	Holding company with internal vertical and horizontal separation	Amalgamation into four railway companies	*Sondervermögen* with director-general	Public corporation operating as part of British Transport Commission	*Sondervermögen* with executive committee

Allocation of regulatory authority	Economic regulation with Office of the Rail Regulator, service regulation with Franchising Director, safety with Railway Inspectorate at the HSE	No economic regulator, *ex post* control via Federal Cartel Office, safety and technical supervision via Eisenbahn Bundesamt	Ministry of Transport, Railway and Canal Commission, Railway Rates Commission	Ministry of Transport, International Railway Commissioner, International arbitrator, tribunal for domestic conflicts	Ministry of Transport, Transport Tribunal	Federal Ministry of Transport and Supervisory Board
Public services	Franchising of passenger services	Regionalization and franchising	Rejection of development fund	DRG objective to serve the national economy	Debate how transport services can be made financially self-sufficient	Federal and *Land* powers to veto line closures with limited compensation arrangements

such as the long-distance passenger operations, and those of the Treasury that favoured a vertical separation of infrastructure and transport services as well as an extensive fragmentation of the industry. The Treasury's view was shaped by prior experience in the privatization and regulation of network industries, including the diagnosis that structural solutions to introduce competition were to be preferred over regulatory activity in achieving efficiency gains, and further shaped by sensitivity to criticism that previous privatizations had achieved too little financial return for the state. Although some commitment to the Treasury's preferred policy option had been reached prior to the 1992 general election, serious consideration concerning the regulatory design of the privatized railways only began after the Conservative Party's election victory. Despite some attempts, on the grounds of 'saleability' to the wider electorate, to favour a vertically integrated structure on the lines of the 1920s British railway system (discussed below), the Treasury view eventually succeeded.

The 1993 Railways Act signalled, cautiously, the creation of a vertically integrated railway structure, initially, however, within British Rail. A franchising system was to allow for the provision of non-commercial services, while an economic regulator was to assess access to the infrastructure. In terms of timing, only after the transfer of all passenger franchises was the privatization of the railway infrastructure, Railtrack, to take place. However, political considerations, in particular the administrative desire to 'hardwire' the regulatory regime prior to a general election (due to be held by 1997), meant that the intended policies were amended: Railtrack was privatized before the franchises had been let; the intended open-access regime was compromised in order to reduce payments to the franchise operators; instead of a sale to a number of parties, the rail freight industry was sold to a single operator; the sale of the rolling stock companies was criticized for its low sale price; and the rail regulator's functions overlapped with those of the Franchising Director, as the latter's authority had been carved out of the initial blueprints for the regulatory office and designed as a 'creature of government' to be told 'what to do' and to sell and then later monitor the passenger railway franchises. The overlap and the partly contradictory objectives between these two offices led to continuous fights over responsibilities. Overall, the industry had been substantially fragmented, not only in its core businesses and regulatory functions, but also in its subsidiary businesses, such as maintenance companies.

Although occurring at roughly the same time and under the same European legislation (Directive 91/440), the privatization of the (West) German railway, the Deutsche Bundesbahn, followed different policy priorities. Initial demands for reform of the (West) German Bundesbahn emerged from the operator itself that demanded a debt refinancing and a vertical separation of its accounts (while undertaking a 'divisionalization' that coincided, but did not represent a read-across from the simultaneous organizational reforms by British Rail during the 1980s). The then opposition Social Democrat and Green parties as well as business associations made similar demands.

In January 1989, the government decided to set up a 'commission' that would investigate ways to make the Bundesbahn more 'competitive' while reducing the threat to the federal budget from the Bundesbahn's debts. Unification in 1990 meant that the unification of railway operators became a further priority (which reinforced the political interest in proposals that potentially reduced the federal government's exposure to the railways' financial demands). The 'commission' lacked any 'psychological predisposition' to any particular policy template and was also uncertain of its potential in setting the agenda for regulatory innovation. In its final report of 1991, the commission proposed the vertical separation of the railways operations under (at least temporarily) a holding company (not unlike the British Rail of the immediate period after the 1993 Railways Act) and the regionalization of regional and local passenger services. These services were to be franchised by the *Länder* (which received a block payment from the federal government for these services). The idea of a sectoral regulator was rejected (*ex post* control was to be exerted by the Federal Cartel Office). A supervisory authority, the Eisenbahn Bundesamt, dealing with safety and technical aspects, was established (activities previously regulated by the Bundesbahn itself).

The federal government accepted these suggestions, in particular the proposal to establish the railways as a limited company. As this required an amendment to the federal constitution, subsequent modifications to the reform proposals were mostly motivated to secure the extra-large two-third majorities among federal parliamentarians and *Land* governments. Thus, the 'new' Article 87 in the Basic Law established that railway administration was the responsibility of the federal government, restricted however to the oversight of legality and, more importantly, the provision of infrastructure. Furthermore, besides the watering-down of proposals that would have fixed a transition period for the separation of rail freight, long-distance passenger and local-passenger services as well as infrastructure and stations by dissolving the overarching holding company into an indeterminate intention, a provision was inserted that constitutionally hardwired a requirement that the federal government was to maintain majority ownership over the infrastructure operator. Far from selling any shares, initially (and until the time of completing this book in late 2004), privatization meant a transfer in legal status, but, unlike the British case, no transfer to the private sector (although some regional and even long-distance services were provided by private operators, most prominently, Connex, which also operated in Britain).

The comparison of the two episodes of regulatory innovation in the age of privatization points to some similarities at one level, but also considerable variety in terms of the way in which the industry was structured, the way in which regulatory authority was allocated and in terms of different approaches towards privatization. At first sight, these differences seem to support many of the claims in the different worlds of regulatory innovation literatures, ranging from those that stress the more wholehearted endorsement of the 'neoliberal' paradigm in Britain than in Germany in the last two decades of the twentieth century and the difference between Britain as the 'fastest law in the West' (Dunleavy 1995) to the German 'gridlock' state in affecting the extent to which regulatory innovation could take place. Innovation was informed, in the British case, by experience of the regulation of network industries; in contrast, in the German case, the railways were regarded as a transport domain, with no reading across from other domestic sectors, such as telecommunications (see Lodge 2003).

While these initial observations will be further discussed below, such claims need also to be considered in the light of two further questions. First, were these diagnosed patterns of 'radical' British versus German 'incremental' change typical for these two states across time? Second, were those issues that were diagnosed as 'radical' new to the railway domain in the 1990s or had they been part of contests between templates for regulatory innovation in early time periods?

Regulatory Innovation and the First Age of Nationalization

As already noted, the regulatory approach of the 1920s briefly returned to the policy debate during the negotiations over the British privatization of the 1990s, as part of an attempt by the prime minister, John Major, and his personal policy advisors to make the overall policy more 'saleable' to the wider electorate by referring to a 'golden age' of the railways. Regulatory innovation following World War I led to a 'nationalization' of British railway policy, in the sense of the setting up of a national Ministry of Transport and moving away from a largely oligopolistic industry towards the eventual creation of four regional monopolies. Similar to the four 'great' railway companies that were temporarily advocated as a template for railway privatization in Britain in the 1990s, the 1924 Deutsche Reichsbahn Gesellschaft (DRG) law has continued to attract substantial enthusiasm within German academic circles. In certain ways, railway privatization of the 1990s was said to bring the German railways back into the future of the 1920s law (see, for example, Fromm 1994). However, a closer analysis does not suggest that the 1924 law represented the emergence of a commercially autonomous operator or that the law emerged as part of the Versailles 'Diktat', as was often argued in the German literature of that period (see Heiber 1981, p. 157; Kolb 1999, pp. 114–15).

In Britain, regulatory innovation during the post-First World War period was mostly a history of defeat for proposals for more far-reaching regulatory innovation. Given the pre-war financial decline of the industry, its market concentration, its economic and financial position due to the so-called trading interest's veto against outright mergers,[3] the extensive wartime demands on the industry, and the positive experience of co-ordinated railway management during the war, a consensus existed that some form of state involvement was inevitable (and which had started to emerge even prior to the war), ranging from trade unions (organized in the Railway Nationalization Society), business (hoping for lower rates) and academics, such as Sir William Acworth (of the London School of Economics), who had previously opposed any major form of state involvement in the railways.

While there was little contestation regarding the notion of enhanced state involvement, there was substantial disagreement regarding the degree of that involvement. Initial proposals, inspired by the, at the time, strong support from the prime minister Lloyd George (see Abrams 1963) and put forward by the eventual transport minister and former railway manager, Eric Geddes, reflected a view that the railways should play an active part in the reconstruction effort that would see the emergence of well-connected 'garden cities' which would alleviate problems of urban squalor.[4] Organizationally, this involved, for example, the inclusion of organized labour in the management of the railways (in a so-called Joint Industrial Council). Initial drafts of the 1919 Ministry of Ways and Communications Bill included clauses that provided for the taking into ownership of railway operators whose operation was then to be delegated to third parties (Geddes could 'not conceive of anything more disastrous' than direct ministerial control[5]). Among the powers of the proposed ministry were, apart from the railways themselves, all modes of transport (harbours, docks) as well as electricity. The railways were to promote agricultural and housing development as well as industry through preferential rates. A central ministry was to take a strategic and activist role, particularly in dealing with what was perceived to be the inefficient industrial and social conditions in which the railways operated, including powers to construct, manage and maintain railways as well as being able to authorize rates and determine employment conditions and wages. Put differently, the role of the ministry was to move from the traditional functions of 'criticism, regulation, conciliation and arbitration' to the 'inspiration and control of the development of a public sector . . . in all methods of commercial movement'.[6]

However, rival approaches, led by 'deflationatory interests', especially the Board of Trade and the Treasury, succeeded in dismantling these initial proposals in the legislative process. It scaled down the powers of the ministry considerably by reducing its authority to covering railways alone, eliminated powers to take railway companies into state ownership and the initial name, reflecting the reduction in powers, was altered from Ministry of Ways and Communications to Ministry of Transport.

The subsequent negotiations on the 1921 Railways Act that closely involved the railway companies' industry association, the RCA, and the Ministry of Transport, did not involve such disparate sources of ideas for regulatory innovation. State ownership was not considered, as Geddes regarded state ownership as 'corrupting', whereas a regulatory arrangement would allow the government 'to exercise all the powers we require'.[7] Amalgamation of the different companies into seven companies (eventually resulting in the creation of four railway operators) was to allow for 'economical working' that would avoid the 'illusory benefits' of 'wasteful competition'.[8] In terms of regulatory authority, there was an overall fragmentation of authority in order to avoid political influence over rate-setting. The Ministry of Transport was provided with powers of standardization and co-operation. These powers were, however, checked by review powers of the Railway and Canal Commission. In addition, a Railway Rates Commission was established to monitor rates and establish classification schemes for merchandise. A further example for the disappearance of the 'reconstruction' ideas of the immediate post-war period was the rejection of the idea of establishing a 'development fund' that would utilize surplus profits for the development of infrastructure in less well-connected regions.

In sum, the example of the 1919 and 1921 Acts suggests a considerable amount of regulatory innovation, in terms of amalgamating railway companies and the creation of a national ministry of transport. However, in contrast to the initial proposals, the two Acts represented rather cautious developments that reflected mostly existing tendencies within the industry in that restructuring costs were minimized. Alternative ideas concerning regulatory innovation were rejected by the increasingly dominant 'anti-waste' and deflationary interest within the British government that vetoed the original proposals, and by the initially insulated group of former railway managers, led by Geddes.

Nationalization in the German case included a move from a mixture of ownership patterns at the state level to Reich ownership (a move that had been highly contested and vetoed since the foundation of the German Reich in 1871) mainly as a consequence of the deteriorating revenue position of the respective states and the run-down post-war condition of railway operations; nevertheless, larger states, in particular Bavaria, sought to maximize their discretion over regional railway policy. The railways were to be run as a *Sondervermögen* (special property), i.e. as a supposedly autonomous commercial undertaking in Reich ownership (as prescribed in Article 89 of the Weimar constitution) which was to finance its own expenditures and its debt repayments. The Ministry of Transport took control of the railways in May 1920. Modelled on the Prussian Ministry of Public Works, from which it also took most of its staff (Mierzejewski 1999, p. 23), it became the world's largest enterprise, as well as Germany's biggest employer and largest procurer of industrial products.

Economic and political turmoil in the early years of the Weimar Republic, as well as the negotiations with the victorious states on the extent of reparation payments, resulted in considerable debate about the appropriate regulatory framework for the Reichsbahn. Regulatory innovation occurred in the context of mainly financial considerations. Following the government's request for financial support from industrial circles to cover reparation payments, business interests demanded a reorganization of the railways on a corporatist basis (as a *gemeinwirtschaftliches Unternehmen*) in order to fulfil their 'commonweal' function. This function was to include a prioritization of German economic interests, while allowing for 'efficiency gains' of private rather than public ownership. In addition, the role of the Reich ministry was to be restricted to that of safety and overall transport policy. In contrast, the Reich transport ministry advocated continuing Reich ownership, given that it was better able to 'make sacrifices', while entrepreneurship rather than legal form was said to offer the key for better operational performance. During the period of hyperinflation in 1923, the finance ministry stopped all financial support to the Reichsbahn and declared it autonomous. A subsequent *Verordnung* established the Reichsbahn as an independent commercial undertaking with its own legal personality, although not as a special property. The Reichsbahn remained in Reich ownership and administration, with the minister maintaining his supervisory and leadership functions over it.

International reparation negotiations added further pressure for particular forms of regulatory innovation (compatible with the preferences of the Reich finance ministry), demanding an increased distancing of the railway operator from the Reich government. The so-called Dawes Commission had been set up to establish the extent and conditions for reparation payments. As Paragraph 248 of the Versailles Treaty had made all publicly owned enterprises liable for reparation payments, the Reichsbahn became an immediate target for international reparation payment demands – although the Reich government itself had offered the use of Reichsbahn receipts for reparation payments in 1923. A special committee, constituted by the international railway experts Sir William Acworth and Gaston Leverve, was to establish the details of the reparation regime as applied to the Reichsbahn. The two experts asserted that the Reich government was mostly to blame for the poor performance of the railways. It was claimed that the Reichsbahn would be profitable as a profit-maximizing and expenditure-minimizing joint stock company. However, they also noted that 'we do not believe that any German administration will have the necessary strength to battle successfully against the traditional predisposition, unless there is a permanent pressure exerted by an expert, established and maintained by the Allies in their own interest in order to supervise the management with regard to rates and expenditures'.[9] Such a view was strongly contested by German experts, who emphasized that rate-setting had to remain in purely national hands, regardless of ownership.

The eventual 1924 law emerged therefore in a context of international negotiations that saw considerable compromise in favour of German interests. The 1924 Law established the Deutsche Reichsbahn Gesellschaft (DRG), headed by a Director-General, with regulatory control fully separated from the operational and managerial functions. The railways remained in Reich owner-ship as a special body of public law with some private law applications. While the Reich government had the right to appoint nine of the 18 administrative board members (unless an inability to pay reparations forced it to sell shares), the transport minister's authority was restricted to so-called *hoheitliche Funktionen* (sovereign functions) that included technical and safety regula-tion. An independent international commissioner was to act as a regulator, operating as a potential counterbalance against the perceived 'statist predispo-sitions' of German civil servants. The international commissioner's powers, less extensive than initially envisaged by Acworth and Leverve, were limited to those of an observer without voting rights but with full access to informa-tion. The commissioner was only enabled to exercise powers, ranging from the restriction of expenditures to the taking-over of the Reichsbahn management in cases of non-payment of reparations. A separate 'international arbitrator' was to deal with conflicts between Germany and the allied states over repara-tion payments as such, while a special railway tribunal was to resolve conflicts between the DRG and the Reich government.

However, despite the widespread praise in the late twentieth century for the 1924 law's extent of regulatory innovation (also said to have provoked signif-icant procedural innovations, for example, in terms of locomotive repairs, vehicle maintenance and the introduction of technologies, such as brake-systems, but, because of its high cost, not electrification), there were also significant examples of continuity in terms of the German understanding of the railway system. The railways were, according to the law, to have 'due regard' to the German national economic interest despite their autonomy, the government could request rate reductions as long as they did not threaten repa-ration payments and the DRG was to maintain equipment that represented the 'state of the art'.

Regulatory Innovation and the Age of the 'Positive State'

If the 1920s have been widely regarded as a golden period of railway regula-tion, the innovation of the 1940s were generally held, from the perspective of the innovators of the 1990s in both Britain and Germany, to be the dark ages.

In the British case, regulatory innovation, hailed by William Robson (1962, p. 95) as embodying 'the most grandiose scheme of nationalisation so far witnessed in Britain', was defined by the creation of a single publicly owned monopoly in the form of a public corporation. The main benefit was seen to lie in the co-ordination of different modes of transport, given also the poor financial state of the railway operators, especially due to the rise of unlicensed road haulage (Aldcroft 1968, pp. 105–6; Tivey 1973, p. 50; Tivey 1982; Foster 1992, p. 73). The subsequent debate centred on the extent to which the eventual public corporation was to become an instrument of government or a largely autonomous and commercially oriented organization. In the German case, the 1951 Bundesbahn Law was mainly a reaction to the 1924 Law, which was widely seen as having provided the Reichsbahn with too much organizational autonomy.

In the context of the application of the 'public corporation' idea in the interwar period and the absence of any major advocacy that the railways should play a role in 'reconstruction' (as had happened, as noted above, in the interwar period), discussions about the appropriate design of the regulation of the railways had already emerged during the war and had taken little note of the wider debates regarding public ownership. In July 1943, the permanent secretary at the Ministry of War Transport, Sir Cyril Hurcomb, noted that a 'definite view' had to be taken with regard to the railways in order to avoid 'competitive chaos'.[10] This provoked proposals ranging from the vertical separation of the railways (with the railway infrastructure being taken into ownership by the state) to the creation of a publicly-owned monopoly. While Labour Party and Trades Union Congress proposals advocated a 'public corporation' model, the ministry at the time was sympathetic to a 'clearing house' model which would see a central organization setting rates and allocating traffic. The railway industry was, naturally, opposed to being nationalized, but argued that any return to the pre-war age of regulation was financially nonviable. One proposal was therefore to split the running of services from track operations, with the latter to be run by the government.[11]

Once the newly elected Labour government had decided that the railways should be taken into public ownership under a 'unified financial machinery' for 'central direction of policy', contestation over different ideas concerning regulatory design focused on the extent of power the corporation should have *vis-à-vis* the minister, the allocation of regulatory authority, and the co-ordination of different modes of transport. The minister, Alfred Barnes, decided to rename the 'National Transport Authority' into 'National Transport Commission' (and subsequently the British Transport Commission, BTC), in order to signal a lesser degree of independence from political discretion, as 'commissions' were seen to act as agents of the minister, following the minister's general directions. Furthermore, the BTC was to be vested with the transport industries' assets and be responsible for the co-ordination and controlling of the operating executives. In order to avoid disruption, these operating boards were structured on a modal basis, despite arguments that these boards should operate on a regional, cross-modal basis.

Similar tensions emerged in the allocation of regulatory authority. Great emphasis was placed on restricting the ability of ministerial interference to issues of general policy – and appointments. Morrison, in a policy document, noted that ministries' functions were to be reduced to those of supervision and regulation, while boards were to act 'professionally' – or, as expressed elsewhere, as 'high custodians of the public interest' (Morrison 1933, pp. 156–7). A comparable emphasis on arrangements that were supposed to prevent political considerations was guiding the creation of rate-setting arrangements. A Transport Tribunal replaced the Railway Rates Tribunal and the Railway and Canal Commission was to monitor and apply rates set initially by the BTC. The absence of any interest – very much in contrast to the ideas of the 1920s – in a major integrated transport policy was also evident in the debate regarding the licensing of road haulage, in particular over so-called C-licences for short-distance traffic (up to 40 miles). A proposal to regulate these services was eventually dropped.

Thus, what is widely criticized as a regulatory innovation that paid too little attention to the specification of regulatory objectives, the extent of public control and the reliance on informal relations and trust as main regulatory techniques (Majone 1996, pp. 11–5) was characterized by considerable debate regarding exactly those issues. Moreover, regulatory innovation was largely oriented towards the transport domain, rather than seeking a 'read across' from other socialized industries, that also prioritized economic efficiency considerations.

In contrast to regulatory innovation in Britain, with its underlying assumption that socialization would promote efficiency, the German 1951 Bundesbahn Law sought to prevent a return to the formal degree of autonomy of the 1924 Law by maintaining the principles of a railway law of 1937 which had *de jure* made the railways part of the Reich government.[12] In contrast, some actors, including the French administrative zone and, from 1949 onwards, North Rhine-Westphalia,[13] sought a return to the 1924 law. Their proposals sought to strengthen the operational autonomy of the operator *vis-à-vis* the federal ministry, the latter's task being limited to 'classical sovereign tasks'.[14] The conflict over the degree of operational autonomy was particularly evident in a battle over the legal interpretation of Article 87 that defined the railways as part of the federal administration. Whereas the federal Ministry of Transport stressed that this clause ruled out any form of delegation, given the implied extent of ministerial accountability, North Rhine-Westphalia (and railway officials) regarded the clause as merely establishing federal rather than subnational competence for railways.[15] Particular disagreement emerged with regard to the extent to which the railways were to be made to perform *commonweal* functions. Similar conflict divisions were replicated across the differing types of advice that were received from the various national and international railway experts.

These debates to a large extent reflected the various parties' interest in ensuring institutional access to decision-making, given the perceived importance of rail infrastructure development and rate-setting for regional economies, and they were carried through into the eventual law. While the *Bundesbahn* was established as a *Sondervermögen* with budgetary and relative operational autonomy and independent borrowing powers on capital markets, its decision-making was checked by an administrative board (constituted of members from the *Länder*, the trade unions, business and 'free' appointments) that took final decisions in politically sensitive areas, such as major expenditures, economic planning and rate-setting. However, the federal minister of transport was granted veto powers. Such a structure was seen as a substantial move away from the proposed 'presidential' structure that had characterized the 1924 DRG and that was perceived to have granted the DRG too much personalized autonomy.

Regulatory innovation as a compromise between competing institutional interests was also evident in the allocation of regulatory authority. The federal transport minister was granted the right to give 'common ministerial directions' and to enforce 'political imperatives' regarding transport policy in general, business, finance and social policy, including the 'ability' to 'co-ordinate' the various means of transport to establish 'harmony', and to ensure health and safety as well as technological development. The *Länder* had veto powers over proposed line closures (which were not matched by financial responsibilities). The rate-setting machinery similarly sought to ensure that the Bundesbahn was to promote the interests of the wider economy. Rate-setting was therefore defined as part of the 'classical sovereign tasks' which included the federal ministerial right to impose rates on the Bundesbahn with only limited compensation rights being granted to the operator.

RECONSIDERING WORLDS OF REGULATORY INNOVATION

Having briefly set out the history of regulatory innovation at three critical junctures, this section discusses to what extent the claims of the different literatures on regulatory innovation 'fit' with the observed regulatory innovation in the three episodes in the two countries.

The World 'of the Innovation': did Paradigms Matter?

As noted at the outset, according to this type of explanation international policy trends are said to lead to narrowing differences ('convergence') or, in the case of existing similar starting points, similar policy tendencies across states. At the same time, these paradigms would originate as a consequence of continued disappointment with the previous policy approaches. Regulatory innovation in all three periods could to some extent be seen as examples of 'narrowing differences' between countries.

In the inter-war period, the two countries moved from different starting points – in Britain, an oligopolistic private railway industry, in Germany, a partly (sub-national) state-owned, and partly private-owned railway industry – to 'nationalized' railway regulation in terms of creating national ministries of transport. As contemporary observers suggested (Witte 1932), these developments represented a convergence of approaches – from commercial towards greater state regulation (Britain) and from state administration towards greater delegation and commercialization (Germany). Similarly, regulatory innovation following World War II revealed substantial similarities. In both countries, the operators were organized as state-owned monopolies, with the national transport ministry acting as the regulatory authority. Finally, in the 1990s, both countries witnessed 'privatization'. Regulatory authorities were established (albeit with different remits) and market-type instruments (franchising) were used for the procurement of subsidized services (a requirement that related to EU obligations). In both countries, the railways were privatized at least in legal form.

However, at a more detailed level, the three episodes appear more as a case of a joint language of regulatory innovation divided by different policy assumptions. Across all three eras, the common regulatory themes offered only a 'limited number of accepted truths' as Norman Chester suggested in the specific case of the socialization of the British railways in 1947 (Chester 1974, p. 44). In the inter-war period, apart from 'nationalization', there was little similarity. In Britain, four private regional monopolies were established, whereas in Germany a formally autonomous operator under Reich ownership was created. Different motivations and policy environments guided regulatory innovation; the British examples – the 1919 Ministry of Transport Act and the 1921 Railways Act – represented cases of a rejection of initial proposals that placed the railways at the heart of an activist economic policy of 'reconstruction'. In the German case, the regulatory regime for the Deutsche Reichsbahn Gesellschaft represented a compromise between interests in the Reich government that sought to continue the 'commonweal' function of the railways and an international policy environment, represented by the two railway experts William Acworth and Gaston Leverve, who demanded a more commercial orientation of the operator.

In the post-Second World War period, regulatory innovation differed considerably in both their degree and their objectives. In Britain, reliance was placed on informal relations between the minister and the chairperson of the public corporation. The need to maximize delegation and commercial orientation of the operator were stressed, a requirement furthered by the addition of the Transport Tribunal to provide an extra safeguard against ministerial intervention. In short, 'socialization' was to enhance the efficiency of the operator. In Germany, in contrast, regulatory debates concentrated on how to maximize leverage (by both federal and *Land* governments) over the economic behaviour of the operator. In contrast to the informality of the British approach, the regime relied on a formal allocation of roles and legal competencies. Finally, the 'privatization' era was also marked by distinct differences. In Britain, regulatory innovation was based on previous experience with the privatization and regulation of utilities, whereas in Germany, privatization meant a (at least temporary) continuation of public ownership under public law with the explicit objective of increasing the competitiveness of the railway sector.

An argument that largely relies on disappointment effects in driving regulatory innovation, either in an 'arrow' fashion or in terms of 'pendulum swings' (Hirschman 1982), also receives only mixed support. At all three critical junctures, it was widely argued that any return to the default position was not financially viable for railway operations. Nevertheless, despite the non-viability of a return to state-run railway systems, the initial 'nationalization' of the German railways was far more a 'carrying over' than a 'rejection' in that the Prussian ministry was simply relabelled as the Reich ministry. In the case of the 1951 Bundesbahn Law it was only the federal Ministry of Transport and a number of railway experts that explicitly rejected the 1924 law establishing the Deutsche Reichsbahn Gesellschaft for granting the operator too high a degree of operational autonomy. However, this rejection was far from universal. The British 1993 Railway Act was mostly a response to utility regulation of the previous decades (which arguably moved in an 'arrow' fashion in increasingly applying principles of industry fragmentation to the privatization of network industries) and less a response to diagnosed failings of a monopolist. In addition, the contests of policy templates at each critical juncture also highlight that the diagnosed patterns of regulatory innovation were more differentiated than a simple 'pendulum swing' analysis would suggest.

In sum, while at some level, there is some mileage in the claim that particular economic paradigms affected the way in which the two states' railway systems were nationalized or privatized, closer analysis exposes considerable differences that hardly support an understanding of an international policy bandwagoning effect of anything but broad labels.

Findings that point to contestability of policy templates and an absence of 'narrowing difference' at any deep level also throw some light on claims about

the supposed 'rise' of the regulatory state in Western Europe as a major innovation of the late twentieth century. Across all three time periods, there were
substantial debates regarding the appropriate regulation of the railway domain,
in terms of industry organization, the allocation of regulatory authority and the
provision of non-commercial services. Demands that ministries should be
merely supervisory or regulatory occurred in Germany and Britain in the
1920s, 1940s and 1990s, and administrative agencies charged with aspects of
safety, but also with economic regulation, were not unfamiliar to the British
administration. Even if one were to accept the historical peculiarity of the
1990s, the different national (and sectoral) understandings of regulation and of
the appropriate role of economic regulation suggested that there was very little
that unified the different national experiences that would suggest a single type
or 'age' of the regulatory state that suddenly emerged in the last quarter of the
twentieth century.

The 'Organizational' World of Regulatory Innovation: did Sectoral Ideas Matter?

One core claim of the organizational world of regulatory innovation is that
innovation is successful if it fulfils a certain sectoral logic of appropriateness.
Accordingly, there should be an interest in applying 'railway' templates rather
than other policy templates, either over time or over space, given their perception as being successful or legitimate.

Despite the evident existence of a 'railway profession' and diplomatic visi-
tations of other countries' railway industries in the 1920s – and widespread
support for the Japanese railways in the British case of the late twentieth
century following the 1993 Act (as an example of a punctual railway that was
organized on a vertically integrated basis), there was little evidence that at any
of the three critical junctures there was a particular idea about how 'railways'
as such should be regulated.

The argument that the railways, as an inherently technically complex
system, require the integration of infrastructure and track services is one of
those key ideas that are often promoted as an inherently 'appropriate' policy
template for the railways. In contemporary times, it was suggested (especially
by the incumbents) that the complexity of railway technology, in particular the
interplay between locomotive and track, signalling systems and the like,
required an integrated organization. Thus, vertical integration was argued to be
'natural' to the railways – and the example of Japan, with its vertically integrated railways was used as a case of a successful example (and, if one was to
believe a private consultancy report produced for the Deutsche Bahn, a further
successful example of a vertically integrated railways was the United States).
Regardless of the validity of such comparison (both Britain and Germany were

characterized by an inter-running of services over different tracks that was not the case in Japan (or the USA)) such claims of the 'unnaturalness' of vertical separation of track and services seem less persuasive when considering the historical record. In Germany, the Bundesbahn was actively proposing the idea of vertical separation from at least the 1980s, whereas in the British case, railway companies floated the vertical separation idea during and after the Second World War in order to prevent full-scale nationalization. Across time and countries, the argument that road traffic did not have to pay for its infrastructure in contrast to the railways was used to advocate some form of separation (although usually in the combination of state-owned infrastructures and commercially autonomous services). In the 1990s, this argument was supplemented by the idea that infrastructure and rolling stock investments appealed to very different financial market products given the different duration of expected financial return (opponents of privately owned infrastructures suggested that financial markets were biased against providing sufficient resources for long-term investments in essential infrastructures, given their emphasis on short-term returns).

While the idea of railways as a naturally integrated industry seems therefore less persuasive in the light of historical debates, there was also very little evidence of cross-national sectoral awareness. In the British post-war cases there was no evidence of any interest in 'lesson drawing' from other jurisdictions. In contrast, in the 1990s, some comparisons were made. However, these qualified at best as 'awareness raising' as the widespread attitude across British officials and politicians was that the British railways were at the spearhead of regulatory and organizational reform and therefore had very little to gain from explicit comparison. In contrast, the German cases of the 1920s and 1990s offered evidence of attempts at cross-national comparison. In the 1920s case this was restricted to receiving information from German embassies and these experiences were filtered to suit the domestic policy preference – for example, the British 1921 Act was interpreted as a first step to state ownership. Similarly, in the 1990s, there was both academic and ministry interest in international railway reforms. The Japanese reforms were used as an illustration of similar institutional processes for the consideration of policy options (although the idea of a Commission had been widespread in Germany in the past in order to establish a technocratic consensus without any political commitment by the government, commissions were nonetheless seen as government attempts to reduce the veto-power of parliaments and bureaucracies); the Swedish case was also examined in terms of its approach towards vertical separation. However, that experience, in particular the fact that the infrastructure was owned by the state, was actively rejected. Instead, regulatory innovation emerged largely from domestic policy preferences.[16]

In sum, this suggests that certain taken-for-granted assumptions about

policy sectors should be considered with extreme caution. As in numerous
other areas of public policy, many supposedly long-standing traditions are of
rather recent incarnation, allowing for the selective drawing on historical and
cross-national examples. At least this limited area of railways in two countries
in three time periods, regulatory innovation was not determined by particular
sectoral assumptions as to how to regulate the railways.

To What Extent did the 'State' World of Regulatory Innovation Matter?

As noted at the outset, the 'state' world is associated with three claims, namely
the impact on regulatory innovation of state structures, of national 'styles' and
of distinct institutional mechanisms. The 'national style' of innovation explanation to some extent coincides with a sectoral idea account (especially in a
non-cross-domain study such as this), the main difference being that national
style accounts usually rely on an interaction between sectoral and national
governance patterns which establish the commonalities across policy domains
(see Kitschelt 1991, 1994).

Turning to state structures first, the German case seems to confirm to some
extent the importance of institutional structures. The political institutional
system generated federal as well as corporatist policy-making patterns that,
usually, included 'experts' across all three time periods, even at times of non-
sovereignty following world wars. In contrast, against expectations, the
British cases seem to be either unrepresentative or to motivate further probing
into the accuracy of the argument that its political system generates strong
unitary government which facilitates rapid policy change and adversarial politics. The inter-war government that was responsible for the 1919 and 1921
legislation was weak, leading to corporatist and bureaucratic decision-making
patterns with little party-political input. Some elements of party-politics were
evident in the British privatization case, but these were driven mainly by a
weak government that sought to make policy reversal as difficult as possible.
However, while these macro-institutional decision-making rules provided for
opportunity structures for different actors, they, at best, facilitated certain
types of regulatory innovation rather than others, but did not explain why. For
example, Christoph Knill (1999, 2001, p. 94), in an argument that follows
well-known claims about weak and strong states, has suggested that the British
civil service has been characterized by an 'instrumental' pattern in relying on
external sources of influence, whereas the German bureaucracy is said to be
characterized by 'autonomy' and self-generated (and incremental) reforms
(which are generated in agreement with expert advisors attached to departments). *Pace* Knill, the main sources for regulatory innovation in the 1990s
were within the British bureaucracy. During this episode, the British civil
service operated on a more autonomous basis than the German federal bureau-

cracy, where regulatory innovation followed more closely the pattern predicted by Knill. An argument that emphasizes the importance of the 'reading across' from domestic experience in the regulation of network industries in the British case qualifies to some extent Michael Moran's suggestion that the British railways privatization of the 1990s was a pure example of 'high modernism' – at least it requires a more differentiated perspective regarding the source of the 'radical measures' which in this case drew largely on bureaucratic interpretations of and experience in network regulation than (rapidly fading) party-political convictions.[17] And it was not only in the 1990s case of railway policy where Knill's account did not hold (the period he particularly emphasizes) – also during the post-World War II socialization, policy in Britain emerged largely as a product from an autonomous bureaucracy, while the 1921 Act was characterized by extensive negotiations with the railway companies, which arguably more resembled the German 'corporatist' bargaining style characteristic of the 1990s reforms that led to the formation of the Deutsche Bahn as a limited company.

There was also only limited evidence of regulatory innovation resulting from a particular 'national style', especially in the British case. Instead, the observed patterns across the three critical junctures revealed substantial variation and contestation. In terms of organizational form, Britain experienced a privately owned oligopolistic market prior to the First World War, regional private monopolies in the inter-war period, a single, publicly owned monopoly following the Second World War and a fragmentation into separate private undertakings in the 'age' of privatization. In contrast, the German case offered somewhat more continuity in terms of organizational form. In all periods under investigation in this chapter, the railways were under federal ownership, although there were differences in organizational structure ranging from formal autonomy in the inter-war period, limited operational autonomy post-Second World War and a unified private law undertaking after 'privatization'.

Arguably more national continuity existed at the ideational level – in the British case, there was a persisting assumption that the railways should operate on commercial lines, while in Germany regulatory innovation was driven by the assumption that the railways should operate in the wider interest of the national and regional economy. Regulatory innovation sought primarily to safeguard these functions; for example in terms of infrastructure provision. Nevertheless, such a perspective on ideational national persistence that is linked to processes of filtered problem perception and solution generation, much promoted by sociologists such as Frank Dobbin (1994) who claims that sectoral policy paradigms 'fit' with national industrial policy paradigms, misses out the substantial debates illustrated in the earlier section. Across both countries and time periods, there was no deterministic policy continuation; in contrast, neither were there distinct understandings of the policy problems requiring attention, nor was there a deterministic generation of distinct policy solutions; instead there was considerable contestation with similar ideas being put forward in both countries, for example, the 'corporatist' proposals in Britain following World War I.

At another level, however, institutional mechanisms generated certain actor constellations that were decisive in shaping the character of regulatory innovation. Thus, in the 1990s case, the 'lateral transfer' system within the British civil service (Hood 1996) allowed for a 'herding' of senior officials with experience in utility regulation and privatization to apply their lessons in the railway domain, therefore leading to a type of innovation that was oriented at previous domestic utility privatizations. In contrast, in the German 1990s case, regulatory innovation was oriented towards a 'transport'-type regime, reflecting the composition of the expert commission as well as the dominance of the federal ministry of transport. This pattern was also reflected in the other two German cases. In contrast to the British 1990s case, the public corporation model that was applied in the British post-1945 case was hardly a 'reading across', apart from the dominance of Herbert Morrison. Most proposals had already emanated from within the Ministry of Transport, even during the war. In contrast, in the case of the 1919 Ministry of Transport Act, the recruitment of railway managers for the administration of wartime and post-war transport was countered by the rise of the 'deflationary' interests, in particular the rise of the Treasury (Lowe 1978).

In sum, broad statements regarding state structures, national innovation styles or institutional mechanisms facilitating regulatory innovation offer some insights into the way in which railway regulation developed in the various episodes and states. However, a closer look reveals that a more differentiated analysis is required. Institutions, and therefore the 'state' world of regulatory innovation, matter, but not necessarily at the macro-level so often emphasized by accounts on national political institutions and national policy styles, and hardly in deterministic ways.

CONCLUSIONS

More than a decade after 'privatization', the railways in both countries were back in the headlines once again. In Britain, legislative proposals returned considerable administrative powers to the ministry of transport; in Germany, major disputes existed between politicians, business and trade union interests and Deutsche Bahn's executive, the latter having initially sought a partial flotation as a vertically integrated company on the stock exchange by 2006. However, in the latter case, there were no major proposals for major regulatory upheaval. In that sense (of stability) at least, regulatory innovation in Germany in the 1990s seems to have been more successful than in Britain.

This chapter has investigated a selected number of claims drawn from three 'worlds of regulatory innovation'. The empirical account points to the need for a differentiated analysis instead of taking the broad 'worlds' for granted, any analysis of regulatory innovation requires a move towards the analysis of specific mechanisms or factors (drawn from the various worlds of regulatory innovation) and how they impact on processes of regulatory innovation. In addition, this chapter has attempted to show that there is considerable contestation among potentially legitimate policy templates. The railway domain, as with any policy domain, is surrounded by a number of policy environments which offer competing policy templates. Therefore, a claim that particular organizational forms are likely to become more similar to other forms facing the same environment are relatively meaningless, as the important question is why particular environments are chosen as legitimate rather than others, not that such institutional processes occur in the first place. At the same time, the empirical pattern has suggested that while certain ideas did indeed return – seldom put forward by the same institutional actor – there was only to some extent a 'back to the future' effect in that old and rejected proposals for regulatory innovation were returned to the agenda-setting process.

Traditional accounts of historical railway regulation have often emphasized the importance of the railway industry (Kolko 1965) or of political entrepreneurs (McLean and Foster 1992). According to the interpretation put forward here, these factors (and therefore also distinct claims drawn from the 'worlds of regulatory innovation') did not matter much in influencing the shape of regulatory innovation. Entrepreneurs, where they were evident, vanished over the course of the policy episode and were dependent on political support – whether it was the two railway experts, Acworth and Leverve, in the case of the 1921 DRG law, Geddes in the case of the 1919 Ministry of Transport law or the role of Deutsche Bahn chief executive Heinz Dürr in the 1990s; in the other three cases, there was hardly any noticeable impact of any one individual, even in the case of Herbert Morrison and the 'socialization' of British transport policy. Similarly, while railway interests were certainly not uninfluential, they were mostly influential when negotiating the details of intended innovations, but not in setting the key parameters of regulatory innovation. For example, they succeeded in the British inter-war case in persuading the government over the number of amalgamated companies and succeeded, together with the railway unions, in vetoing proposals for union membership on the industry board, or in maintaining the Bundesbahn as a vertically integrated operator for an indeterminate period in the 1990s. In the other cases, the railway operators did not feature largely in debates concerning regulatory innovation   and the same holds for the supposed powers of the railway unions, even at the time when their power was widely held to be a threat to the stability of the state as in the early 1920s.

A perspective that emphasizes the importance of contestation of policy templates for regulatory innovation also suggests that far from stability, any regulatory innovation is likely to face considerable instability over time. Once there is a noted difference between perceived and expected performance, actors are likely to emerge and offer competing policy solutions drawn from alternative policy environments. Such a view also points to the importance of considering side-effects and unintended consequences (Hood and Peters 2004) in the analysis of regulatory innovation (which was not attempted here). The notion of 'regulatory innovation' is often associated with an engineering perspective that implies progress and stability; however, such a view is in the face of the contestability of policy templates inherently illusionary.

Nor at the same time did the observed patterns reveal a 'pendulum swing' or 'nothing new under the sun' pattern. While respective reforms were often justified by contrasting the anticipated benefits of the future with the perceived failures of the past, regulatory innovation did not follow a 'pendulum swing' pattern in that regulatory proposals were put forward that were on the lines of provisions which had been replaced in the previous reform era, despite some (mostly superficial) enthusiasm in both states in the 1990s for the regulatory regimes of the 1920s. Such a focus of selection of templates for regulatory innovation puts the contending arguments of the different worlds of regulatory innovation in perspective. In a somewhat similar way to the literature on technological innovation and the evolution of large-scale technical systems, regulatory innovation does not appear as a straightforward product of particular state or sectoral structures or national and sectoral policy styles, but rather as a product of interactions among self-interested (individual and composite) actors within particular institutional constellations that are surrounded by diverse policy environments that offer competing policy templates.

NOTES

1. More broadly, this interpretation of the 'state' world of regulatory innovation arguably links to the 'internal determinants model' for explaining policy diffusion, as defined by Berry and Berry (1999, pp. 178–83).
2. This section draws on Lodge (2002).
3. 130 companies were under government control at the time of the war; 12 companies controlled 75 per cent of the network.
4. House of Lords Records Office (HoL RO) 4/45/9/21, 9 November 1918.
5. Public Records Office (PRO), MT45/235, 10 March 1919.
6. PRO MT45/226/5 March 1919.
7. HoL RO F/18/4/10, 9 December 1920.
8. HoL RO F/18/4/10, 9 February 1920.
9. Bundesarchiv R5 2045, 26 March 1924.

10. PRO MT 74/1, July 1943.
11. PRO RAIL 1007/606, 1 May 1942.
12. Early proposals by the then Administration for Transport in 1947 had, unsuccessfully, proposed the transfer of unlimited powers over the railways to the Director of the Administration for Transport (Nicholls 1999, pp. 274–5).
13. At the time, the federal and the NRW governments were headed by rival factions of the Christian Democratic Union.
14. BA B108/28541, no date. 'Stellungnahme zum Entwurf eines Gesetzes über die Deutsche Bundesbahn von Nordrhein-Westfalen'.
15. The federal Ministry of Justice eventually concluded that Article 87 required that the possibility of ministerial influence had to be ensured.
16. This is not to deny the existence of drawing from international sources. The legislative provisions allowing for the collective administration of the railways in Britain during wartime was a direct response to the successful use of the railway system in the 1871 Franco-Prussian war.
17. Arguably, a situation where the administration was more 'high modern' than party politicians could be defined as an illustration of the success of this ideology in penetrating the state.

5. Sale of the century: 3G mobile phone licensing in Europe

Mark Thatcher

INTRODUCTION

The licensing of 3G (third generation) mobile phones in Europe represented a major change in the regulation of mobile communications. Discretionary allocation of licences to favoured domestic national champions was replaced with auctions or formalized high-cost beauty contests. Although auctions are an 'old instrument', their application in 3G mobile phone licensing can truly be termed a regulatory innovation as it saw major alterations of instruments, the degree of formality, competition, interests served, cost, cross-national learning the positions of incumbent suppliers. Modification of 3G mobile phone licensing represents at least a 'second-order change' whereby instruments and techniques are altered, and approaches a third-order change in which policy goals and paradigms are altered (Hall 1993).

This chapter analyses 3G mobile phone licensing by drawing primarily on the perspectives offered by the 'state world' of innovation, namely the decisions of the state. Its starting points are the claims by interest group and industrial policy literatures that public policy-makers act in the interests of large suppliers and arguments by comparative institutionalist studies that inherited institutional arrangements result in major cross-national differences in innovation. However the analysis also has implications for the individual world of entrepreneurs who are argued to lead innovation and for the 'world of the innovation' since it considers how the features of 3G licence auctions in Europe affected their cross-national spread.

This chapter explores four general issues that relate to these worlds. First, it discusses the conditions for regulatory innovation – in this case, responding to major technological change. It helps us to consider the opportunities for policy-makers to innovate, looking in particular at the interests served by innovation. 3G mobile phone licensing offers a case in which policy-makers faced very large, entrenched and concentrated 'national champion' suppliers. The central argument is that new technology offers new opportunities for actors to alter long-standing policies, instruments and relationships. The chapter shows how and to what extent policy-makers were able to seize the opportunities provided by a new technology to reshape the interests that benefit from regulation. At the same time, it emphasizes the role of political factors – notably learning (both cross-national and domestic) – which led policy-makers to question and modify their traditional strategies. As a result, regulatory innovations were pursued that ran counter to interest group theories which predict state regulation favouring large, concentrated supplier interests.

Second, the case provides a rare clear-cut case for cross-national policy comparison of regulatory innovation, since all European countries faced the same question – issuing 3G licences – and took decisions in rapid sequence between 1999 and 2001. The licensing of mobile phone networks was very public and provided apparently simple lessons about institutional design and outcomes. The chapter shows how a combination of a new technology, fiscal pressures and cross-national learning counteracted inherited institutional differences and led to policy-makers following similar innovations despite operating in diverse national institutional contexts. However, the degree of diffusion and convergence varied, a common aim of generating high revenues spread across nations, but there were considerable cross-national differences in outcomes of the licensing process. Thus although regulatory innovations took place across four institutionally diverse nations, the degree of similarity varied by the aspect of innovation considered.

Individual economists were involved in 3G licensing and hence the analysis touches on the role of individual entrepreneurs. Strong claims have been made for economists who 'invented' auctions for 3G mobile phones and allowed governments to break out of 'inefficient' inherited methods of licence allocation. The case study shows that although entrepreneurial individuals played their part, they had supporting roles. Rather their place must be set within a context transformed by new opportunities offered by technology and by the role of large organizations – government bureaucracies and firms. Indeed, initial entrepreneurs were often state organizations and officials rather than external individuals.

Finally, auctions are apparently simple to understand and their fundamental purpose – to maximize revenue from sales – was attractive to governments. The chapter argues that these features contributed to cross-national policy learning. However, that learning was selective. In particular, it was easier to 'learn' about the large sums of money that 3G licensing might raise than about the full institutional, political and market conditions that influence auction outcomes. Selective learning was partly responsible for variations across the four nations notably in the use of instruments for allocating licences and in the outcomes of licensing.

The chapter compares the experiences of four countries (Britain, Germany, Italy and France – taken in that order due to the chronology of 3G licensing).

It begins with a brief discussion of puzzles for regulatory innovation in mobile communications derived from past experience in the sector and expectations derived from work on the three worlds of innovation, notably capture, policy learning, varieties of capitalism and the role of policy entrepreneurs. Thereafter it analyses the first innovator – Britain, before turning to the other three countries. Finally, it looks briefly at some of the consequences of 3G licensing for telecommunications operators before drawing some broader conclusions about regulatory innovation.

3G MOBILE TELEPHONY AS A CASE TO STUDY REGULATORY INNOVATION

Until the 1980s, mobile telephony was small, expensive and technologically unreliable. Limited public services were provided by monopoly national suppliers (e.g. BT, France Télécom, Deutsche Telekom, TIM). However, from the late 1980s onwards, second-generation networks were developed that offered much more reliable services at lower costs with small handsets. Most European countries licensed a small number of suppliers – initially creating a monopoly or duopoly, then licensing three or even four networks. These suppliers were almost all national companies, including the historic incumbents and consortia led by well-established companies such as CGE (now Vivendi) or Olivetti. Licences were attributed, at very low cost, and often with few formal rules governing selection.

Mobile telephony grew extremely rapidly in the 1990s. From being a rare luxury, mobile telephones became an everyday item, often an essential one for business and private use. Profits from 2G telephony were extremely high, driven by falling costs, rising usage, high prices and low licence fees.

The late 1990s saw the development of a new form of mobile communications – '3G' or UMTS (universal mobile telecommunications system). This promised a broadband (i.e. high capacity) digital network capable of transmitting voice telephony, data and video material. It thus offered not only a technologically advanced form of an existing service but also the addition of many new services. Examples of new applications included Internet services, sending digital images, and geographically tailored services such as maps or restaurants or shops in the vicinity of the phone. 3G mobile telephones involved a further step towards the integration of telecommunications, computing and broadcasting.

The appearancce of 3G thus represented a rapid technological development. It required substantial investment, notably in networks but also in developing handsets. However, it offered the prospect of being used for a myriad of services. The late 1990s were the years of the high-technology 'boom' or bubble, marked by great optimism about the profitability of the 'new economy' and information and communications. Moreover, 3G stood in a subsector of telecommunications that had enjoyed very rapid growth and high profits. When licensing decisions were being made (from 1998 onwards), 3G seemed to face excellent prospects.

UMTS was based on an international allocation of a common spectrum bandwidth, whilst common standards were also being developed across nations, thereby offering the prospect of Europe-wide and indeed international markets. Nevertheless, national governments in Europe had much discretion over licensing. EC Directive 97/13/EC, passed as a council directive and Decision 128/1999/EC of the European Parliament and Council specifically on UMTS, obliged member states to allocate licences in a fair, transparent and non-discriminatory manner. Their provisions were general and often contradictory. Thus for instance, member states could only limit individual licences to the extent necessary to ensure the efficient use of radio frequencies, but where scarce resources were to be used, they were allowed to impose charges which reflect the need to ensure the optimal use of these resources. Those charges were to be non-discriminatory and to take into particular account the need to foster the development of innovative services and competition. Member states were to achieve a broad competitive offering but also to achieve coverage of less populated areas and to take social and societal needs into account. Thus EC law allowed member states to choose the exact number of licences, the method of licensing and the cost of licences.

Worlds of Regulatory Innovation and Expectations Derived from Theory

The state world of regulatory innovation focuses on the strategies and interests of governments and public policy-makers. A key group for 3G mobile phone network licensing are regulators – be they in governments or regulatory agencies. A well-established American literature on capture theory, rents and interest groups argues that concentrated interests, especially suppliers, are likely to capture regulators and earn 'rents' from regulation, because they face low organizational costs and enjoy potentially high benefits, whereas other interests such as consumers are too diffuse and would gain only limited benefits; regulatory change is likely to favour concentrated interests, which 'trade' money and support with regulators, including politicians (e.g. Stigler 1971; Peltzman, 1976, 1989; Becker 1983). Work on the protection of 'national champions' in Europe supports such a view, underlining how national governments have aided powerful public and private companies, through, *inter alia*, regulation (Hayward 1995; Cohen and Bauer 1985).

Cross-national comparative studies of industrial and economic policy-making in Europe provides a large literature claiming that policies are strongly marked by national institutions (Hall and Taylor 1996; Hall 1986; Thelen 1999; Dobbin 1994; Immergut 1998; Thelen and Steinmo 1992). Existing institutions such as state structures, links between the state and society, the organization of society and state traditions also influence national innovatory capacities (cf. Cortell and Peterson 1999; Hall 1986, 1983). For instance, the structure of the state, particularly the form of the executive and legislature, rules governing relations between political leaders and their officials, and the number of veto players/points in making decisions, affects the ability of political leaders to formulate policies (cf. Tsebelis 2003; Immergut 1992). Moreover, nations have differing state traditions and policy styles that influence the acceptance of state leadership and power (Richardson 1982; Dyson 1980). Hence we would expect cross-national variations in the degree of regulatory innovation. In the 1970s, France was argued to be much better able to change than Britain or West Germany thanks to its institutions that allowed political leaders to mobilize resources to overcome inertia (Hayward 1976; Hall 1983, 1986). In the 1980s and 1990s, the roles appeared to be reversed. Italy has been claimed to be blocked by political fragmentation and a weak state (Locke 1995; Cassese 2000).

Recent comparative work on 'varieties of capitalism' (e.g. Hall and Soskice 2001; Schmidt 2002) focuses on how nations maintain the competitiveness of firms. It argues that countries have different 'institutional complementarities' whereby they derive comparative institutional advantages for their national firms. As a result, they are 'locked into' specific patterns of adjustment to changed economic conditions: existing institutional and firm structures mean that the most efficient responses to economic change differ from one nation to another. In particular, Britain tends to choose a 'liberal' approach based on competition, whereas Germany opts for a coordinated approach in which government and firms cooperate. France has perhaps moved somewhat from its dirigiste traditions, but the state remains very active in promoting the prosperity of national firms. Italy suffers from a weak state and many veto players and hence alteration of institutions and policies is difficult.

Thus applying work on the strategies and interests of public policy-makers would lead us to expect regulators to favour large, powerful, national champion firms in 3G mobile phone licensing. This would merely have been following the pattern seen in 1G and 2G licensing. Cross-national comparative studies would also predict that different nations would favour their national champions in diverse ways, following existing institutional arrangements and complementarities. In particular, one would expect British policy-makers to use tools appropriate for a liberal market economy – ones that do not discriminate between individual firms but aid overall competitiveness. In contrast, one would expect German policy-makers to cooperate closely with existing individual suppliers in designing new rules. French public policy-makers could be expected to lead change, with the explicit aim of aiding national champions. Finally, innovation in Italy would be expected to be difficult, because of multiple veto players and points, that change.

A second 'world' of regulatory innovation investigated is that of policy entrepreneurs. Work by Kingdon (1984) suggests that such entrepreneurs take advantage of 'policy windows' offered by the concatenation of policy problems, policies and politics to catapult new items onto the political agenda and alter policy. Entrepreneurs may include policy experts. In 3G mobile phone licensing, economists have claimed to have played a crucial role in regulatory innovation (Klemperer 2002, 2004). This perspective thus focuses on heroic individuals who climb through policy windows to break through (or into) staid, stable and perhaps inefficient closed policy communities.

Auctions allow some discussion of the 'world of the innovation'. At first sight, they are simple to understand, are usually public and they are easy to copy. Their effects are open to analysis and theorization. In 3G mobile phone licensing, economists have explicitly set out theories as to how auctions should be designed and work and theorized why they produce superior outcomes to other forms of licence allocation such as beauty contests (see notably Klemperer 2004). These features of auctions should aid their diffusion, especially if successful, if the characteristics of an innovation are important for its spread.

How does the experience of 3G mobile phone licensing in Britain, Germany, Italy and France match the predictions and perspectives offered by these three worlds of innovation?

BRITAIN AS AN EARLY MOVER IN 3G LICENSING: PROCESSES, INSTRUMENTS AND OUTCOMES

In Europe, 3G mobile phone licences were allocated within a two-year period between 1999 and 2001. The first countries to issues licences, Finland and Spain, did so through a 'beauty contest' (i.e. choosing the best bidder according to several criteria, with bidders presenting their diverse plans for a network) at very low fees (0.5 billion euros for Spain). However, in 2000, the UK auctioned 3G licences.

In 2000, telecommunications in Britain seemed a good sectoral example of a liberal market economy. Since 1984, the incumbent, BT, had been majority privately owned and an independent regulatory agency, Oftel (the Office of Telecommunications) had existed and indeed grown in strength and reputation (Thatcher 1999). Policy had been directed towards enhancing competition, notably by regulation. Nevertheless, auctions had not previously been used to allocate licences in telecommunications in Britain. Although economists had argued for auctioning of the radio spectrum since the late 1950s (cf. Coase 1959), the 2G licences had been awarded through a very closed beauty contest. Following by the Broadcasting Act 1990, auctions had been introduced for allocating ITV licences in 1991. They had met considerable resistance by broadcasters and indeed the experience was marked by a number of problems. The method used was a one-round 'sealed bids'. The outcome was that some licences were allocated for very small sums, becoming 'licences to print money', whilst others attracted very high bids; moreover, very well-respected or innovative broadcasters such as Thames Television and TV-AM lost their licences. Thus, the climate for ambitious 3G mobile phone licenses seemed unpropitious.

The process that led to the choice of auctions for 3G mobiles phone licensing involved a combination of factors, several of which had been at work well before 2000. Although by the late 1990s there were four competing 2G mobile phone networks (Vodafone, Cellnet – owned by BT – Orange, and One2One), the operators were earning very large profits, thanks to low fees, prices above costs and rapidly increasing demand. Limitations on the spectrum available restricted the number of networks that could operate. Yet until 1998, legislation only allowed licence fees to be set at levels to recover the costs of licensing. A specialist organization, the Radiocommunications Agency (an executive agency of the Department for Trade and Industry), was responsible for spectrum management. In the 1990s, it argued that a new approach to spectrum management was needed because there was increasing demand, but prices set at licensing costs did not give any incentives to use the spectrum efficiently (Radiocommunications Agency 1994). In 1996 the then Conservative government, having consulted with the Radiocommunications Agency, issued a White Paper (DTI 1996) that pointed out the economic importance of radio communications. It argued that pricing based on licence costs undervalued spectrum and had been devised at a time when demand for spectrum was low, whereas now there was increased demand and spectrum shortages. It therefore announced a new approach whereby spectrum pricing should reflect the value of the spectrum and should also be used to promote policies such as efficient use of spectrum, enhancing competition and access. A predictable, transparent, comprehensible and workable framework of progressive spectrum pricing was needed.

The 1996 White Paper was highly favourable to auctions, which it described as the government's preferred method of spectrum pricing. It claimed that auctions aided economic efficiency, allowing prices to be set by the market rather than administratively, transparency, speed, and incentives for using the spectrum efficiently. It suggested that auctions could be especially useful for high-value services for which there would be a reasonable number of bidders (to prevent collusion). It pointed to experiences in using auctions for spectrum in the US and New Zealand (DTI 1996, s. 6.4). Indeed, in 1994, the Federal Communications Commission (FCC) had auctioned radio spectrum for mobile telephone networks using an 'ascending auction'; the experience seemed to work well, raised $20 billion and attracted favourable attention in Britain (Binmore and Klemperer 2002, p. 75). The White Paper accepted that auctions had drawbacks and underlined the need for good design, citing the advantages of the FCC simultaneous multi-round auctions, especially compared with single-round sealed-bid auctions (DTI 1996, ss. 6.9–6.11).

The process of regulatory innovation continued and was implemented under the new Labour government after 1997. Its consultative document (DTI 1997) reaffirmed the views of the 1996 White Paper, including the use of auctions. Responses to the 1997 document revealed sometimes reluctant acceptance of the use of auctions, also by established suppliers (cf. BT 1997). Thereafter the government passed the Wireless Telegraphy Act 1998 which allowed the Secretary of State (for Trade and Industry) to make regulations for the sale of licences and hence set prices above licensing costs. (S)he had to do so having regard to: the availability of the radio spectrum for the licences to be granted; future demand for that part of the spectrum; the desirability of promoting the efficient use and management of the spectrum, economic benefits, the development of innovative services and competition in the supply of telecommunications services (Wireless Telegraphy Act 1998, s. 2). In May 1998, the telecoms minister, Barbara Roche, announced that licences for 3G mobile phones would be allocated by auction and emphasized that:

> the Government's overall aim is to secure, for the long term benefit of UK consumers and the national economy, the timely and economically advantageous development and sustained provision of UMTS services in the UK. Subject to this overall aim the Government's objectives are to (i) utilise the available UMTS spectrum with optimum efficiency; (ii) promote effective and sustainable competition for the provision of UMTS services; and (iii) subject to the above objectives, design an auction which is best judged to realise the full economic value to consumers, industry and the taxpayer of the spectrum. (DTI 1998)

The design of the auction had been identified as a major issue for its success. The government sought advice from several parties in designing the 3G mobile phone licence auction. It set up the 'UMTS Auction Consultative Group' in 1998, which comprised most interested parties, including suppliers and users. At the same time, it retained the merchant bank NM Rothschild as its financial advisor; interestingly, Rothschild's fee increased as the number of bidders increased (Binmore and Klemperer 2002, p. 90, fn. 49). However, it also commissioned advice from two academic economists, Ken Binmore and Paul Klemperer, who were well known for their work on auctions. Policy advice was also given by the semi-independent telecommunications regulator Oftel (the Office of Telecommunications) and consultants.

Key issues for the auction included: entry by new suppliers; the number of licences; the form and rules of the auction; the form of payments. The European-wide UMTS Forum, representing operators and manufacturers, together with national regulators, had recommended a minimum spectrum for each licence such that only four licences would be available in the bandwidth allocated to UMTS (Börgers and Dustmann 2002), a position followed by the UK UMST Auction Consultative Group. However, after initial hesitations, and then reports by consultants, the Radiocommunications Agency and the government decided to issue five licences (Börgers and Dustmann 2002; Binmore and Klemperer 2002, pp. c 84–c 85), thereby increasing competition; the five licences were of three unequal sizes, and hence value, further aiding entry for operators with lower financial capabilities. Moreover, following advice from its economic and financial consultants, the government reserved one licence for a new entrant to the UK market– i.e. a bidder who did not already possess a 2G licence (Binmore and Klemperer 2002, pp. c 80–c 81). Finally, a 'simultaneous ascending' form of the auction was chosen, strongly modelled on the design used by the FCC; this meant rounds undertaken simultaneously for the five licences, with bidders obliged to exceed the highest bid of the previous round by a minimum percentage set during the auction, or else drop out;[1] in addition, low reserve prices and minimum payments (relative to the bids in fact made) were set (for details of the auction, see Binmore and Klemperer 2002; Börgers and Dustmann 2002).

The results of the auction were quite unexpected. Thirteen bidders were attracted. The auction ran for 150 rounds between March and April 2000. The five successful bidders included the four existing 2G licence holders.[2] However, the total bids were £22.5 billion (€37 billion), approximately 15 times the original estimates of the auction revenues to be raised and representing a payment of €642 per head of population (for details and analyses of the bids, see NAO 2001; Börgers and Dustmann 2002).

Four related points are worth underlining in the decision to choose auctions and its design in Britain. First, the fundamental reasons for using auctions were to increase efficient use of the radio spectrum and to enhance competition. This fitted with the overall direction of policy adopted in Britain after 1984, a policy led by Oftel and that had become increasingly accepted by the government (Thatcher 1999). It would seem that initially spectrum efficiency issues were paramount, but that the aim of increasing competition became more prominent in the auction design phase. 3G mobile phone network licensing thus offered an opportunity to extend existing policies into mobile communications. The policy of seeking competition fits with claims by the literature on 'varieties of capitalism' that Britain is a 'liberal market economy'. Second, the decision to use auctions and choices over its design arose from a combination of factors. Some had been factors that had been present for many years, notably the views of academic economists and high profits of 2G licence holders, but became more powerful in the 1990s. Others were newer, especially increasing demand for scarce spectrum; advice by the specialist Radiocommunications Agency and looking to overseas examples, especially the USA, rather than European nations or past UK experience in a related field such as television. The confluence of several factors led to the choice of auctions despite unfavourable terrain in terms of past UK experience (the ITV auctions and the lack of use of auctions in British and European telecoms licensing). Third, initial policy entrepreneurs appear to have been state agencies and officials within them, notably the Radiocommunications Agency. Outside economists entered later, and although important for specific details of the auction design were not responsible for the decision to use auctions. Finally, estimates of the sums raised were relatively low; thus for instance, the radiocommunications advisors estimated in April 1999 that perhaps the auction might raise £1.5 (NAO 2001, p. 17). Hence raising revenue was not the primary consideration in the decision to use auctions. Thus the sums raised were greatly unexpected.

LATER INNOVATORS: GERMANY, ITALY AND FRANCE

The British example created great interest in other European countries. However, the effects of the UK auction and the choices made over licence allocation systems varied across nations.

Germany

Telecommunications supply had traditionally been marked by close state involvement in supply (notably through public monopoly and ownership of the Deutsche Bundespost) and in manufacturing (via cooperation between Deutsche Bundespost and German manufacturers, especially Siemens) (cf. Werle 1999). By 1999, Germany had only moved away partially from that. The state still had a majority stake in Deutsche Telekom and hence significant incentives to support its value. Moreover, the independent regulator, the RegTP (Regulierungsbehörde für Telekommunikation und Post), was seen by many as facing considerable pressures from the government and Deutsche Telekom (Coen et al. 2002).

Despite these institutional features, Germany allocated 3G licences through an ascending auction, the same method as in Britain. However, its decisions to use an auction and on the design of its auction were taken between January 1999 and February 2000, before the UK auction took place. Its choice of an auction arose from previous domestic experiences of licence allocation rather than overseas experiences (Scheurle 2002; personal interviews). In particular, there had been difficulties in attracting new entrants. In 1997, bids were invited for a fourth 2G licence (the first three having been allocated through political decisions); only one offer was received. Moreover, Germany had already used an auction for the 2G mobile phone spectrum in 1999; again the outcome was disappointing in terms of entry in that the four licences were taken by the four existing networks.

The rules for 3G mobile phone licensing by the independent sectoral regulator were designed by the independent sectoral regulator, the RegTP, and differed in important respects from those used in Britain (for a description and analysis see Grimm et al. 2002; for a UK-centred critique, see Klemperer 2002). The number of licences was not determined in advance. Instead, 12 equal spectrum blocks were created; bidders were allowed to make offers for either two or three blocks (at least two were needed for a 3G system), so that, depending on the bids, the number of licences could have varied between four and six. This rule allowed a trade-off between the number of licences and prices, since four bidders could 'crowd out' two potential operators by each bidding for three spectrum blocks each; such a strategy was likely to drive up prices. Initially, the RegTP proposed rules to discriminate in favour of new entrants, but in the final version no spectrum blocks were reserved for new entrants. A second auction for any unallocated spectrum was also planned. If two bidders bought three blocks each, resulting in four licences, it was highly likely that, as in the 1999 auction for 2G spectrum, existing operators would take all the licences. The rules were strongly criticized by economists who argued that this was a likely outcome and hence there would be no new entrants (Grimm et al. 2002, p. 125). Moreover, the rules were similar to the auction used in the Netherlands, although that auction, taking place a few months before Germany's, was largely a failure, attracting the same number of bidders as licences available.

In the event, the 3G auction in Germany attracted seven bidders (reduced from an initial 12 who had registered). These were the four incumbents in the German market plus three new entrants backed by overseas operators.[3] Hence only one bidder had to drop out to allow six licences, but bidding could continue if other companies sought three spectrum blocks (there being 12 spectrum blocks). During the auction rounds (July–August 2000), one bidder (Debitel) dropped out in round 127 when bidding had reached circa DM5 billion (approximately €2.5 billion), but bidding continued as other firms still sought three blocks rather than two. Finally, however, all bidders reduced their offers to two blocks and hence six licences were allocated. The costs were extremely high – the six licences raised €50.5 billion, representing €615 per head of population (for figures, see Cartelier 2003).

The German case shows clear regulatory innovation in the use of auctions.

Interestingly, policy learning concerning the new policy instrument was largely domestic – drawing on experiences of past German failures (although the sums raised appear to have been influenced by the UK auction). The aim of maximizing revenue ran counter to the tradition of protecting incumbent suppliers, and also to expectations generated by the state's holding of shares in Deutsche Telekom and the perceived weakness of the sectoral regulator. Thus although less pro-competitive than Britain (in that the rules allowed crowding out of operators and did not discriminate in favour of new entrants), the auction marked a major move towards a liberal market approach to the allocation of licences. Finally, innovation was led by state agencies and officials, rather than outside economists.

Italy

Traditionally, Italian telecommunications offered a classic example of the effects of a weak and fragmented state. No fewer than five operators existed until the mid-1990s. All were majority state-owned, but they had diverse organizational bases. Political parties were closely involved in decision making both by the telecommunications ministry and by the operators. Attempts at reform during the 1980s mostly failed, due to vetoes by political parties. The position altered in the mid-1990s, when the operators were united in Telecom Italia, of which a large majority was privatized during the late 1990s. In 1997, a sectoral regulator, AGCOM (the Autorità per le Garanzie nelle Comunicazioni) was created; but many of its members were linked to political parties and it was a recent creation, seen as weak and vulnerable to party politicization (Perez 2002; Thatcher 2002). Moreover, Italy remained subject to multi-party governments, whose continuation was threatened by intra-coalition crises.

After a short period of uncertainty in 1999, Italy had originally planned to use a beauty contest to issue 3G licences. One reason was continuity with previous methods of licence allocation (*Il Sole 24 Ore*, 1 October 1999). In addition, policy-makers sought to protect the Italian market from powerful foreign entrants and safeguard the profitability of Italian suppliers (*Il Sole 24 Ore*, 15 March 2000). The use of a beauty contest was strongly supported by AGCOM (*Il Sole 24 Ore*, 1 October 1999). It appeared to be accepted by most Italian policy-makers including the government then led by Massimo d'Alema (*Il Sole 24 Ore*, 16 January 2000, 20 February 2000, 15 March 2000). A committee of ministers was set up which would choose the successful bidders, chaired by the Prime Minister (*Il Sole 24 Ore*, 20 February 2000). Five licences would be granted, the number being justified by AGCOM on the basis of the maximum number of profitable operators that the market could support (*Il Sole 24 Ore*, 28 March 2000). Moreover, relatively limited sums were

envisaged from the sale of the licences (perhaps 1750–2500 billion lire, or
€0.9–1.3 billion). Thus the original design followed traditional policies, leav-
ing considerable discretion in the hands of elected politicians and seeking low
fees from operators, who were likely to be mostly domestic companies.

However, after the UK auction, the position began to change (cf. Perez
2002, pp. 269–79). Initially, its appetite whetted by the financial success of the
UK sale, the government considered merely raising the cost of licences but
keeping a beauty contest (*Il Sole 24 Ore*, 14 April 2000). The UK example of
an auction was explicitly rejected by politicians, AGCOM and suppliers as
unsuitable for Italy due to being too costly and threatening Italian operators (*Il
Sole 24 Ore*, 14, 19 April 2000, 3 May 2000). Italian suppliers continued to
press for a beauty contest (*Il Sole 24 Ore*, 29 April 2000, 5, 24 May 2000).
However, new voices began to call for an auction – most notably the influential general competition authority, the Autorità per le Garanzie nelle
Communicazioni (*Il Sole 24 Ore*, 9, 24 May 2000, 17 June 2000). In addition,
political parties such as the Allianze Nazionale and the Greens called for an
auction (*Il Sole 24 Ore*, 5 May 2000). Several months of discussions took
place within the government seeking to balance increased receipts, avoiding
'excessive' prices and protecting Italian suppliers through a modified form of
beauty contest (*Il Sole 24 Ore*, 11 May 2000, 15, 16, 17 June 2000). By the
summer of 2000, the government, now led by Guiliano Amato, a university
professor and former head of the competition authority, changed its choice. It
decided to hold a two-stage sale (cf. Perez 2002, pp. 275–9). First there would
be a qualifying stage for candidates, based on their suitability as an operator
and the viability of their business plan. Thereafter five licences would be sold
through an ascending auction with a substantial reserve price being set.
Following the Dutch experience, provisions were made to reduce the number
of licences if the number of bidders was inadequate.

In late 1999 and early 2000, a large number of potential bidders had
expressed interest in the Italian 3G market. This was not surprising given that
the mobile telephony market was one of the largest markets in Europe, especially in terms of penetration. But, during the summer of 2000, the telecom-
munication and Internet crash began and financial market sentiment towards
telecoms operators and especially 3G licences altered. When the auction took
place, only six companies participated, and one (Blu) rapidly withdrew, bringing the auction to a swift end, and preventing the safeguard clause of reducing
the number of licences from being used.[4] The result was that the five licences
raised €14 billion, just above the reserve prices but considerably below the
sums hoped for or raised in Britain and Germany. Per head, the total revenues
represented €210.

The Italian case shows how a new technology allowed the opportunity to
break with past policies of low-fee licences for incumbents. Entrepreneurs

from within the state – both elected politicians and regulatory authorities – played a major role in regulatory innovation, drawing on cross-national experiences, especially in terms of revenue objectives. However, the Italian experience also indicates that existing institutions influence regulatory innovation: the form of auction chosen was a compromise, due to the twin aims of offering some protection for domestic suppliers and maximizing revenue; the delays in getting agreement meant that Italy was late in the queue of nations selling 3G licences and indeed was hit by unfavourable stock market conditions.

France

Telecommunications offers a prime example of an activist French state. During the 1970s and 1980s, a strategy of *grands projets* was pursued, led by the state-owned operator France Télécom, in cooperation with the government (Thatcher 1999). The result was a powerful national operator, engaged in an extremely close relationship with governments and officials. Mobile communications had formed part of French strategy to develop 'national champions', if necessary by allocating licences at low cost to domestic operators who would then have the ability to grow and establish themselves as leading companies in the field. Expectations of continuing government protection of French suppliers were increased by the fact that in the late 1990s, only a minority of France Télécom had been privatized, other operators had close links with politicians and although a sectoral regulator, the Autorité de Régulation des Télécommunications (ART), had been established, its birth was recent (1996).

France was one of the last countries in Europe to sell 3G licences. By the late 1990s, there were three 2G mobile networks – France Télécom, SFR (a subsidiary of Vivendi) and the small Bouygues Télécom, a subsidiary of the family-run Bouygues firm. All had considerable political influence – their senior personnel had strong personal and professional links to policy-makers, France Télécom was the publicly owned national champion and Vivendi and Bouygues owned politically important newspaper and media companies.

A vigorous but rapidly one-sided debate emerged on the choice of allocating licences by an auction or a beauty contest (for a critique, see Curien 2002). The existing mobile phone suppliers opposed an auction. They were strongly supported by the ART. The main explicit arguments were that the costs of an auction would reduce investment, cripple suppliers, and raise prices for consumers. In the background however were two other factors: the danger of foreign entrants, who might crowd out French firms; the desire of policy-makers to protect the financial health of the three French firms. Bouygues was especially vulnerable due to its small capital base. Moreover, in 1999–2000 a host of overseas firms had expressed interest in entering the French market, appearing to represent a foreign threat to French suppliers.[5]

Initially, the debate was highly 'technical'. Interest in auctions grew after the UK and German experiences. In particular, the Finance Ministry was greatly attracted by the prospect of high revenues, especially given the sums raised in Britain and Germany (*Les Echos*, 12 April 2000, 3, 5 May 2000). However, attempts by the Industry Ministry and then the Finance Ministry to toy with auctions rapidly met with sustained and high-level opposition by the suppliers and indeed almost the entire telecommunications sector, including trade unions and user associations (*Les Echos*, 5, 10, 26 May 2000). Importantly, the ART argued consistently and very strongly against an auction (*Les Echos*, 13 October 1999, 12 May 2000). It sought to protect the existing French suppliers (*Les Echos*, 5 April 2000). Only a few 'liberal economists' supported an auction, together with potential new entrants such as Deutsche Telekom (cf. Chamoux 2000; Penard 2002, pp. 50–2; *Les Echos*, 19 May 2000). Faced with powerful resistance by the entire telecoms sector, the Finance Ministry sought to both raise revenues and avoid an auction.

The choice was thus made to run a high-fee beauty contest. High fixed licence fees (€4.9 billion per licence) were set in order to raise €19.6 billion – which would aid the government's debt and pensions policies but would also allow the ART and government to select candidates and to ensure that existing French suppliers obtained a licence. The fees were claimed to be those that would have resulted from an action as calculated from the sums raised through auctions in the UK and Germany! (Penard 2002, p. 51; cf Curien 2002, pp. 150–1). The 'beauty contest' conducted by the ART was based on points allocated to criteria such as the coherence and credibility of the project and business plan, scope and speed of service deployment and employment. These were all rather vague and hence left much room for ART discretion (Penard 2002, p. 51).

Another issue concerned whether four or five licences should be offered. The question at stake was again foreign entry and the financial viability of the operators versus increasing competition. Existing French suppliers pressed for a choice of four licences to offer maximum protection against entrants, a position supported by the ART (*Les Echos*, 13 October 1999, 26, 30 May 2000). There were few voices calling for five licences. The government followed the views of the suppliers and ART and decided to issue only four licences.

In choosing a beauty contest, the government had planned to protect French suppliers from competition by foreign entrants whilst ensuring substantial revenues for the state. However, events soon took unexpected turns. By 2001, the telecoms and Internet stock market boom was over. Moreover, the high prices paid by operators for 3G licences (both directly through their bids for licences and indirectly through expensive acquisitions of companies with 3G licences) were weighing on company balance sheets. As a result, by late 2000, potential and previously interested foreign applicants had decided not to make offers. Worse still, potential French suppliers, such as La Lyonnaise des Eaux, did not proceed with bids. Most strikingly, Bouygues Télécom, faced with the high cost of the licence, withdrew a few days before the deadline for submissions. The result was that only two operators submitted bids (both existing operators – France Télécom and SFR). Not only had the French government failed to achieve similar revenues to those in Britain and Germany, but it found itself facing a potential duopoly in 3G mobile telephony, with an existing French supplier (Bouygues) lacking a 3G licence! Moreover, it only raised €9.8 billion (from two licences) in revenue. Although the two companies were granted UMTS licences in June 2001, the government's difficulties did not end. Instead, when it sought to attract a bid for the third licence, it was obliged to offer a lower price to Bouygues and to renegotiate licence fees with SFR and France Télécom; the new terms, such as longer licences and lower prices, greatly reduced the revenues to almost one-eighth of the original licence fee (each licence was now priced at €0.619 billion each or €41 euros per head – Cartelier 2003, pp. 79–80).

Attempts at regulatory innovation in France were led by state officials (notably the Finance ministry). They looked at overseas examples, especially concerning possible revenues. However, the French case also shows how existing institutions and interests can limit innovation. Those seeking an auction faced strong opposition from existing domestic interests and other state officials. The result was a compromise in terms of objectives and form of licensing. Timing then meant that licensing took place at a highly inopportune moment for telecommunications and 3G in particular; however, in the face of difficulties, the French government decided to make significant concessions to existing operators, limiting the extent of change.

THE AFTERMATH OF 3G: THE CONSEQUENCES OF REGULATORY INNOVATION

The 3G mobile phone licence bids were rapidly followed by difficult times for telecoms companies in general, with the end of the stock market high-tech boom. Moreover, 3G rapidly became seen as a white elephant: costs were high, handsets unavailable and worst of all, rival networks (e.g. $2^{1}/_{2}$G) that offered similar capabilities to 3G began to not only be developed but arrive on the marketplace. After 2000, national champions such as BT, France Télécom and Deutsche Telekom were faced by cash crises that obliged them to have firesales of assets and indeed for FT, almost drove it bankruptcy. Their senior managers (for instance, Sir Peter Bonfield and Michel Bon) were forced out.

3G costs played a part in the higher debts of 'successful' bidders – either directly through licence fees or indirectly when companies bought expensive overseas mobile phone companies in an attempt to build pan-European mobile phone services (for instance, France Télécom's purchase of Orange). However, national governments obliged the companies to pay out bids for 3G – only in France were licence costs effectively reduced (by altering payment terms and lengthening licence lengths). The results of regulatory innovation was thus highly costly for incumbent national suppliers, in sharp contrast to previous protective policies that had offered cheap licences for mobile telephony networks offering high revenues.

CONCLUSIONS

In Britain, Germany, Italy and France, regulatory innovation took place in 3G mobile phone licensing compared with previous mobile phone licensing, in terms of the instruments used, degree of formality in allocating licences, extent of competition introduced, reduced protection of national champions, processes and perhaps most visibly, the cost of licences and their effects on supplier profitability. Thus although auctions have existed for centuries, their use in 3G mobile phone licensing represents a significant regulatory innovation. Even when beauty contests were used, their rules were radically altered away from the traditional low-cost, informal, nationally closed process designed to protect the incumbent operator. Table 5.1 indicates how the regulatory regime for 3G licensing was innovatory compared to the previous regime. It also allows cross-national comparisons of different aspects of innovation. Greater cross-national details of regulatory outcomes are offered in Table 5.2.

Whilst the changes introduced match those expected by a 'varieties of capitalism' approach for Britain, the results for other countries are surprising. Germany and Italy responded with considerable innovation. Indeed, in terms of cross-national choices of instrument, Germany and Italy, usually classified as having many veto players, engaged in more regulatory innovation than France. They moved sharply away from licence allocation systems designed to protect national suppliers and give discretion to policy-makers over the choice of licensees to using competitive auctions that facilitated entry, including that by overseas entrants. Several factors were responsible for the extent of innovation in Germany and Italy. First, both engaged in considerable policy learning – Germany from its failures in the 1990s with 2G licensing and Italy from the examples of auctions in Britain, Germany and Holland. Second, governments were eager to maximize revenues – seen in the case of Germany by a complex system allowing bidders to in effect reduce the number of licences,

Table 5.1   Regulatory innovation in mobile phone licensing over time and cross-nationally

Regulatory regime feature	Previous regime	3G licensing	Cross-national variations
Instrument	Government decision or very limited beauty contest	Auction or full-scale beauty contest	UK and Germany: auctions; France: beauty contest; Italy: mixed system
Degree of formality of rules (thickening/ thinning) and discretion	Low – much discretion left for governments	High – legal rules for allocation; low discretion once rules set in auctions	Much more discretion in France than auction systems in UK and Germany
Competition	Small number of licences	Higher number of licences – 4–6	Highest number in UK and Germany
Protection of national champions	High protection – 1 licence to incumbent, others to consortia led by domestic companies	Low – deliberate efforts to attract entrants	Highest remaining protection of national champions in France
Cost to companies	Low	Very high	Costs higher in Britain and Germany than in France and Italy

Table 5.1   continued

Regulatory regime feature	Previous regime	3G licensing	Cross-national variations
Learning	Little cross-national learning	Much cross-national learning; also learning from past domestic experience	Britain failed to copy earlier examples in Europe; least copying of British example in France
Outcomes	Very high profits for licensees	Very damaging to licensees	Some aid given in France through licence fee reductions

and in Italy by the move away from a low-cost beauty contest to an auction chosen in the hope of high revenues (based on overseas experiences) with a relatively high reserve price.

France offers the example of least regulatory innovation among the four nations. Significant regulatory innovation did take place, especially in terms of attempts to raise high revenues, but existing institutions and market conditions placed stronger constraints on change. Thus after the debate following 'learning' from 3G licensing in Britain and Germany, policy-makers chose a licence allocation system designed to protect national suppliers, but also imposed high licence fees based on overseas experiences; they were then forced to lower fees when the first licensing round failed to attract more than two bidders. The key constraints in France appears to have been the attitude of the government, which chose not to confront both the sectoral regulator and established suppliers, and then market conditions (due to discouragement of bidders, arising in large measure from altered market conditions).

Finally, the outcomes were surprising in terms of the initial expectations and aims of national policy-makers. The enormous sums raised by the British auction were unexpected, especially for a process designed to increase competition rather than revenue. The Italian auction failed to produce the high bids for which it had been specifically designed, whilst the French beauty contest failed to attract even domestic suppliers or raise the substantial revenues desired. The outcomes cannot be entirely explained by national institutions: Italy and France faced very different market conditions to those in Britain and

Table 5.2   Outcomes of 3G mobile phone licensing

	Total government revenues from mobile phone licences (billion euros)	Licence revenues per head (euros)	Number of licences allocated
Britain	*c*.37 (£22.5b)[a]	*c*.642	5
Germany	50.5	615	6
Italy	14	210	5
France[b]	(a) first round: 9.8	(a) 163	(a) 2
	(b) second round 1.86	(b) 31	(b) 3

Notes

a   Depending on exchange rate used; figures cited for € from NAO (2001), Börgers and Dustmann (2002).

b   Figures exclude future tax on turnover; since in the second round prices were reduced for previous bidders, total revenues fell sharply.

Germany, as telecoms companies had already paid vast sums in the 3G bidding round and the high-technology stock market boom had ended, but nevertheless policy-makers in those two countries continued to apply lessons from British and German experiences that were no longer valid. At the same time, political battles in Italy and France over the balance between protecting domestic companies raising revenue played significant roles, both through the slowness in licensing and in design features that limited the number of bidders.

Four broad conclusions can be drawn related to the three worlds of regulatory innovation. First, with respect to the state world of innovation, 3G mobile phone licensing in Europe shows that technological developments offered opportunities for regulatory innovation, particularly for debates on choice of policy instruments, allocation of new property rights and the interests pursued by governments. They gave rise to sharp debates about how to regulate and policy-makers broke with past policies of protecting national incumbents through low-cost assured licences.

However, the chapter does not argue that technology on its own led to innovation. Other contingent factors were also needed for such opportunities to be taken. The analysis has paid particular attention to the politics of innovation, underlining the roles and strategies of governments. It shows how learning and examples contributed to governments rethinking their role in protecting domestic suppliers and hence altering traditional 'national champion' industrial policies in mobile phone communications.

The case of 3G mobile phone licensing thus suggests that the appearance of a new technology gives policy-makers, and especially governments, opportunities to alter regulation and to act contrary to the interests of powerful concentrated suppliers. Hence it permits governments to break out of inherited relationships and capture by incumbents, somewhat contrary to the expectations derived from the literature on how regulators will favour strong, established private interests and also on specifically European industrial policy studies on how governments support 'national champions'.

From a cross-national institutionalist perspective, a second broad conclusion is that the case of 3G mobile phone licensing shows how the combination of a new technology, fiscal pressures on governments and policy learning led very different nations to adopt similar policy aims and instruments. In particular, auctions were adopted by Germany and Italy as well as Britain, despite these countries having very diverse political institutions and representing distinct types of 'varieties of capitalism'. France adopted the aim of high revenues, although not an auction. Thus it seems that policy-makers can engage in major regulatory innovation – at least when there are favourable conditions, such as the appearance of a major new technology, learning from past domestic experiences or the availability of overseas examples of change. Hence even 'coordinated market economies' or those with many veto points, such as Germany or Italy, can introduce major regulatory innovations that run counter to those expected given their institutional frameworks. At the same time, there were important variations in the extent of change and cross-national convergence. Policy aims converged around high-cost licences. Policy instruments saw some convergence – around auctions or at least high-cost formalized beauty contests opened to new entrants and overseas bidders. However, the use of those instruments differed. Thus policy-makers in Italy and especially France sought greater discretion and higher protection of existing suppliers than in Britain and Germany. Licensing outcomes saw greatest differences – in terms of numbers of bidders, revenues raised and new entrants. In part dissimilarities are explicable by timing and alterations of market conditions. However, they are also linked to the ways in which existing institutions constrain or shape regulatory innovation. Thus Italy and France introduced less innovation than Britain, limited in large measure by strong links between government and suppliers. Overall, important movements in directions that run counter to those expected by much of the general comparative institutional literature on industrial and economic policy took place, but these were greatest for revenue aims and least for regulatory outcomes. Cross-national comparisons thus need to distinguish between different aspects of regulatory innovation.

For the world of individual entrepreneurs, 3G mobile phone licensing is a disappointment. Innovation was led by governments and state officials. Individuals outside the state, including economists, played a supporting role, adding detail to decisions driven by organizations. However, for those who believe that states can learn and innovate, the case of 3G mobile phone licensing is a welcome example that innovation is not a monopoly for the private sector – public officials too can be innovatory.

A final note concerns the world of the innovation. Auctions appear to be simple to understand and to copy. However, it was much easier for policy-makers in France and Italy to try to 'copy' the lesson that 3G mobile phone licensing offered high revenues than other features of the British and German examples. Introducing competitive auctions met stiff domestic opposition, to such an extent that they were not introduced in France. Moreover, more subtle features of the operation of an auction were more difficult to understand. These included factors such as the importance of timing, prevailing market sentiment, firms as well as governments learning from overseas experiences and incompatibility between aims of achieving high prices and also protecting existing domestic incumbents. The failure to understand these more difficult aspects of auctions contributed to the fact that the consequences of 3G mobile phone licensing were largely unexpected in terms of the aims and expectations of policy-makers. Early movers obtained many bids, very high revenues and greater competition. Policy-makers in nations that were later movers faced changed market conditions but applied learning that had become inappropriate to their aims of high revenues and also failed to introduce mechanisms to attract many new entrants. Thus British and German policy-makers were faced with unexpectedly large receipts for licences, a surprise compared with their past national lessons; in contrast, Italy and France had disappointing numbers of bidders and 3G licence revenues compared to their expectations derived from the experiences of Britain and Germany. The case thus serves as an antidote to beliefs that the outcomes of innovation can be controlled and predicted.

NOTES

1. They were allowed three waivers from this rule.
2. In addition to the four existing 2G network operators, a Canadian company, TIW obtained Licence A, reserved for a new entrant; soon afterwards it sold the subsidiary that owned the licence to Hutchinson Whampoa, based in Hong Kong.
3. The four incumbents were: T-Mobil, a subsidiary of Deutsche Telekom, Mannesmann-Vodafone, e-plus and Viag Interkom, backed by BT; the entrants were Mobilcom, supported by France Télécom, debitel, supported by Swisscom, and 3G, supported by Telefonica and Sonera.
4. Indeed, collusion between Blu and other bidders was suspected, leading to an ultimately unsuccessful legal action against the company – Perez (2002, p. 276–7).
5. For instance, Telefonica, Sonera, NTT DoCoMo, Virgin, Jazztel, Global Crossing, Worldcom, Tele 2 – see *Les Echos* (5 April 2000).

6. Between the old and the new: innovation in the regulation of Internet gambling

Colin Scott

INTRODUCTION

The takeoff of the Internet in the mid-1990s, linked to the development of the World Wide Web, has spawned a wide variety of new practices and applications of computing for both commercial and non-commercial purposes. These social and economic innovations have raised a variety of new challenges for governments, destabilizing, to some extent, state interests not only in regulation and law enforcement, but also taxation. Gambling on the Internet presents these challenges in a particularly acute form. The state is central to the nature of the market, and the existence, shape and activities of the (legal) market are determined by the regulatory framework to an extent which is unusual with other market activities (Collins 2003, p. 1). The destabilization effects are thus likely to be high. Paradoxically, perhaps, there is a high degree of dependence on non-state actors to provide solutions to regulatory problems (Scott 2004).

In this chapter we investigate the regulatory response to the challenges presented by the Internet to public policy in the area of remote gaming. We compare the recent policy history of three jurisdictions, New York State, Australia and the UK and use this comparison to elaborate on the analysis of the nature of regulatory innovation. Innovation to meet new policy conditions might be explicable by reference to the capacities of key actors to consider the various options and put the best solutions into effect. But in this case the diverse patterns of regulatory innovation appear to owe more to contingent factors in the institutional and cultural make up of the governmental units responsible for making and implementing policy on Internet gaming, set within the wider relationships and social and economic activities affecting policy implementation. In particular we find the individual world of the policy entrepreneur to be central to the capacity for particular types of innovation in regulatory enforcement in New York State, whereas policy developments in Australia and the UK are dominated by the organizational world in which policy is processed by government departments to reach workable solutions to identified problems which in some cases are innovative and in other instances not. It is striking that though the inter-jurisdictional dimension to the Internet is a key part of the policy problem presented by Internet gaming, the global world of interactions between governments, regulatory and policy entrepreneurs at the international level has only a limited role which is rarely decisive in shaping policy change. This may change as battles over Internet gaming regulation are won and lost at domestic level and key actors attempt to build international constituencies for policy or legal positions which support their interests.

The New York story represents a matching of conservatism in substantive policy with innovation in the instruments of regulatory enforcement, while the UK case offers a contrary pattern within which a radical policy shift is effected through the reinforcement of well-established policy instruments. Only in the Australian case are both the substantive policy and the methods of implementation radically reconceived so as to offer innovation in both dimensions. The bottom line for purposive regulatory reform is concerned with the effects and effectiveness of change. Effects may not be those which were intended, and responses may reveal the determination of outcomes to be outside the control of policy-makers and enforcement officials. Patterns of innovation in enforcement in Internet gaming suggest some recognition among officials concerning the limits of the state's regulatory capacities.

INTERNET GAMING AND REGULATORY INNOVATION

Internet gambling is big business. An official Australian report, while recognizing the difficulties of measurement, has adopted figures which suggest that global Internet gambling revenue nearly doubled between 2000 and 2002 from $A 3.1 billion to $A 5.6 billion, with an estimate that by 2006 the market will be worth $A 17.6 billion (DCITA 2004, p. 6, citing Balestra and Cabot 2003, p. 56). One could argue that this activity presents few new policy issues. 'Remote gambling' using telephone and fax pre-dates the Internet and most OECD countries made legislative responses to the issue long ago. Nevertheless the development of Internet gambling has caused governments to adapt regulatory policies and practices in response to perceptions that new or accentuated problems are presented (cf Collins 2003, chapter 7).

Two main forms of Internet gambling have emerged and grown very rapidly in popularity. Interactive wagering involves the use of the Internet as the medium for taking bets on 'real world' events such as horse races and soccer games. This commercial application of the Internet is seen within policy circles as essentially similar to the use of telephone or fax for the placing of bets on

such sports events, which is already legalized and regulated in all three jurisdictions. Internet gaming, in which punters are simply pitting themselves
against a computer, offers both traditional activities such as poker games and
slot machine activities, and new types of game. With Internet gaming the
outcome is determined by the computer using a random number generator
(Australian Senate 2000, paras 1.7, 2.3). The development of such Internet
gaming (or Internet casinos) cuts across national and state policies which seek
to regulate or ban certain forms of gaming transactions. The provision of
Internet gaming is attractive to businesses because the start-up and running
costs are much less than those of a bricks and mortar operation (McMillen
2003). An official Australian report has suggested that government should
support Internet gambling operations on the basis that they achieve higher
productivity both in terms of capital and labour costs (DCITA 2004,
p. 36).

Internet gaming has the potential not only to replicate but also to magnify
some of the policy problems associated with gambling, because of its immediacy, the potential for anonymity for the punter, and the inter-jurisdictional
reach of the Internet. Internet gambling, it has been suggested, offers a 'quantum leap in accessibility' for punters (DCITA 2004, p. 41). The immediacy of
Internet gaming creates risk that players will act irrationally in spending on
gaming well beyond what they can afford given the risks of substantial losses.
The anonymity of gaming on a computer in one's own home is thought to
reduce the effects of inhibitions and processes of social control which prevent
some from taking up gaming and encourage others to gamble only moderately.
Thus commentators anticipate an increase in 'problem gambling' (McMillen
and Grabosky 1998, p. 2). The inter-jurisdictional reach of the Internet greatly
reduces the effects of traditional controls over gaming that were oriented
towards the presence of the punter in a licensed premises and now enables
punters to deal with firms offering gaming from potentially any country in the
world. This last feature makes application of domestic regulatory rules highly
problematic, while immediacy and anonymity may increase the potential for
causing problem gaming. There are also risks to consumers in dealing with
overseas sites that games could be rigged or that winnings might not be paid
(McMillen 2003).

The interest of the state in gambling has various dimensions. The social
problems generated by gambling are but one aspect. Law may be considered
to have an expressive function, expressing, *inter alia*, the morality of society.
In societies where gambling is considered immoral, laws which prohibit
gambling reflect and reinforce that disapprobation. A more pragmatic reason
for controlling gambling is linked to wider criminal enforcement functions. A
major longitudinal study of crime rates across all US states suggests that the
operation of casinos was a significant factor in increasing levels of crime in

counties where casinos are located (Grinols et al. 2000). Additionally large-scale gambling operations create opportunities for organized crime to engage in money laundering (Miers 2004, p. 503), and Internet casinos are identified by the OECD Financial Action Task Force on Money Laundering as a key risk area falling within the OECD guidelines on controlling transactions which may permit money laundering (OECD 2003a). Large-scale gambling is also connected to the development of other criminal rackets such as the provision of private protection services in competition with state law enforcement authorities.

Prohibitions on gambling do not, by themselves, necessarily alleviate these problems. Indeed prohibition may create enhanced opportunities for corruption and a consequent undermining of confidence in the probity of law enforcement agencies. The growth of police corruption in twentieth-century New South Wales and Queensland, an endemic problem for many years, has been partially linked to attempts by the states to suppress off-course 'starting price' (SP) bookmaking from the 1930s (Dixon 1996, pp. 87–9). Decriminalization of off-course SP began in Britain at about the same time as the Australian crackdown and was partly targeted at reducing both police corruption and incentives to link gambling to organized crime (Dixon 1996, pp. 90–1).

State interest in gambling also extends to the collection of taxation revenues, which may be linked to the introduction of legalized gambling, but which are threatened by the flight of gambling money to overseas firms connected with their punters by the Internet. In the United States liberalization in respect of bricks and mortar operations for reasons of raising tax, tourism and lottery revenues has apparently outstripped changes in social values which have traditionally frowned on gambling while doing little to stem the growth in illegal gambling activity and the problems it brings (Abt 1996, p. 182).

Internet gaming provides a new dimension to the old policy problem of how stringently to control gambling and what techniques to use. Thus it is a newly configured problem to which both old and new solutions have been applied. Following the usage of Julia Black in the first chapter we conceive of regulatory innovation as the application of new solutions either to new problems or to old problems. Some innovations take the form of second-order change in which new processes or techniques are applied to the policy problem. A third-order change involves a reconceptualization of the policy domain or a paradigm shift in the approach deployed. In all three jurisdictions there were well-established policies on regulation of gaming prior to development of Internet gaming. Internet gaming is itself a second-order innovation within the world of gambling operations, representing a new technique for delivery of an old product. We might expect the policy response in areas where public policy is well established to be biased towards the incremental and this appears to be the case most strongly with the New York State case. The Australian case exhibits incrementalism in one dimension of the policy – permitting the continuation of licences of Internet gaming operations within the jurisdiction but prohibiting licensees from serving customers located in Australia and prohibiting the states and territories from issuing further licences. But in respect of punters located in Australia the approach is more radical – imposing a prohibition. With the UK the approach combines the regulatory technology of a commission, well established in other regulatory domains, with a radical liberalization of substantive policy so as to permit the licensing of online gaming operations in the UK for the first time.

The focus of attention is on the regulatory structure – the basic legal rules governing Internet gambling – and on techniques of enforcement. The introduction of new enforcement techniques represents a second-order innovation, while significant changes to the regulatory structure, and in particular the stringency of control, exemplify third-order innovation. What is striking is that innovation in one of these dimensions is accompanied by non-innovation in the other, though in a different mix, in both New York State and the UK. The Australian Federal Government alone of the three jurisdictions examined in this chapter innovates to a significant degree in both dimensions.

Notwithstanding the revolution associated with the Internet, the position of the New York State Attorney-General's Department is one in which they hold to the familiar paradigm of prohibition over gambling but, recognizing the limits to state enforcement, deploying new instruments, and in particular the targeting of payment intermediaries – second-order innovation.

The UK story shows a government responding to change with third-order innovation – a paradigm shift away from a restrictive policy, suspicious of gaming, to an embracing of the possibilities of being a world leader in the regulation of legitimate gaming activities. New instruments, second-order innovations, are deployed only at the margins, as with the application of new technologies to permit punters to self-control their own usage. Overall the UK case reasserts the classical model of state regulation as a solution to the Internet gaming policy problem, along with the regulatory competition which the policy engenders.

But, of course, one could argue that the very deployment of new mechanisms of control is, in itself, a paradigm shift in the New York case, a move away from state-centric control and both a shifting of responsibility and recognition of the capacity of key firms to act as gatekeepers over the Internet. From the perspective of the instruments of the regulatory state there is little that is innovative about the UK story. The Australian story is, perhaps, the most unequivocally innovative (second-order change – new instruments of enforcement linked to third-order change – rethinking the nature and objectives of control over gaming), in the sense that federal legislative policy represents a departure from traditional liberal approaches in the states and territories, and in that it also engages a systematic targeting of intermediaries centrally among the instruments for delivering the policy.

THE CONTINGENCY OF REGULATORY INNOVATION

The pattern of innovation investigated in the previous section requires explanation. While the United States was a pioneer of classical regulatory agency models from the creation of the Interstate Commerce Commission in 1887 through to the more extensive use of this model of regulatory independence during the New Deal era, it is not regarded as a leading innovator today. Yet the New York State Attorney-General's office has been the pioneering innovator in the enrolment of the gate-keeping capacity of banks to support government policy on the control of Internet gaming. Conversely many analysts regard the UK as offering the leading case of sustained regulatory innovation (and even hyper-innovation (Moran 2003)) over the past 25 years. But in this case the instruments deployed for the implementation of UK policy were of the tried and tested rather than the innovative variety. Each of the three cases suggest that attempts to explain regulatory innovation as a product of rational consideration of options and selection of optimal instruments have little power. Taken together the three stories suggest that the nature and extent of innovations was contingent upon such factors as the existence of policy entrepreneurs (particularly in the New York case), the structuring and allocation of tasks within governmental departments, the wider constitutional setting, and particular perspectives on the globalization of competition in Internet gaming. In each case these factors affected not only the policy response, but also the way the policy problem was characterized, as shown in Table 6.1.

As with other areas of public policy it is possible to construct contrasting but overlapping worlds within which debates about regulatory policy and implementation occur. Policy on Internet gambling involves complex interaction between social and political actors involving both moral and fiscal dimensions. It is striking that, notwithstanding this complexity, the worlds of the individual and the organization appear to be quite significant in fostering innovation in the regulatory response to Internet gaming in New York State. In Australia and the UK we see more of what we might expect by way of policy dominated by the state world of bureaucracies, public and private, seeking to work through their various interests in the issue. The inter-jurisdictional aspect of the Internet, and the diffuse locations of both Internet gaming operators, punters and governments willing to license operators adds an important global dimension which none of the three states examined in this chapter can ignore.

Table 6.1 Comparison of policies on Internet gaming in three jurisdictions

	New York State	Australia (Federal)	UK
Characterization of policy problem	Enforcement of law constitutional prohibition on unauthorized gaming in face of Internet	How to minimize harm to Australian punters associated with growth of Internet gaming	Given the increase of gaming opportunities associated with Internet how to minimize harm to UK punters while increasing tax revenue
Substantive norms	Prohibition and criminalization of offering of Internet gaming within New York state and to persons located in New York State	Prohibition and criminalization of of offering of Internet gaming services to persons located within Australia; state/territory licensing and regulation of Internet gaming services supplied to punters outside Australia permitted	Provision of Internet gaming services within UK to persons within or outside UK permitted subject to licensing and regulation by new Gambling Commission
Enforcement	Prosecution of any person located in New York offering prohibited gaming	Prosecution of persons within Australia offering prohibited Internet gaming	Main monitoring and and enforcement effort focuses on licensed UK

services; targeting of financial intermediaries (banks, Internet payment systems) in respect of offshore Internet gaming services

services. Agency monitoring of provision of prohibited services to Australia; targeting of intermediaries (financial – voluntary; ISPs – code of practice and potential for mandatory blocking of access to sites

operators; offshore operators targeting UK punters regulated by competition from regulated UK operators

The New York state story is part of a wider policy under which Attorney-General Eliot Spitzer is seeking to lead the world in policies that seek to protect consumers from the problems of the Internet. The restrictive approach to Internet gaming which this concern engenders is supported also by a tradition within the United States of doubt about the morality of gambling generally, which is relaxed somewhat in respect of wagering and state lotteries, but which leads to widespread condemnation of commercial gaming.

The power of Spitzer's personality, and the extent of his identification with aggressive enforcement policies (particularly in the area of financial services) has generated a new word in the American lexicon. To be 'Spitzered' is to be investigated for financial services legislation offences.[1] The New York State story is one of enforcement within a bureaucracy with little transparency, giving a significant role to the initiative of the Attorney-General. The relative opacity of policy-making and implementation, linked to a paucity of formal consultation, give space for a form of entrepreneurship which is connected more to the ambitions and ideas of the policy-makers than to any identified needs among the public. This has been characterized as 'empowered entrepreneurship' (Bartlett and Dibben 2002). To the extent that staff in the Attorney-General's department have sought allies, these have been with the wider enforcement community in the United States. The alignment of state enforcement policies with wider federal legislation on wire communications reinforces the centrality of the enforcement function to the definition of policy.

Within the Attorney-General's office key staff are located in the Internet Bureau, which was established in 1998 to address a wide range of enforcement issues largely relating to consumer protection. Thus the strategy for enforcing criminal law against gaming operators has been spearheaded by an assistant Attorney-General, while the targeting of information intermediaries is a strategy devised by Kenneth Dreifach who heads the Internet Bureau. Vigorous assertion of the ban on Internet gaming may, of course, act to protect both state and non-state actors and their legitimate and illegitimate activities. The state has a legitimate interest in raising revenue through lotteries. New York state devotes all lottery revenues to education, and lottery funds comprise 5 per cent of the state funding of schools. It may be hypothesized that Internet gaming and lotteries are to some extent in competition with each other in the gambling market and the prohibition on the latter assists in maintaining the revenue of the former. The prohibition on gaming in New York state also supports a market in illegal gaming. While such illegal gambling creates a significant enforcement problem for enforcement agencies it also creates opportunities for corrupt officers to receive payments for protecting such operations. The development of policy within an enforcement paradigm in New York State has been a significant factor in encouraging a variety of private sector intermediaries to cooperate with the Attorney-General's strategy for addressing Internet gaming, notably in providing resources for what amounts to private enforcement of prohibitions on Internet gaming. This policy has involved the use of the state's coercive power to enrol financial intermediaries in the enforcement tasks.

New York State has been an early mover on tightening enforcement of gaming laws against Internet casinos. The Australian federal government has sought directly to adopt the New York model, but in an environment where US adversarial legalism (Kagan 2000) is much less significant within dominant enforcement styles. The need for uncoerced cooperation in the Australian context has forced the Australian government into a rather different strategy and a different organizational focus for its enforcement efforts, though recognizably of the same family of enforcement innovations which are dependent on intermediaries for their effects.

The UK and Australian stories involve state worlds dominated by policy-making in government departments and a shift in the underlying moral imperatives which have permitted a relaxation of controls over gaming since World War II. The shift in responsibility for gambling within UK government in June 2001 from the Home Office (traditionally responsible for the criminal justice system and supervision of law enforcement) to the Department for Culture, Media and Sport (DCMS) represented a form of convergence since this UK department mirrors some of the responsibilities of the Australian federal Department of Communications, Information Technology and the Arts, the department with responsibility for policy on interactive gambling. This shift in responsibility is significant since the Home Office conceives of itself as largely concerned with criminal justice matters, whereas the DCMS is oriented chiefly towards policy on entertainment.

A key difference between the UK and Australian policy worlds is the split jurisdiction over gambling in the Australian federal system and the potential for a dialectical process between the two levels of government which has resulted in an apparently contradictory policy of regulated liberalization of Internet gaming for the rest of the world but prohibition for Australians. This story may reflect the desire of federal government to involve itself in a policy domain generally reserved to the states and territories. State stewardship of gambling policy has seen the states competing with each other to liberalize gaming rules, encouraging massive growth in expenditure by consumers on gambling, and also very substantial tax contributions to state coffers. Organized interests, both from gaming firms and groups opposed to gaming, play a much stronger role in the development of Australian policy, a reflection of a longer history of liberalization at state and territory level. The widespread legalization of gaming in the Australian states has also targeted problems of corruption of law enforcement officials (Dixon 1996).

There are international pressures on national policies, particularly because of the inter-jurisdictional reach of Internet activities. Governmental policies on Internet gaming globally are highly diverse, but must each address the effects on national economies and societies of the policies of others. These policy externalities are a key driver for all three cases examined in this chapter. A number of states have sought to promote Internet gaming from their jurisdictions in order to collect licensing revenue and have accordingly applied minimal regulatory requirements. Antigua is a leader in this market licensing of Internet gaming. The firms offering Internet gaming services are highly mobile and capable of moving their operations to favourable regulatory and taxation regimes.

These pressures notwithstanding, the global world of policy development found in regulatory networks, intergovernmental organizations, and the juridical capacity of supranational orders, though not immune from a need to address the impact of Internet gaming, has had little impact on national policymaking. Interactions between regulators in the global world provide support for a restrictive approach, but policy positions within the key international policy-making institutions do not command support among all governments and to the extent that prohibitions on Internet gaming have been tested in international legal fora the outcomes have been mixed.

Among the supranational governance institutions the OECD has developed a strong interest in the regulation of e-commerce generally (OECD 2003b) but has limited its engagement with Internet gaming to the development of norms to control money laundering through this medium (OECD 2003a). The Gaming Regulators' European Forum (1998) have set down a principle of respect for the policy decisions and national lawmaking in respect of Internet gaming. Accordingly they recommend that Internet gaming should be directed only at persons within the jurisdiction in which it is licensed and regulated or at persons in other jurisdictions with which bilateral or reciprocal arrangements exist. The UK government has rejected this position in favour of a free market approach, noting that the governments of Australia and New York State are free to attempt to block access to prohibited gaming sites or use other means such as the targeting of payment intermediaries (DCMS 2003a, p. 24). A WTO appellate panel has upheld a claim by the government of Antigua that the US policy of extraterritorial application of criminal law breaches international trade rules.[2] The European Court of Justice (ECJ) has been asked on a number of occasions to rule on the legality of laws establishing restrictions which protect national lotteries and gaming operations from international competition. Ladbrokes have been key players in challenging national restrictions through litigation. In the first decision on remote gaming, the ECJ applied its earlier doctrine that restrictions may be justified on moral or social grounds, such as the wish to inhibit the growth of problem gaming, where the legal measures adopted are proportionate to the objective sought.[3]

THE EXTENT OF INNOVATION

In this section of the chapter we evaluate the extent of innovation in the three jurisdictions, comparing the structure of the legal norms on Internet gaming first before moving on to compare old and new enforcement mechanisms. The analysis is suggestive not of any systematic pattern of innovation (or hyper-innovation) but rather of limited and institutionally specific instances of regulatory innovation. If there is a claimant to hyper-innovation this is provided by the Australian case in which the federal government changed both the policy paradigm, through abandoning the historically liberal approach to gaming adopted by the state and territory governments, while seeking innovative mechanisms through which to enforce the new prohibitions.

Old Norms

The Constitution of the State of New York prohibits all gambling within the state which is not authorized by the state legislature (Article 1, section 9(1)). New York's penal code further criminalizes unlawful gambling (New York Penal Law, s. 225). In practice the state has pursued a very restrictive approach to gaming generally. The UK similarly took a quite restrictive policy approach to controlling the availability of casinos and gaming machines more tightly than was the case with ubiquitous wagering operations such as betting shops. It is pretty clear that within both jurisdictions it is unlawful to establish a gaming operation such as an online casino without a licence. Indeed the UK Gaming Act 1968 requires punters to be physically present on the premises of the licensed operator (Miers 2004, p. 502). These legislative requirements, which pre-date the Internet, make the operation of an online casino illegal in the UK but have not been applied to the provision of online gaming services to persons located in the UK from other jurisdictions.

In Australia responsibility for regulation of gambling generally falls to the state and territory governments. These governments have adopted increasingly liberal approaches to casinos and gaming machines (McMillen 2003). The initial response of the states and territories to the development of Internet gaming was to offer licences to Internet gaming operators analogous to those held by bricks and mortar casinos. These policies were reflected in a joint report issued in 1997 which set out a 'Draft Regulatory Control Model for New Forms of Interactive Home Gambling' (Australian Senate 2000, appendix 6). The draft regulatory control model has had wide influence and underpinned a report from a Committee of the Australian Senate published in 2000. The Senate Committee highlighted the difficulties associated with enforcing a prohibition on Internet gaming and recommended the adoption of a raft of innovative regulatory strategies aimed at 'harm minimization'. The Senators were concerned, in particular, that a prohibition would drive Australian gamblers to online gaming sites located in reputable jurisdictions, but which did not have in place harm minimization measures of the kind they proposed for Australia (Australian Senate 2000, para 1.27). It may be added that strict prohibition creates considerable enforcement costs for a government while gambling revenues would 'continue to flow to another jurisdiction' (McMillen and Grabosky 1998, p. 3).

The measures proposed by the Senate Committee included the development and application of technology to identify and exclude problem gamblers; time limits on gambling; use of hot links to problem gambling information; and requirements of better information for customers about odds of winning and losing and amounts won and lost (Australian Senate 2000, para 1.28 and table 1.2). These proposed measures were substantially modelled both on the draft regulatory control model and on the existing voluntary practice of Lasseters Online, a major Australian gaming operation located in the Northern Territory. No doubt keen to ward off prohibition, Lasseters provided detailed assistance both to government and the Senate in drawing up their policies. The Senate Committee noted its belief that strict regulation would be of value to Australian firms seeking to market their services in other jurisdictions (para 2.43). This market effect of credible regulation would in turn be expected to bring additional tax revenue.

New Norms

In the face of the new commercial activities facilitated by the Internet, New York State has responded by reasserting its traditional highly restrictive approach. This conservatism is in part a reflection of the fact that the issue has not been considered as a matter of legislative policy, but is asserted rather as an adaptation of existing enforcement policy within the office of the state Attorney-General's Internet Bureau, a unit charged with protecting consumers from the evils associated with the Internet.

The position in Australia is more complicated. The states and territories hold to the diverse, but substantially liberal approach to gaming, licensing and regulating gaming machines and casinos and deriving substantial tax revenues from them. This is unsurprising. The popularity of gambling together with the advantages to governments of the revenues appear to make it a win–win policy. However the interstate (and international) dimension to Internet gaming has given the federal government a legitimate interest in the issue. The Liberal government in power since 1996 under John Howard has been socially conservative and has seized on the opportunity to assert greater restrictions on gambling, developing a policy markedly at variance from the states and territories. The federal government substantially rejected the approach of the draft regulatory control model and adopted a policy which permitted wagering on the Internet (gambling on real-world events such as sports) but prohibited persons located in Australia from engaging in Internet gaming, while permitting existing licensed Australian operators to offer Internet gaming services to persons located elsewhere in the world. The exception of existing licensed operators dealing with offshore customers can be seen in two possible ways. It may be that the government was reluctant to withdraw existing licences completely, facing possible allegations of confiscation, but anticipated that in practice the existing operators would wither when starved of Australian customers. Alternatively the government might have been seeking to permit Australian firms to compete in the global marketplace, trading on the reputation of Australia for stringent regulation and consumer protection. The issue is discussed further in the section on effects and effectiveness below.

The use of its legislative power to implement this policy in the Interactive Gambling Act 2001 has been described as 'unprecedented' in terms of the federal government grab over powers to regulate gambling, and was implemented despite the fact that the National Office for the Information Economy report on the issue could not recommend a feasible mechanism for making a ban effective through either legal prohibition or physical blocking of transactions (McMillen 2003). Lying behind the policy was a concern to protect Australian citizens from what were perceived as accentuated risks of problem gambling associated with the Internet, while at the same timer permitting less problematic Internet gambling activities (such as wagering) and permitting Australian firms (and the Australian Tax Office) to benefit from the profits available from offering Internet gaming from Australia to punters in countries where it is permitted.

Like Australia, the UK has engaged in a major review of gambling policy, partly in response to issues raised by the Internet, but also with a view to liberalizing gambling more generally. The Gambling Review, which reported in 2001, recommended that UK companies should in future be licensed and regulated to provide online gaming services from servers located in the UK using UK domain names. Regulation by a new Gambling Commission would entail routine random checks and audits of software systems, mandatory requirements that firms provided set limits and capacity for self-banning of punters and requirements that licensed providers display the Gambling Commission kitemark (DCMS 2001, recommendations 137–151). These recommendations have been substantially adopted by government and incorporated in a draft bill (DCMS 2003c, DCMS 2003b).

Old Enforcement

The NY Attorney-General's Office Internet Bureau has adopted a multi-pronged approach to its attempts to enforce the ban on Internet gaming within the state. The case which initially prompted an action for enforcement through the courts landed within the policy world tangentially. In 1998, the Internet Bureau had referred to a complaint from the state of Nevada about an online gaming operation for which the servers were licensed and located in Antigua, but the parent company was physically located in Suffolk County, New York State. The initial complaint against the World Interactive Gaming Corporation (WIGC) was not about Internet gaming but rather investment fraud. The New York State Supreme Court held that the creation of 'a virtual casino within the user's computer terminal' in New York State was in breach of the ban on Internet gaming within the state, irrespective of where the company's servers were located and imposed substantial penalties and granted an injunction.[4] The granting of remedies against the firm was a key aspect of the development of the Internet Bureau's juridical strategy for tackling Internet gaming. In this particular case the firm was physically located in New York State making the application of remedies more straightforward, but this was not a precondition to the success of the Attorney-General in claiming remedies as it was the action of the punter in communicating with the gaming servers and not the location of the firm which gave the New York courts jurisdiction over the matter.

The exact position in federal law is uncertain. The Wire Act of 1961 prohibits the knowing use of wire communication for 'the transmission of interstate or foreign commerce of bets and wagers or information assisting in the placing of bets or wagers' (18 USC 1084(a)). The New York State Supreme Court held that the use of the Internet for gaming across state and international border was a violation of this legislation[5] but there is some uncertainty whether the provisions of the legislation really extend beyond sports betting to gaming. A bill introduced by Senator Jon Kyl was intended to put the matter beyond doubt in favour of prohibition by putting into federal law a prohibition on the acceptance of virtually all forms of payment other than cash for Internet gambling transactions generally ('restricted transactions').[6] The Bill proposed rules requiring that all such restricted transactions be coded so as to be readily identifiable and establishes a new agency (the Office of Electronic Funding Oversight) to monitor and enforce both the new procedural requirements and the core prohibition. Notwithstanding the doubts as to the position in federal law it is reported that federal prosecutors have begun investigations into whether US firms trading with offshore Internet gaming providers are illegally 'aiding and abetting' criminal activity. In response to these investigations it is reported that a number of major corporations have ceased advertising online gaming operations.[7]

The approach of New York State, and United States authorities generally, applying state criminal laws to offshore gaming operations, is widely contested. The UK government has rejected the US legal doctrine to the effect that online gaming takes place within the 'virtual casino' created by the punter's computer, in favour of an understanding that the activity occurs where the operator is based (DCMS 2003a, p. 25, DCMS 2003b, para 4.67). Thus one of the main brands in the UK betting industry has established an online casino in Gibraltar which is targeted chiefly at UK punters.[8]

The main legal instrument of control in Australia is the Interactive Gambling Act 2001. The Act prohibits and criminalizes the provision of Internet gaming services to persons in Australia by means of a general prohibition on interactive gambling (ss. 5, 6, 15), subject to exceptions (s. 6(3)) for telephone betting services, wagering on events, series of events and contingencies (s. 8A(1)), gaming in public places (s. 8B(1)) and the provision of some, but not all, lottery services (ss. 6(3), 8A(1), 8B(1), 8D). The prohibition can be extended by ministerial declaration to the provision of Internet gaming to persons located in other jurisdictions (ss. 9A, 15A). The Act additionally prohibits the advertising of Internet gaming services in Australia (s. 61 EA). Monitoring of the availability of prohibited services falls to the federal regulator, the Australian Broadcasting Authority (ABA). The ABA is required to consider complaints about availability of illegal gaming services to persons located in Australia. Where investigation reveals that the servers are located in Australia the matter is to be referred to Australian Federal Police for criminal enforcement. In contrast with the US doctrine, which seeks to enforce New York State criminal law internationally, the 2001 Act triggers novel and non-criminal enforcement mechanisms in respect of services provided from outside Australia, discussed in the next section.

New Enforcement

Having established the criminal status of the activities of offering Internet gaming services to persons located in New York State, wherever the provider may be located, the next headache for the Internet Bureau was conceived as a problem of enforcement. In the test case against WIGC it was fortuitous that the firm operating Internet gaming from abroad nevertheless had its corporate offices within New York State. This characteristic does not hold true for most Internet gaming operations.

The key innovation in the enforcement strategy occurred when the Internet Bureau decided to target the payment intermediaries rather than the online casino operators. The targeting of financial intermediaries was already established in policy initiatives in a number of jurisdictions, including New York State, directed at money laundering activities. It is a precondition for operating an Internet gaming service that the service provider is able to receive payments from punters anywhere in the world. Most of these payments are electronic and provided through payment intermediaries such as banks which issue credit cards and specialist Internet payment services such as Paypal. The targeting of financial intermediaries exploits the practice of Visa and Mastercard of coding all credit card transactions in such a way that the issuing bank can know what kind of transaction is being made before granting approval. This practice, combined with various technologies for monitoring customer expenditure patterns, is used in attempting to combat credit card fraud. Thus gaming or gambling transactions are assigned a merchant category code and, a separate indicator will show where there is an e-commerce transaction (DCITA 2004, p. 80). It appears quite simple in principle for card issuing banks simply to reject all e-commerce transactions which involve gaming or gambling.

The Internet Bureau highlighted to payment intermediaries the criminal nature of the enterprise offering Internet gaming and asked the banks and others whether they wanted to be associated with supporting such activity. In at least two instances the contacts between the Internet Bureau and the payment intermediaries took the form of a formal investigation, resolved only by voluntary assurances from the payment intermediaries that they would refuse to accept payments for online gaming.

The first such 'assurance of discontinuance' was given by Citibank in June 2002. Citibank is a national banking operation which issued Mastercard and Visa credit cards to consumers with New York State billing addresses. In 2001 it was the largest issuer of bank cards in the USA. While denying any breach of the law in providing general purpose credit, Citibank nevertheless gave in to the pressure from the Internet Bureau and agreed to decline all transactions identified as Internet gaming, whether the consumer was located in or billed to New York State or not. It is indicative of the degree of pressure which Citibank faced, and in particular a reluctance to push the issue to litigation, that it also agreed to pay the state's investigation costs of $100 000 and a sum of $400 000 to charitable organizations offering support to those harmed by compulsive or problem gambling. Perhaps even more extraordinary is an acknowledgement by the Attorney-General that neither Citibank nor its regulator (the Office of the Comptroller of the Currency (OCC) accepted the jurisdiction of the Attorney-General to seek or enforce the assurance given by the bank.[9] In the second assurance, given by Internet payment system operator Paypal in August 2002, the decision by Paypal not to accept payments for online gaming from New York State residents was said to be a matter of voluntary cooperation with the Internet Bureau. In this instance Paypal agreed to pay $200 000 to the state as 'disgorgement of profits related to online gambling, penalties and costs of investigation.'[10]

From this platform of criminalization of Internet gaming through litigation and formal enforcement actions (falling short of litigation) and voluntary penalties for payment intermediaries, the Internet Bureau has targeted further payment intermediaries to secure their cooperation in refusing to process payments to online gaming service providers. Ten further banks signed up to blocking online gaming transactions and payment of the state's investigative costs in February 2003. Attorney-General Eliot Spitzer said of the settlements that they 'mark a trend in law enforcement to focus on intermediaries in combating illegal online activity' (Office of New York State Attorney-General Press Release, 11 February 2003).

Evasion of the 'voluntary refusal' to process Internet gaming transactions takes a number of forms. First, it may be possible for consumers to sign up to payment intermediaries in other jurisdictions and beyond the persuasive forces of the New York State Internet Bureau or US federal prosecutors. Thus Internet payment services outside the USA are liable to be attractive to US citizens seeking to gamble online, and it may be possible to secure credit cards from overseas providers. A second possibility for consumers seeking to evade the controls is simply to make pre-payments by cheque.[11]

Enforcement of the prohibition on Internet gaming within Australia is pursued using a number of approaches. The Australian government has sought to take up the New York State practice of persuading the banks to decline identifiable Internet gaming transactions on their customers' credit cards, through substantially private and apparently unsuccessful negotiations. The Australian banks simply do not accept that the provision of general purpose credit to fund illegal activities renders the banks themselves subject ultimately to prosecution and, in the absence of such a threat, they are unwilling to restrict the services they provide their customers. Additionally the practice of the Australian banks is not to check the merchant category code prior to authorizing transactions (DCITA 2004, pp. 81–2). Accordingly the government has considered using powers to require banks to decline such transactions and/or to make prohibited transactions under the IGA unenforceable, making credit offered to consumers unrecoverable. The Australian banks oppose the proposed ban on the grounds that the provision of general purpose credit can be used for a wide range of activities which the government might like to ban and it is wrong to turn the banks into moral arbiters. ('Banks oppose net bet card ban', *The Australian*, 4 May 2004). The government has apparently accepted the case against a statutory ban, but on the grounds that it would likely damage legal gambling activity through over-inclusive application (DCITA 2004, p. 76). The government has additionally rejected the option of making debts incurred in Internet gaming unenforceable on the grounds that it might be counterproductive. First this might encourage consumers to gamble more, in the knowledge that the banks could not pursue the debts. This in turn might cause the banks to refuse all Internet gambling transactions, whether prohibited or not, and thus damage legitimate businesses.

More promising are other mechanisms for targeting key intermediaries located in Australia. A key innovation to deal with the accessibility of Internet services which are illegal in Australia but located overseas has been the development of a co-regulatory code of practice. This approach was initially developed in other legislation targeted at undesirable Internet contents provided on overseas servers (Broadcasting Services (Online Services) Amendment Act 1999) (Airo-Farulla 2003) and is, accordingly, an indigenous solution. Under the code the Australian Broadcasting Authority collects information about illegal sites and has the power to require all Internet service providers (ISPs) to 'take all reasonable steps to prevent end-users from accessing the content' (IGA 2001 s. 24(1)(c)). Though this power of direction is apparently quite intrusive, it is questionable whether it is technologically feasible for ISPs to implement bans on access to particular sites (DCITA 2004, p. 67). The draconian power of direction can be avoided through the creation by the ISP industry of an industry code of practice under which ISPs are obliged to provide filtering software to exclude access to the prohibited sites (s. 24(1)(b)). Prohibited sites are defined by reference to the provisions of the Interactive Gambling Act 2001. Up to March 2004 the ABA had identified ten overseas sites as offering prohibited services to Australia and required their inclusion in filtering software (DCITA 2004, p. 49). Central weaknesses in the code are that the take-up of filtering software is optional for consumers and that ISPs are permitted to charge users for it (Internet Industry Association 2001). Thus the co-regulatory model appears unlikely to be effective. It is possible that the threat of more coercive action to block access to sites might encourage ISPs to make the code workable in practice, an application of the pyramid of regulatory technique within the theory of responsive regulation (Ayres and Braithwaite 1992, chapter 2; Gunningham and Grabosky 1998, p. 398).

While the UK government is substantially seeking to rely on traditional licensing and inspection, the current reform proposals also make use of technological and other means to reduce potential harm to punters. For example in respect of displays, government is seeking to prohibit the use of the whole screen for a game so that punters can always see the onscreen clock of their operating system. Similarly links to problem gambling advice and to the Gambling Commission are to be visible at all times (DCMS 2003b, p. 14). The government suggests that good practice will be for online gaming operators to register their URL with filtering services so that users of filtering services (such as Netnanny) can opt to have access to gaming sites blocked. Punters should be able to restrict or limit their own expenditure by registering with the operator and operators should build in natural breaks in play after each hour (DCMS 2003a, pp. 12–13). The government's intention is that the regime should have a reputation for very high standards of regulation such that UK punters will choose to gamble only with readily identifiable UK operators (DCMS 2003a, para 4.69).

REGULATORY EFFECTS AND EFFECTIVENESS

In this section we distinguish regulatory effects, as the consequences of regulatory actions, from the subset of effects which are aligned with the objectives of those responsible, from the regulatory regime which we label 'effectiveness'. The wider set of effects includes consequences which were not intended but which are consistent with the objectives of the regime, unintended consequences which are neither positive nor negative for the objectives of the regime and counterproductive or reverse effects (Grabosky 1995).

There is some evidence that the hostile regulatory environment for Internet gaming, and in particular in the United States is reducing projected growth in revenue for online gaming operators (DCITA 2004, p. 7). The US jurisdictions, of which New York state has been a leader, appear to have persuaded the majority of banks to refuse credit card transactions involving Internet gambling. An official report suggested that 80 per cent of the purchase volume of cards is covered by what is in essence a voluntary prohibition (DCITA 2004, p. 15). In Australia the legislative regime introduced in 2001 has inhibited the licensing of new Internet gaming operations and, through the ban on taking custom from persons located in Australia, forced the closure, on commercial grounds, of all but one of the existing licensed operations. One Australian firm which ran Ausvegas Casino online from Australia cited the risk of breaching the legislative prohibition inadvertently as an additional reason for ceasing its operations (DCITA 2004, pp. 42–3). The attempt to transfer from the USA the policy of targeting financial intermediaries to Australia has not been successful because it was not embedded within a wider capacity for enforcement and because the Australian banks appeared to have greater political clout in resisting compulsion. The indigenous Australian strategy for targeting ISPs (which would likely call forth howls of protest from organized US groups such as the Electronic Frontier Foundation) appear more promising because they are embedded within the wider legislative capacities for directing ISPs.

It is more difficult to gauge the effects of the Australian and New York State bans on Internet gaming on levels of Internet gambling by citizens of those jurisdictions. Some data from Australia suggests that while legal Internet wagering is growing, illegal Internet gaming is declining. Official data in Australia suggests that between 1999 and 2003 the number of users of Internet gaming within Australia declined from 56 000 to 18 000 (DCITA 2004, pp. 43–5), but comparisons between levels of legitimate and illegitimate activity are notoriously unreliable.

The liberal regime proposed for the UK, 'an interesting exercise in regulatory arbitrage' according to a leading commentator (Miers 2004, p. 503), is intended to encourage operators targeting the UK to subject themselves to UK regulation. The stated objective is to maintain high standards so as to permit

UK firms to compete for business on the basis that they are tightly regulated. The minister has explicitly ruled out any participation by the UK in 'race to the bottom' in regulatory standards (Joint Parliamentary Committee on the Gambling Bill 2004, p. 146). However, there is some suggestion that firms will choose to locate offshore in order to avoid the 15 per cent tax levied on gambling transactions in the UK, and take advantage of their capacity to market themselves to the UK legally from low-tax offshore jurisdictions.

Nothwithstanding the liberal approach of the UK government there is some evidence that the effects of the targeting of intermediaries in the United States are spilling over into other jurisdictions. Thus Citibank's UK operation is reported to be proposing to apply its ban on processing Internet gaming transactions to holders of its credit cards in the UK, to the irritation of the UK government which feels its liberalization policy may be undermined.[12] Conversely, and illustrating the problems of unintended effects, the targeting of financial intermediaries appears to be creating incentives to organizations other than banks to establish themselves as financial intermediaries. The creation of this new non-banking market in supplying payment mechanisms creates the risk of generating a substantial market in payment mechanisms which are more difficult for the state to monitor and control. Thus their emergence may amplify the problem that targeting of intermediaries was designed to address and create other problems, for example creating new mechanisms for money laundering.

CONCLUSIONS

The Internet gambling case offers a number of insights into issues of regulatory innovation more generally. First it offers an image of regulatory innovation as a solution to the limited capacity of the state for regulatory enforcement. Notwithstanding the fact of apparently uniform pressures for policy change presented both by technology and internationalization, the structures within which the policy response occurs has yielded markedly different approaches. The regulatory innovations associated with these diverse policies seek to address the perceived limits of the state to enforce domestic laws, but are mediated by contingent factors which shape both what is thinkable and what is workable as a policy change.

In New York State the novel approach to the enrolment of financial intermediaries was driven by the commitment of individual policy entrepreneurs responsible for enforcement of restrictive gaming laws within the Attorney-General's Office, deploying criminal law enforcement in such a way as to coerce powerful banking interests to support the policy. Thus the individual world of the policy entrepreneur with power to implement change with little dependence on others is very much to the fore. The Australian government substantially adopted the model developed in New York State, but found itself impotent to enrol the banks and other financial intermediaries in the enforcement mission, and switched its focus to the rather weaker Internet service provider industry (with effects that are difficult to determine). The UK policy of liberalization presents fewer enforcement problems. Rather innovations are located at the level of the switch from highly restrictive controls to a more permissive regime, linked in part to the transfer of responsibility away from the government department responsible for law enforcement to a dedicated culture ministry. In the UK gaming was reclassified from crime to entertainment. In the UK case innovation occurs largely through the operations of the organizational world in which there is systematic processing of a new policy problem presented to government within the wider policy reforms over gambling more generally.

In principle, the international and commercial environments in which policy-makers are operating are similar for all three jurisdictions. A key international pressure is created by the willingness of small countries to licence online gaming operations with relatively lax regulation, creating potential problems for consumers within the USA, Australia and the UK. With highly mobile operators and the prospect of global markets we might expect to see a 'race to the bottom' as the product of regulatory innovation in this domain. In fact, the picture is much more complicated with the willingness of states to permit participation in the market or not, and the nature of regulatory controls is shaped as much by ethical and cultural considerations as by pressures of competition. But the response was again mediated by national institutions. Thus it has been jurisdictions in the United States which have exhibited the most restrictive approach to Internet gaming, apparently at odds with the dominance of a free market ideology, but consistent with a moral imperative to restrict access to commercial gaming generally. The point is driven home by the fact of Antigua's successful claim before the WTO to the effect that US policy is contrary to international trade rules.

The US response to this policy problem is substantially juridical – applying a well-established and ambitious strategy of extraterritorial application of domestic criminal law and rejecting regulatory competition. Australia and the UK are operating (or in the UK case proposing to operate) a radically different strategy of offering competition to gaming operators licensed in less reputable jurisdictions. The provision of high standards of regulation within the UK is intended to draw UK and other consumers to deal with UK-licensed operators, reducing consumer harm and raising tax revenue. Set against this objective the Australian strategy, which drives Australian punters to offshore gaming services, appears perverse. The UK government may be concerned chiefly to establish the UK as a trusted and credible base for provision of regulated

Internet gaming services to citizens in the UK and abroad. The UK government line is that it is futile to attempt to prohibit Internet gaming in the UK, because such a policy will simply send punters into the hands of potentially less regulated overseas providers from one of the other 75 countries which offer some form of Internet gaming licence.[13] The Australian government seeks to promote take-up of services provided by Australian firms abroad while cutting off the provision of services by Australian and other suppliers to Australia. An official report has highlighted the ethical contradictions within this position of attempting to reduce an identified harm within Australia while permitting Australian companies to profit from the harm caused to persons overseas (DCITA 2004, p. 47). For both the UK and Australia, a key concern is to promote the collection of taxes from those offering services from within their jurisdiction.

Overall the analysis in this chapter questions the capacity for developing and transferring regulatory innovation across jurisdictions as a policy mentality fitted to the resolution of policy problems old and new. Rather we find a pattern of contingent responses to pressures, mediated by national institutions (including in this case moral outlook), in which alternative (more or less innovative) solutions were not available. The one instance of a rather clear policy transfer – the attempt by the Australian government to implement a New York State-style approach to enforcement through the gate-keeping capacity of banks – failed because it was unsuited to the particular configuration of institutions (and in particular national approaches to enforcement) and interests (the relatively more powerful position of the banks to resist such innovation in Australia). Thus, if innovation is to be both a policy prescription and its extent a measure of performance, then the Internet gaming story suggests that in both cases sensitivity to national institutional structures and configurations of interests is required.

ACKNOWLEDGEMENT

I am grateful to the other contributors to this book and to David Miers for comments on an earlier draft of this chapter.

NOTES

1. A search on Google hit 32 separate instances of the term being used, 2 December 2004.
2. *United States – Measures Affecting the Cross-Border Supply of Gambling and Betting Services*, Report of the Panel, 10 November 2004, WT/DS285/R.
3. *Gambelli* [Case C-243/01 ECJ 2003] **ECR** I (6.11.2003).
4. *People of New York* v. *World Interactive Gaming Corp.* 185 Misc. 2d 852, 714 N.Y.S.2d 844 (N.Y. County Sup. Ct. 1999).

5. *People of New York* v. *World Interactive Gaming Corp*, above.
6. 'The Kyl Bill' – Bill S. 672 108th Congress, 2003.
7. 'US Pursuing Abettors of Internet Gaming', *New York Times*, 15 March 2004.
8. www.ladbrokescasino.com.
9. Office of New York State Attorney General, Press Release, 14 June 2002. http://www.oag.state.ny.us/press/agpress02.html, visited 17 December 2004.
10. Office of New York State Attorney General Press Release, 21 August 2002. http://www.oag.state.ny.us/press/agpress02.html, visited 17 December 2004.
11. 'Crackdown Just an Irritant to Net Gamblers', *New York Times*, 22 March 2004.
12. 'Credit card firms ban gambling on the internet', *The Times*, 21 October 2004.
13. http://www.gamblinglicenses.com/licensesDatabase.cfm, visited 10 September 2004.

7. Pavlovian innovation, pet solutions and economizing on rationality? Politicians and dangerous dogs

Christopher Hood and Martin Lodge

INTRODUCTION

On 29 May 1991, six-year-old Ruckhsana Khan suffered severe chest and head injuries as a result of an unprovoked attack in a public place by an American pit bull terrier (called 'Dog'), which had broken loose from its 21-year-old and pregnant 'dog walker'. The attack took place in Manningham, a run-down area of Bradford in the North of England, and it came on the heels of similar dog attacks in Bolton and Lincoln. The result was intense media interest and concern with dog attack dangers (for example, the now-defunct tabloid newspaper *Today* carried about 40 articles on dangerous dog risks in the subsequent month) and demands for prompt and decisive action from the responsible Home Secretary, Kenneth Baker (see Hood et al. 2001, p. 91). The minister's first response was to stress the difficulty of crafting effective legislation to deal with the problem, but that response led to vicious media criticism and as a result, legislation intended to curb dangerous dog attacks was rapidly drafted and passed through all its legislative stages with cross-party support and strong backing in opinion polls. The Act (the much discussed Dangerous Dogs Act of 1991) made it a criminal offence to have any dog dangerously out of control in a public place and introduced additional controls that were targeted at the American pit bull terrier plus some other exotic types of fighting dogs (that were mostly either little known or hardly present in the UK). Additional controls included compulsory neutering, insurance, registration, tattooing, identification by the insertion of microchips and the obligation to be muzzled and on the leash in any public place. Controversially, the Act provided for the mandatory destruction of any of these specified dogs that were found to be in breach of these provisions, with no discretion available to law courts.

A few years later, in June 1995, 19-year old Nicolas Pons set his American pit bull terrier on two schoolboys of African origin outside a school in Evry, a 1970s *'ville nouvelle'* in the south of Paris, well-known for its run-down estates and gang culture. The two boys suffered severe bite injuries, and the attack led to political demands for legislation to curb dangerous dogs (*Le Monde*, 31 January 1996), especially as it took place against a general backdrop of increasing use of vicious dogs by French criminals and a massive increase in the estimated population of fighting dogs in France (rising from between 2 to 3000 in 1993 to between 20 to 40 000 in 1998). After an initial attempt to respond to these pressures mainly by incremental changes in existing laws and at regional rather than central-government level, the French government eventually decided to introduce national legislation to curb dangerous dogs in 1999, targeting fighting dogs as well as guard and defence dogs. The subsequent ministerial decree by the agriculture and interior ministries under their ministers (Jean Glavany and Jean-Pierre Chevènement respectively) targeted crossbreeds and dog types that had not been officially recognized as breeds via a compulsory sterilization programme.

While these debates were going on in France, on 22 October 1998, five-year-old Chantal Versteeg was savagely attacked by an 85 kg Mastino Napolitano in the mixed neighbourhood of Amsterdam-North. That attack brought the issue of dangerous dogs regulation back onto the Dutch political agenda, and the responsible ministers – Hayo Apotheker, and his successor and D66 party colleague Laurens Jan Brinkhorst – faced criticisms on the grounds that the existing dangerous dog legislation, dating from 1993, did not effectively protect innocent victims like Chantal Versteeg. That 1993 law had itself been passed in the aftermath of a series of fatal attacks on children (from 1990–1992). The Dutch government's first response to those earlier attacks was a proposal to destroy all American pit bull terriers (plus American Staffordshire bull terriers and two other fighting breeds), but after predictable opposition to compulsory mass execution from dog owners and ministerial worries about public acceptability of that policy, the law as passed was aimed only at dogs of the pit bull terrier type and aimed for long-term elimination via compulsory sterilization rather than mass execution. The attack on Chantal Versteeg led to political pressure to extend legislation to other types of dog, such that more types and breeds of dogs were subjected to special measures under the dangerous dogs law (and indeed for a time, compulsory 'dog character' tests were proposed by the Dutch government).

Shortly after the French and Dutch legislation, on 26 June 2000, six-year-old Volkan Kaya was killed by 'Gipsy', an American pit bull terrier, and 'Zeus', an American Staffordshire bull terrier, while playing on a school playground in Wilhelmsburg, a working class district of Hamburg known for its high unemployment rate and high immigrant population. Volkan Kaya's death led to media-driven political pressure that caused 14 of the 16 German *Länder* to change their laws and regulations governing dogs. Fifteen *Länder* made the legal obligations on dog owners depend on the breed of their dogs (in contrast to an earlier position in which all German dogs had been equal before the law), with the laws mainly targeting the American pit bull terrier, the American Staffordshire bull terrier, the Staffordshire bull terrier and the Japanese Tosa Inu. *Land* governments also developed a widespread, if short-lived interest in compulsory character tests, both for dogs and their owners. This uncharacteristically rapid German legislative response – with new legal provisions to curb dangerous dogs being brought forward within weeks (and in many cases days) of Volkan Kaya's death – took place in a context of concerns about the growth in the population of dogs that were seen as particularly aggressive, a series of attacks preceding Volkan Kaya's death, and a history of largely unsuccessful attempts by the *Länder* to negotiate a common framework for *Land* legislation on dangerous dogs.

Four different countries with distinct and different state traditions, political institutions and legal cultures, but four very similar responses to a series of tragedies involving unprovoked dog attacks on innocent victims in public places culminating in a particularly serious case. Against that backdrop, all four of those countries moved away from their traditional legislation governing dogs (involving in all cases a notion of all dogs being equal before the law and some version of the traditional notion that every dog is allowed 'one-free-bite' before it is confirmed as inherently dangerous), towards a risk-based approach that singled out particular dog types and breeds as being particularly aggressive. Moreover, as can be seen in Tables 7.1 and 7.2, it was not merely the four states picked out earlier that responded to the political stimulus of media-salient dog attacks in this way. The same behaviour pattern is shown by other European states too.

Table 7.1   Dogs selected for special measures in different countries

		Pit bull terrier	Tosa Inu	American Staffordshire bull terrier	Staffordshire bull terrier	Other dogs
Britain	1991 & 1997	Y	Y	N	N	Y
Ireland	1991	Y	Y	Y	Y	Y
Denmark	1991	Y	Y	N	N	N
Netherlands	1993	Y	N	N	N	N
Netherlands	1998 (not passed)	Y	Y	Y	Y	Y
France	1998	Y	Y	Y	Y	Y
Most German Länder	2000	Y	Y	Y	Y	Y

Note: Y = yes; N = no

Table 7.2 *Special measures for selected dogs*

	Identification	Neutering	Muzzle and leash	Registration	Insurance	Character test
Britain	M	Y	Y	Y	Y	N
Ireland	B	N	Y	N	N	N
Denmark	N	Y	Y	N	N	N
Netherlands (1993)	T	Y	Y	Y	Y	N
Netherlands (1998, initial prcposals)	T	Y	Y	Y	Y	Y (for dogs)
France	T	Y (for most dangerous category)	Y	Y	Y	N
Most German Länder	M, T, B (varied across *Länder*)	Y	Y	Y	Y	Y (for owners and dogs)

Notes
Y = yes; N = no
M = microchip, T = tattoo, B = badge

PAVLOVIAN REGULATORY INNOVATION?

Welcome to the world of 'Pavlovian' regulatory innovation – a world that seems to cut across some of the worlds of innovation sketched out in the introductory chapter. By Pavlovian regulatory innovation we mean a style of politico-bureaucratic behaviour that exhibits patterns similar to those found by Ivan Pavlov in his well-known psychological experiments of the 1920s, which showed that dogs could be conditioned to behave in a particular way (salivating to the sound of a bell) by a set of circumstances (being exposed to food along with the bell). The question that this chapter explores is whether or how far we can understand regulatory innovation in the case of dangerous dogs as representing a roughly analogous conditioned response by politicians, with legislative changes instead of salivation, dog bites instead of a bell and the expectation of reduced media pressure and public criticism instead of food. We do not, however, wish to push the Pavlovian analogy too far, beyond arguing that the observed legislative response is conditioned rather than a reflex of the kind represented by a 'knee-jerk' and that the behaviour is a low-intelligence response rather than the kind of intelligent learning represented by several of the 'worlds' of innovation discussed at the outset.

Thus one central element in our world of Pavlovian regulatory innovation is that the political response is a conditioned rather than a direct reflex, even though the metaphor of 'knee-jerk response' is often loosely invoked to describe unreflective 'off-the-cuff' policy-making. The conditioning process works through the occurrence of a series of attacks on innocent children in public places that bring policy issues to media and public attention in the absence of any alternative headline-grabbing news story (Lodge and Hood 2002, p. 1). In these conditions, major political crises develop and high-level political and bureaucratic attention comes to be devoted to an issue normally relegated to the sphere of 'low politics'. Media coverage of such incidents may itself be either conditioned or a pure reflex, but politicians are conditioned by the chaining of such incidents to make a response. As noted earlier, the Pavlovian metaphor can be only stretched so far, and we do not want to take in all its possible entailments. All we want to convey by the Pavlovian label is the notion of a low-intelligence form of innovation that takes the form of low-level conditioning rather than a simple reflex, and in that sense cuts across the various worlds of innovation discussed at the outset of this book in a distinctive way.

Pavlovian regulatory innovation may involve pet solutions, in more than one sense. But it is far removed from the Kingdonian world of policy innovation where policy entrepreneurs wait for 'windows of opportunity' to open in order to place their pre-prepared solutions onto the policy agenda (Kingdon 1995). It is also far removed from the institutionalists' world of nationally distinctive institutional processes that shape the nature and type of regulatory innovation in ways that follow state traditions or varieties of capitalism (Hall and Soskice 2001; Hall 1983). Rather, if we characterize the world of Pavlovian policy innovation as a Weberian-style ideal type, it has the following attributes, as summarized in Table 7.3.

- It is a form of regulatory innovation in which little or no horizontal learning and diffusion (Berry and Berry 1999) takes place. In pure Pavlovian conditioning, the various dogs exposed to the stimulus do not learn from one another that the ringing of the bell is associated with food. In what we are calling the Pavlovian world of regulatory innovation, the actors do not engage in significant 'lesson-drawing' (Rose 1993) across jurisdictions or over time. Nor (again by analogy with the pure Pavlovian case) do politicians and bureaucrats in the world of Pavlovian regulatory innovation take much notice of other parties' knowledge, interests or attitudes, even of those that are pivotal for the enforcement of policy goals.
- It is a form of regulatory innovation in which proper names or individual leadership qualities do not seem to be very important to outcomes (in contrast to the individual world of policy innovation where proper names and individual styles are the central feature). In pure Pavlovian conditioning, individual dogs will vary in the length of time they take before they start to salivate to the bell, but once they do respond, they respond in very similar ways. The same goes for what we call the Pavlovian world of regulatory innovation, where politicians and bureaucrats may differ in terms of their response time (though not much, in the cases we reported earlier), but the response to the stimulus is broadly similar.
- It is a form of regulatory innovation in which state tradition or institutional milieu (other than the general characteristics of wealthy liberal democracies) do not seem to be very important to outcomes (in contrast to the institutionalists' world of policy innovation). In pure Pavlovian conditioning, German dogs do not respond very differently from French or British dogs when exposed to the same stimulus. Something similar seems to apply to what we are calling the Pavlovian world of regulatory innovation. Institutions obviously 'matter' in the sense of who has the legal competence to legislate or regulate on the matter in hand (such as the central government in the Netherlands and *Land* governments in Germany), but in the Pavlovian world of regulatory innovation, institutional differences do not make a great deal of difference to either the speed or content of the response.

Table 7.3   Pavlovian regulatory innovation compared with other worlds of regulatory innovation

World of Pavlovian regulatory innovation	Other worlds of innovation
Proper names matter little in the sense that the same response tends to be adopted, with differences only of detail	In some innovation 'worlds', individual policy entrepreneurs make a big difference to shaping the way in which organizations innovate
Learning is minimal in the sense that change is adopted with little awareness of or reflection about developments elsewhere	In some innovation 'worlds', diffusion, benchmarking and intelligent learning over time are critical to the process
The diversity of governance structures does not result in diversity of responses	In some innovation 'worlds', innovation is centrally shaped by structural patterns in economic and political systems

Table 7.3 summarizes these features of the Pavlovian world of regulatory innovation and contrasts them with the received or established worlds of regulatory innovation that were discussed in Chapter 2.

We pursue these themes in more detail in the next section, considering how far the political response pattern to dog bites across selected West European states, with particular reference to Britain and the German *Länder*, represents a 'Pavlovian' form of regulatory innovation, and identifying the limits of that metaphor.

DIMENSIONS AND LIMITS OF PAVLOVIAN REGULATORY INNOVATION

How Far do Proper Names Matter?

As Chapter 2 showed, the proper names and leadership skills of particular individuals are critical factors in some intellectual 'worlds' of policy innovation – whether they be Kingdonian or Schumpeterian entrepreneurs bent on their work of 'creative destruction' or Bardachian craftspersons (Bardach 1998) finding new multi-agency ways of tackling policy problems. But in the

Pavlovian world of regulatory innovation, proper names may not matter very much, and that seems to apply to the dangerous dogs case considered here.

At first sight, an examination of the British case might suggest a different conclusion. The minister responsible for responding to the media firestorm that developed in the aftermath of the attack on Ruckhsana Khan in the summer of 1991, Kenneth Baker, certainly had particular political 'form' and political needs. He had political 'form' in the sense that he had in an earlier ministerial role championed the abolition of dog licensing in Britain and presented it as a triumph for 'deregulation' and getting the state off the backs of the people, and that he did not want to be seen to be reintroducing the sort of universal dog licensing he had abolished only a few years before. And he had particular political needs and problems in the sense that in mid-1991 his political career was under threat following a major riot at a high-security prison (Manchester Strangeways) in the spring of 1991 that had taken a long time to bring under control, such that voters were presented pictures of the burning prison and defiant rioters on its roof for day after day. For a Home Secretary of a government with plummeting poll ratings to be seen as responsible for inept handling of a major prison riot in the run-up to the traditional summer Cabinet reshuffle is a decidedly dangerous political position. So it is not difficult to see why Baker had strong motives to be seen to be championing swift and decisive-seeming action on an issue that chimed with popular preferences in opinion polls. But when we look at the responses to similar crises across several of the European countries considered here, we might conclude that such individual characteristics did not count for much, because similar responses were adopted in other countries by ministers with different backgrounds and in different political circumstances, including ministers who were not in personal political 'distress' in the sense that Kenneth Baker was in mid-1991. Across the German *Länder*, responses to the killing of Volkan Kaya in mid-2000 were not related to party-background (Social Democrat, Christian Democrat and Green ministers alike all demanded 'tough' laws), nearness of election day, poll-standing, or the portfolio of minister (for example whether the lead department was law and order or portfolios dealing with animal protection). And more generally, ministers across the countries considered in Tables 7.1 and 7.2 seem to have responded in broadly similar ways regardless of their personal political circumstances.

How Far do Diffusion and Learning Matter?

At first sight, regulatory innovation over the issue of dangerous dogs might be understood as a case from the 'world' of diffusion and cross-national learning. Within the space of a decade or so, a set of countries crossing the common law/Roman law divide moved away from a traditional position in which all dogs were equal before the law (and some version of the traditional one-free-bite convention was applied in the law[1]) to a risk-based approach which associated specified dog breeds and types with higher levels of aggressiveness and therefore tightened controls. A story of policy diffusion might also be inferred from the innovatory timeline as indicated in Tables 7.1 and 7.2. There seem to have been two distinct waves of innovation on this issue; one in the early 1990s that focused particularly on the American pit bull terrier, and another from the later 1990s that in most cases included more types and breeds.

On closer inspection, however, it is hard to tell a story of the kind of diffusion that involves innovators copying initiatives from other jurisdictions, learning from experiences elsewhere, or even knowing what was going on outside their borders. The politician and bureaucrat innovators in the states considered in Tables 7.1 and 7.2 seem to have had little awareness of experiences elsewhere, any more than Pavlov's dogs were aware of other dogs going through the same conditioning process, and dangerous dogs regulation seems to be one of those cases of an innovation occurring in different places at the same time but without any conscious imitation or knowledge. For instance, the regulatory reforms at the turn of the twenty-first century in France and Germany were characterized by very limited awareness, and certainly not conscious imitation, of the measures taken almost a decade earlier by other states such as Britain, the Netherlands or Denmark. In the German case, that lack of knowledge is brought out clearly by the official report that informed the deliberations of the intergovernmental committee of *Länder* governments in the aftermath of Volkan Kaya's death in 2000 (Ständige Konferenz der Innenminister 2000).

Indeed, even within Germany, there was little diffusion and hardly any policy learning across *Land* boundaries.[2] To be sure, the different *Land* governments were aware of a breed-based dog law which had been introduced in Bavaria in the early 1990s (and which, unlike similar measures in other *Länder*, had survived judicial challenges), but none of them copied it. And while most of the *Länder* went for some variant of a breed-based approach after Volkan Kaya's death, they evidently did not work with a common template about the particular dog types and breeds to be considered particularly dangerous in law or by the instruments to be used in assessing risks and registering dogs. Rather, what took place was a curiously uninformed type of 'race to the top' in which ministers aimed for their own *Land* to adopt the 'toughest law in Germany,' but without being aware of the relative positions of other *Land* governments.

Besides the absence of policy diffusion, there seems to have been a general pattern of economizing on rationality and intelligence. In none of the cases of the shift towards breed-based regulation in Table 7.1 was policy informed by high-level and undisputed scientific understanding of the risk factors involved, and in no cases were there serious steps taken to improve the available data for evidence-based analysis (for instance, by making dog attacks notifiable incidents in law). It may well be argued that uncertainty is a common factor in many kinds of policy situations where innovation is in question (in this case involving a lack of firm knowledge about the total number of dogs of the types being subjected to special measures, or of hard data about attack propensity across different breeds or types). But in this case it is notable that even where evidence existed, it was ignored, and also that regulatory innovation did not generate any drive for more information or better statistics.

Critical gaps in the information base included uncertainty about the incidence of dog attacks – particularly of attacks (probably the majority) occurring at home rather than in public. And where information about attacks existed (for instance in some hospital records, as in the case of the Netherlands and the UK), it often did not include a record of the type of dog involved. In Germany there were limited studies by city governments that informed intergovernmental negotiations which suggested that in absolute terms, most attacks came from German Shepherds, but on attacks relative to the numbers of dogs of different types (based on unreliable estimates of total dog populations), American pit bull terriers and Rottweilers posed the highest risk. Such information, however, does not seem to have informed policy, in the sense that it does not explain the widespread selection of the Tosa Inu for special measures, even though that dog was hardly known in any of the West European countries at the time of the measures described in Tables 7.1 and 7.2, and did not feature in any recorded attacks, in contrast to the exemption of the German Shepherd from special measures in many cases.

Thus the existing knowledge base, limited as it was, seems to have had little influence on the selection of dog types for special measures, and there appeared also to be only limited political interest in utilizing scientifically generated knowledge about how to assess the aggressiveness of individual dogs. In the Netherlands, where (alone in the states considered in Tables 7.1 and 7.2) the government funded scientific work on dog character tests as part of its response to dog attack crises of the early 1990s (Netto and Planta 1997), compulsory dog character tests along the lines recommended by the scientists were removed from the legislative drafts that followed the attack on Chantal Versteeg in 1998, on the grounds that administrative costs would be likely to be high and that the tests might not be immediately effective. In Germany, too, there was some interest on the part of *Land* governments in improving knowledge about canine aggressiveness, particularly where certain breeding lines were, by selective nurturing, associated with higher aggressiveness levels. Accordingly, across various German *Länder*, compulsory dog character tests were included in legislative responses to the death of Volkan Kaya in the dog attack in 2000, based on early work that had been conducted by animal behaviourists. But these responses do not seem to have been heavily informed by the Dutch research or policy response and the way that they were used in practice was often different from what the scientists had recommended (as in the case of Lower Saxony, where the use of character tests to decide about neutering were turned by ministerial demand into tests to decide whether a dog should be destroyed).

That is not to deny that some elements of learning and 'reading across' took place, but it seems to have taken place mostly at the national level, in contrast to the innovatory world of cross-national diffusion. For example, in Britain the idea of compulsorily microchipping particular types of dogs[3] was drawn from earlier schemes that had required the microchipping of racehorses. And the avoidance of court discretion (or even the use of dog character tests) to decide the fate of dogs whose owners had not complied with the legal requirements (prior to 1997), apparently reflected earlier (problematic) experience in psychological assessments of prisoners within the Home Office. In France, the decree of 1999 could be regarded as reflecting knowledge that most attacks were caused by cross-breeds and dogs not bred by licensed breeders by applying the harshest sanctions on non-pure breeds. In Germany too, the diversity of lists that emerged could be seen as different attempts by officials to anticipate later judicial challenges by aggrieved dog owners likely to claim that special measures for particular dogs did not respect the requirement for 'proportionality' in regulation built into European and German law.

In short, in a way that is similar to one of Pavlov's dogs, politicians in the countries considered here seem to have responded, albeit with some detailed exceptions, in the same predictable ways to incidents involving dogs in public – regardless of what type or breed of dog caused the incident. And indeed, while the biggest risks of dog attacks seem to have come from the illegal breeding of particularly aggressive and powerful dogs and the wider problem of stray dogs, especially non-neutered males, the typical policy response to dog attack crises took the form of provisions likely to clamp down hardest on law-abiding dog owners.

To What Extent does 'Place' Matter?

The standard assumption of institutionalists in political science is that institutions are key to shaping different patterns of decision-making and policy choices and that they also affect policy outputs. One of the key stereotypes of the traditional British political system is that it is particularly prone to low quality policy-making given a low number of veto-points arising from a unitary, one-party system of government and a thinned-out hierarchy following a decade of administrative reform (see Dunleavy 1995, also Moran 2003). In contrast, the German political system is said to promote gridlock, given its federal nature and the propensity to generate coalition governments. Even in those areas where the *Länder* possess sole policy authority, there is said to be a tendency towards policy homogeneity (Lehmbruch 2000). However, in the Pavlovian world of regulatory innovation, such stereotype institutional differences do not in fact seem to count for very much. Indeed, if we look at direct response time, in the summer of 2000 the German *Länder* responded more rapidly to Volkan Kaya's death than did the British government to the savaging of Ruckhsana Khan in 1991 or indeed than any of the other states in Tables 7.1 and 7.2 in response to the incidents that triggered their legislative responses.

Perhaps we might nevertheless argue that some elements of the familiar 'hare' and 'tortoise' story applied to the way that different jurisdictions responded to dog dangers over the decade or so considered here. It is true that states such as Germany and France responded much later to the dangerous dogs issue than countries such as the UK, Denmark and the Netherlands. But it may well be that the date of legislation is better accounted for by the time pattern of media-salient attacks across the various states rather than by variations in speed of response to such attacks when they happened. And even if they were not, it is notable that in Germany the *Länder* introduced breed-based legislation that moved away from the traditional all-dogs-equal-before-the-law approach in the early 1990s (all of which were struck down by constitutional and administrative courts, with the exception of Bavaria's constitutional court). So there is a case for arguing that German politicians were not in fact behind their British counterparts in their response to dog-attack crises, and that the institutionalist stereotype of the UK as programmed to produce 'the fastest law of the West' does not really apply. But when it came to the institutional response of the judicial system, place did seem to matter more in that German courts were powerful in repealing major, if not all parts of the regulatory innovations, while in the UK pressure from judges was associated only with the abandonment of the mandatory death penalty for dogs whose owners were not in compliance, rather than the breed-based nature of the legal framework.

Place also did not seem to matter when it came to the selection of breeds for special measures, institutional responses to external pressure and patterns of institutional retreat. Across the different countries, a similar pattern of institutional access mattered when it came to the type and breeds that were selected. Primary regulatory targets were those dogs that could not rely on friends in high places in the sense that they were usually not recognized by the national kennel associations (in particular, the American pit bull terrier), were not owned by influential politicians (or middle-class voters more generally), but enjoyed popularity among criminal and fascist subcultures. The institutional access of associations worked to maintain the canine 'class system' by imposing the most draconian controls (notably forced sterilization) onto American pit bull terriers, while shielding Rottweilers (to some extent) and German Shepherds (fully, apart from Ireland). The latter two breeds had attack records that were not markedly different from those of American pit bull terrier, but could rely on friends in high places (Rottweilers and Dobermans) or large numbers of swing voters (German Shepherds). The 1999 French decree that essentially distinguished between those dogs associated or not associated with the *Société Central Canine* is another example of the same process.

When it came to the way in which 'regulatory retreat' occurred in these cases, place also does not seem to have mattered in important ways. By regulatory retreat, we mean the way in which initial regulatory innovation is scaled back because of hostility in the wider policy environment. Place did not seem to matter for some key aspects of regulatory retreat in the case of Britain and Germany, in that in both cases the innovations were soon challenged and to some extent formally and informally pulled back, and in both cases the police soon lost interest in vigorously enforcing the law. In Britain, the (London) Metropolitan Police quickly abandoned the effective enforcement of the 1991 Act: in 1992, a conscious decision was made to not proactively enforce the 1991 Act and by 1994 the police was said to have widely returned to the traditional 'one free bite' policy, the policy approach that the 1991 Act was supposed to have replaced. Similarly, in the German case, special police units to battle loose dangerous dogs were dismantled within months of their initial constitution, in the face of rival claims on resources and reduced public attention. This rapid dismantling of police resources went hand-in-hand with highly diverse attention given to the dog issue by different local authorities.[4]

However, place did seem to matter when it came to the way in which the hostility in the policy environment was channelled. In the German cases, regulatory attempts were challenged in front of administrative courts and regularly struck down (often on the basis that such extensive interference required the basis of a legislative, and not purely an administrative act). In Britain, regulatory retreat was driven by a mixture of judges unhappy with the lack of discretion to courts in the mandatory death penalty rule of 1991 and of media pressure in the form of stories about family pets on death row making the headlines. This pressure eventually led to the relaxation of the mandatory nature of the 1991 Act in 1997.

We can conclude that, in line with the pure Pavlovian model of regulatory innovation, place seems to have mattered little when it came to 'response times' to the stimulus of a media-salient dog-attack tragedy and to the way that targets for special measures were selected. But, looking at Britain and Germany, place does seem to have mattered to some extent in the way that judicial politics either blocked initial legislation or shaped later stages of regulatory retreat.

THE LOGIC OF PAVLOVIAN REGULATORY INNOVATION: ECONOMIZING ON RATIONALITY AND INTELLIGENCE?

So far, so Pavlov. But what are we to make of the Pavlovian form of regulatory innovation, to the extent that it exists? Is it a pattern of regulatory innovation that is to be counted as an embarrassing fact, but inherently undesirable? Is this a world of regulatory innovation that is only worth investigating in order to show practitioners and academics what to avoid in reshaping regulatory regimes?

Certainly, Pavlovian regulatory innovation seems to be a low-intelligence response in several senses of 'intelligence'. The innovators do not learn from one another, do not invest heavily – or at all – in the gathering and evaluation of systematic information about the likely success of policy, and for some purposes can be regarded as automatons who respond in predictable, deterministic and often self-limiting ways. And their world of regulatory innovation seems primed to produce features of risk regulation noted and heavily condemned by Judge Stephen Breyer (1991), in the sense that it is likely to produce legislation designed more with populist-electoral than scientific considerations in mind, following all-too-predictable low-intelligence responses that are more evidence-free than evidence-based.

But there may nevertheless be a logic in, and a justification for, a Pavlovian style of regulatory innovation, for at least three reasons. First, as in the case considered here, Pavlovian regulatory innovation is a form of innovation that can meet the political logic of opinion-responsive government – that is, legislation and policy that reflects public sentiment and opinion. Regulatory innovations that give the voting public at large what (in aggregate terms) they say they want may not appeal to elite 'policy wonks' in their own worlds of cross-national benchmarking, but they chime with what is often assumed to be a fundamental property of democratic government – response to popular demands – as opposed to technocracy.

Second, Pavlovian regulatory innovation can be argued to be a form of innovation that economizes on the very limited stock of intelligence and rationality available to political and bureaucratic decision-makers even in wealthy and developed democracies. Such an argument can be made in several ways. One is to draw a parallel with the famous argument by McCubbins and Schwartz (1984) about the importance of 'fire alarms' as low-cost ways for political principals to control bureaucratic agents. According to this well-known argument, so-called fire alarms (i.e. cries of pain or anxiety from affected constituencies that then result in political action to rein in bureaucratic agents) represent a way of controlling bureaucracies that is cheaper than, but often at least as efficient, informed and reliable as, systematic monitoring by legislative committees or their agents (so-called 'police patrols'). The Pavlovian image of the bell that stimulates legislative innovation may be the policy equivalent of the McCubbins–Schwarzian fire alarm bell, and for the same reason.[5]

A different version of the 'economizing on intelligence' argument is the case for various kinds of decision-making procedure that cope with sharply bounded rationality by means that avoid the costly option of systematically analysing all the available options. Such procedures include the famous Herbert Simon (1947, chapter 5) argument for 'satisficing' rather than 'maximizing' in problem-solving activity; the argument made by the late Aaron Wildavsky (1964) and others for incremental adjustment rather than 'zero-base' reviews as the norm for making changes in complex budgetary systems, and the argument made by Charles Lindblom and others for 'disjointedness' in policy-making as part of the case for the 'intelligence of democracy' (Lindblom 1965). Just as for Pavlov's dogs, salivating to the sound of the bell is a response that economizes on intelligence and broadly makes sense (in that it is eventually abandoned when the food no longer appears after the bell), simple conditioned responses to media firestorms may have similar properties for politicians and bureaucrats.

A different way of making the same point is to say that Pavlovian regulatory innovation of the type observed here may involve very low information-gathering costs. And while such an approach will tend to be dismissed by those who advocate elaborate decision-advice procedures as a key to good governance, it may make sense for issues, such as our case of dangerous dogs, where such official information as exists is highly unreliable[6] and the cost of supplementing it, in the short term at least, very high. In such circumstances, a Pavlovian response seems more likely to meet immediate political needs than a high intensity search for further information in the face of media pressure for urgent action, although the former does not logically exclude the latter. From the viewpoint of central decision-makers, a quick popular response that passes most of the processing and transactional costs onto other agents in the implementation process (in our case, street-level bureaucrats, police, and judges in handling tricky boundary questions about whether any given dog was of a proscribed breed, what constituted 'failing' behaviour in dog character tests, what constitutes being 'dangerously out of control in public') makes sense.

Third and relatedly, for some purposes, the Pavlovian approach might be argued to be capable of being effective – or at least as effective as any feasible alternative. Low-intelligence as they may have been, the regulatory innovations considered in this chapter were largely successful when seen in the light of the primary political and bureaucratic interest in dealing with any crisis, namely the removal of the story and demands for further action from immediate media attention. The British response also conformed quite well when assessed in the light of the British 'Better Regulation Task Force' principles of 'better regulation' (see Hood et al. 2000). Of course, they created unanticipated side-effects, such as later media campaigns to save much-loved family pets 'on death row' for what were portrayed as technical or trivial violations of the law, but the Pavlovian form of regulatory innovation hardly has a monopoly on unanticipated side-effects, as the other cases in this book show. Indeed, the innovations in dangerous dogs law considered here can probably be considered to be as effective as most innovations in the criminal law, including those introduced in a far from 'Pavlovian' style.

There is therefore a Wildavsky-type case for arguing that the world of Pavlovian regulatory innovation, alien as it is to the normative and empirical assumptions of many received approaches to technological and organizational innovation, has a logic behind it and merits understanding rather than simple condemnation. Paradoxical as it may seem, it may sometimes be 'rational' in a certain sense to economize on rationality as ordinarily understood, and we are far from the first to have made this point, as we noted earlier. Indeed that may be the only way to explain why highly educated politicians and bureaucrats, noted for their finely honed political 'savvy' and surrounded by high-powered advisers, sometimes find it makes sense to make their regulatory innovations in the Pavlovian style.

CONCLUSIONS

This chapter has offered a world of regulatory innovation that is in one way far removed from many of the other worlds of innovation discussed in this book and in another way cuts across those worlds. In contrast to those worlds where individual strategies, lesson-drawing or established institutional features are of primary importance in shaping innovation, Pavlovian regulatory innovation is a much more rationality-light affair which washes out proper names and economizes on intelligence. In the Pavlovian world, when the conditioned features appear, politicians and bureaucrats respond in broadly the same way, regardless of name or place but without much regard to what others are doing.

The Pavlovian metaphor is a beguiling one, and cannot be pushed too far: as the analysis above showed, there are some significant qualifications that need to be entered when the cases are examined in detail in their national context (although from the comparative cross-European perspective, the Pavlovian model does not seem to need much qualification). It may be, too, that the dog control policies considered here represent a special, perhaps unique, case of the Pavlovian style. But even if they do it is a style that merits at least a footnote in the discussion of 'worlds' of regulatory innovation.

Moreover, the Pavlovian perspective adopted here should alert us to the importance of a political conditioning process to regulatory innovation. Frequent (and usually disapproving) references to 'knee-jerk responses' in regulatory policy imply a pure reflex response, but that is not what we observe in the case of dangerous dogs policy. And the importance of conditioning highlights the fact that politicians' incentive to respond to critical stimuli may well be motivated by factors unrelated to the stimulus itself (just as Pavlov's dogs did not respond to the bell because of anything to do with its pitch or musicality, at least within some broadish range).

As noted earlier, the world of Pavlovian regulatory innovation is one where the innovators economize on rationality and intelligence in ways that are likely to be disapproved of by advocates of high-intelligence learning (with rich environmental scanning, contextually-sensitive evaluation and response, an evidence-rich environment), but may have a certain rationality of its own. Just as Pavlov's dogs can be seen as economizing on their limited stock of rationality and intelligence by their response to the bell and the food, politicians may likewise be behaving in ways that make sense within a logic of politics for a certain range of conditions. So it may be that we can add to the many paradoxes and ironies of rationality noted by Max Weber, the notion that Pavlovian policy innovation may reflect a rational strategy to economize on rationality.

NOTES

1. Although featuring prominently in Roman law, especially following the adoption of the Greek practice of having dogs as pets, the 'one free bite' doctrine was strongly influenced by Jewish law. The law of dangerous animals as expounded in the Hebrew Bible, Exodus 21: 28–36, makes the owner liable only after the first attack, on the grounds that the owner might not be aware of the danger from a particular animal before that. Jackson (1978, p. 142) suggests that sixth century Roman law was directly reflected in the English dog laws of the 1970s (see also Marmer (1984, p. 1074, footnotes 51 and 52) who points to the tightening of liability provisions of the owner for her dog's actions in the US context over time).
2. A diversity of policy preference prevented learning and reading across in the German case before Volkan Kaya's death in Hamburg in 2000, and even after that tragedy, little cross-boundary learning seems to have occurred.
3. An idea that was later to become a craze among 'clubbers' in Spain who used implanted chips as 'bar tabs' and means of identification.
4. In Hesse, earlier attempts at legislating against dangerous dogs in the mid- to late 1990s had failed because of resistance by local authorities that were opposed to the anticipated enforcement costs.
5. That is not to deny that such 'fire alarm-type' systems raise issues about whether legislators are biased in their responses, paying more attention to bells ringing from some constituencies (notably swing voters) rather than others (see also Horn 1995, p. 70). But no monitoring system can altogether avoid that sort of problem.

6. Even on such basic matters as the size of the dog population (for which information sources such as dog licensing records or breed association records are seriously misleading because of missing cases) or the incidence of dog-bite attacks (dependent in most states on the quirks of hospital record-keeping).

8. The development of risk-based regulation in financial services: just 'modelling through'?[1]

Julia Black

INTRODUCTION

'Risk-based' regulation is in essence 'problem-based' regulation: regulators seek to anticipate problems and deal with them. As such, there seems nothing novel or striking in this, so why should agencies be celebrating their newly developed approaches? Should they not have been doing this already? This chapter examines the extent to which the introduction of 'risk-based' approaches to regulation in three financial services regulators can be regarded as an example of 'regulatory innovation', the reasons why those agencies were prompted to devise quite distinctive and novel systems of organizational processes and internal management, how they arrived at the systems they devised, and what some of the outcomes have been to date.

The 'risk-based' approaches in question are decision-making frameworks which are used to prioritize regulatory activity, focusing it where it is most needed. The 'risks' they seek to manage are the risks that the regulator will not achieve its objectives. So far, so familiar: any risk management strategy seeks to identify risks to an organization's objectives and to manage them. However, in the risk management frameworks devised by these regulators, the risks are seen to arise not from inside the regulatory organization, as is normal for corporate risk management strategies, but from outside: from the activities of the financial institutions that they regulate and, as mediated by those institutions, from the wider commercial and economic environment that those institutions inhabit.

The risk-based frameworks are articulated in a set of generalized, abstract principles supplemented by detailed internal guidance; they are based on shared, although unarticulated, understandings of cause–effect relations; they seek to emphasize homogeneity and commensurability rather than variability and uniqueness, and they are designed to be frameworks for systematization and for enhanced rationalization of the regulatory process.

The introduction of risk-based regulation in each case is an example of regulatory innovation as defined in both subjective and objective terms. Subjectively, each regulator introduced organizational and decision-making processes which they perceived to be new to the regulatory regime in which they were operating. Objectively speaking, the frameworks are novel in that they mark a break with the individual pasts of each of the regulatory regimes examined, but more significantly, they provide an integrated framework for assessing risks across a range of financial institutions, which has not been done before by any other integrated regulator, or at least not with this degree of harmonization and detail. Thus not only is the development of the risk-based frameworks new to the regulators involved, the UK Financial Services Authority (FSA), the Canadian Office of the Superintendent of Financial Institutions (OSFI) and the Australian Prudential Regulation Authority (APRA) are internationally at the forefront of developing integrated risk-based regulation in financial services.

But why should we be interested in how regulatory agencies organize themselves? This is low level, operational detail; far below the dramatic institutional changes which mark the 'regulatory state' and 'hyper-innovation' theses. What can this case tell us about the questions this book is engaged in answering? First, on the question, 'what is regulatory innovation', the innovation is in the organizational processes of the key regulators in the regulatory regime, as Chapter 1 discusses. However, while the innovation introduces a new 'regulatory technology', more interesting than the technology itself is what it entails. These seemingly technical and largely operational changes in fact involve key choices about risk, more particularly as to the levels of risk that will be tolerated, and those that will not. For risk-based regulation requires us to accept what we all know, but rarely admit: not only that regulators will not prevent every risk or find every breach, but that they may consciously decide not even to try. Competing priorities and limited resources mean choices have to be made as to what aspects of its regulatory remit a regulator will try to achieve, and those it will not. The choice is far from new, nor is it necessarily to be deplored or derided – it is an inescapable fact of regulatory life. What is new is thus not the existence of the choice, but the clear articulation of its inevitability and the terms on which it is being made.

Second, in seeking to explain the innovation, the chapter argues that the motivations for regulatory innovation, and the main influences upon it, arose primarily from inside the regulatory regime. External political pressure may have kick-started the innovation process, but it did not have any direct effect on the form it took. However, one should not downplay the role of external pressures, for the sceptre of political intervention had a great effect, even if politicians themselves played no role. For the frameworks themselves were in part designed to forestall the 'Pavlovian world' of innovation that Hood and

Lodge identify: the 'dangerous dogs' response to financial 'scandals', which is the introduction of yet more regulation. In one sense, regulatory agencies 'juridified' their own procedures to prevent further 'juridification' being imposed upon them. Further, the chapter argues that in understanding the process of regulatory innovation, the organizational world and the world of the innovation are in this case critical, and the world of the global polity also has something to add. In particular, to the extent that they could, regulators 'modelled through': they sought out comparable approaches in other financial regulators in other countries, and only when they felt the possibilities for analogical model-building were exhausted did they begin to construct their own. However, the model-builders were given the political and organizational 'space' in which to conduct this exercise in bounded rationality. They were not swayed off-course by political events. Indeed, the innovation process was marked by an absence of the normal play of regulatory politics, and regulated firms, consumer bodies and politicians are all notable by their absence.

Third, in assessing whether what we are witnessing is 'hyper-innovation', the chapter argues that the innovation is indeed on a 'rationalizing' and 'modernist' trajectory, and that this 'shape' of the innovation may well facilitate its future diffusion. Whether this is a matter for celebration or despair, however, is an open question. This is in part because it is still too early to say, but more fundamentally because how one assesses its 'success' or failure is highly problematic and moreover contingent on what the understanding of the criteria for 'success' should be. Moreover, as the regulation debate suggests, the 'modernist' critique of regulation is too totalizing, assuming that all regulation by its nature takes similar forms. Whilst risk-based regulation has 'modernist' dimensions, it is itself a recognition of the limited capacity of regulators to administer the detailed 'command and control' regimes that are the hallmark of that 'modernism'.

Before analysing in more depth the processes and outcomes of these examples of regulatory innovation, the first two sections of the chapter briefly outline the background and legislative remits of the regulatory agencies and the main elements of their risk-based frameworks.

THE REGULATORY AGENCIES

Each of the agencies considered is an 'integrated' financial regulator; in other words it regulates more than one type of financial institution, for example banks, insurance companies, securities dealers, pension funds or investment advisers. The Canadian Office of the Superintendent of Financial Institutions (OSFI) was one of the earliest integrated prudential regulators, and it was formed in 1987 following the failure of two major Canadian banks in the mid-

1980s on the recommendation of the subsequent Royal Commission (Esty Commission). OSFI regulates all banks registered in Canada, all federally registered insurance companies, trust and loan companies and fraternal benefit (friendly) societies and pension plans, and provides actuarial advice to the Government.[2] Institutional integration has not been matched by legislative integration, and OFSI administers five main pieces of legislation with additional duties under three others.[3] In 1996 the OSFI Act was amended following a second wave of financial crises. OSFI's objectives were clarified and it was given additional powers of early intervention. As well as the usual objectives of maintaining public confidence in the financial system, protecting deposit holders and policy holders, and ensuring that financial institutions and pension plans are in sound financial condition,[4] OSFI was given an 'early intervention mandate': that is a legal obligation to anticipate problems and intervene early in the affairs of troubled financial institutions so as to minimize losses to depositors and policy holders, and an obligation to promote the management of risk within financial institutions and pension plans. Moreover, in regulating insurance companies and deposit-taking institutions, OSFI is to monitor and evaluate system-wide events that might impact on those institutions.[5] Finally, the Act provides that the regulation should be carried out bearing in mind that the primary responsibility for financial institutions and pension plans lies with their management, and that financial failures will occur.[6] OSFI currently regulates around 400 financial institutions and 1200 pension plans, and has a staff of around 450 (OSFI 2003).[7]

The FSA, like OSFI, is an integrated regulator in that it spans more than one financial institution, but it has a far wider regulatory community and a much broader set of statutory objectives. It was formed in 1997, and received its full statutory powers in 2001. The amalgamation of nine predecessor regulators, it regulates those who engage specified activities including deposit-taking, dealing, managing or arranging investments or providing investment advice, and unlike OSFI and APRA it regulates the way that firms conduct their business as well as their financial soundness. Its remit is expanding: in 2004 it will take over the regulation of mortgage advice, and in 2005 the regulation of the sale of general insurance companies (it already regulates their financial soundness). Under the governing statute, the Financial Services and Markets Act 2000 (FSMA), which consolidated and replaces the pre-existing legislation, the FSA was given four statutory objectives, and given seven further elements that it is required by statute to 'take into account' in performing its functions.[8] It regulates firms' conduct of business as well as their financial soundness, and its statutory objectives are the maintenance of market confidence, the provision of the appropriate degree of protection for consumers, the reduction in the scope for financial crime, and promoting public understanding of the financial system. It currently regulates over

10 000 financial institutions (with another 13 000 to be added once it starts to regulate general insurance brokers) with a staff of around 2400.

The Australian Prudential Regulation Authority was also the result of the rationalization of the organizational structure of regulation. Following a Commission of Inquiry into the regulation of the financial system in Australia in 1997 (Wallis Report 1997), the regulation of financial services was reformed and two new regulators were created in 1998, the Australian Prudential Regulation Authority (APRA) and the Australian Securities and Investments Commission (ASIC) (for history see Thompson and Abbot 2000). APRA took over the responsibilities of eleven separate state and federal financial regulators, and is responsible for the prudential supervision of all deposit-taking institutions, superannuation funds and insurance companies in Australia (Palmer Report 2002; Royal Commission 2003). Like OSFI, institutional integration was not accompanied by legislative integration, and it currently administers, and receives powers, under more than ten different pieces of legislation.

There are thus some striking similarities in the backgrounds and remit of the regulators. Each was formed as a result of dissatisfaction of the existing state of regulation, prompted to varying degrees by 'scandals': the failures of financial institutions, or instances of widespread malpractice by financial services providers. Each is the amalgamation of several pre-existing regulators. The design of each marked a shift in each nation state from regulation based on financial institutions (banking regulator, insurance regulator, securities regulator) to regulation based on function (deposit-taking, insurance provision, securities dealing), deliberately shadowing the restructuring of the financial industry itself. Nonetheless there are significant differences in the scale of their regulatory responsibilities and relative resources. OSFI and APRA are the most similar in this respect: they are both prudential regulators, and both regulate a similar set of financial services. Both are operating without consolidated legislation and so receive their powers and functions under several pieces of legislation: whilst their organizational structure is based on functional regulation, they administer legislation based on the old, institutional model. In contrast, the FSA regulates a far broader set of financial functions, resulting in a more heterogeneous regulatory community, and more significantly, has a wider set of statutory responsibilities. These two factors are important, for they explain a large part of the differences between the risk-based frameworks and the patterns of their development.

THE MAIN ELEMENTS OF THE 'RISK-BASED' FRAMEWORKS

Of itself, the adoption of policies for prioritizing regulatory resources is not particularly innovative. However, what is 'new', at least to financial regulation, are two things: the degree of formalization and systematization of regulatory policy based on conceptions of risk, and the development of an integrated decision-making framework for regulating firms which applies across a range of different financial institutions and activities. Whilst they differ often quite significantly in the detail, the organizing principle of each regulator's approach is the same: each looks at the relative risks that different regulated firms pose to the attainment of the regulator's objectives (for details see FSA 2000a, 2000b, 2002a, 2002b, 2003a, 2003b; APRA undated(a), undated(b), 2002; OSFI 1999, 2002).

In each case, the regulator has taken its legislative mandate and translated that into an operational agenda, which it has then implemented through the elaboration of a set of detailed procedural requirements and decision criteria. Each framework involves the assessment of the risks financial institutions pose to the regulatory objectives. These risks are divided into two categories: the risks arising from the nature of the business the institution conducts (inherent risk in APRA and OSFI's terminology; business risk in FSA's approach), and management risk, i.e. the risks posed by the firms' corporate governance structures and systems of internal control. To give some idea of the level of detail involved, inherent risk is in each case disaggregated into between five and nine risks (the FSA further disaggregate their five inherent risks into fifteen separate risks), and include such risks as the types of markets or products being dealt in, the nature of an institution's counterparties, its operational risk, the nature of its business strategy, and its legal and regulatory risk.[9] Management and control risk is divided into five or six categories (in FSA's case further disaggregated into twenty separate risks), and includes assessments of the quality of board oversight, of internal audit, financial and risk management functions, and compliance.[10]

In APRA and OSFI's frameworks, the risks are also assessed in terms of their materiality, or impact on the institution overall. The individual risk scores for each risk are aggregated, and the firm is given one of four ratings (the terminology varies, but these are broadly extreme, high, medium and low). In APRA's, that descriptive rating is then translated into a probability score, and there is a non-linear relationship between the score and the rating (i.e. the difference between the lowest and highest ratings is not four but 256). In all the regulators' frameworks the overall rating is communicated directly to the Board and/or chief executive, together with a set of actions which the regulator requires the firm to take. The ratings are 'non-negotiable' and firms are not allowed to disclose them to third parties save in limited circumstances.

To greater or lesser extents, the risk rating that a firm receives structures the supervisory response. In OSFI and APRA's frameworks, the ratings are tied closely to the supervisory response, which is itself highly structured. In FSA's framework, the coupling is much looser. Again, it helps to give some brief details. In OSFI's framework, the final risk rating is mapped directly onto a supervisory response category (set out in OSFI's *Guides to Intervention*), which can only be overridden by senior management. However, in determining that response, the impact that the realization of any of the risks might have on the financial system as a whole plays no role at all. This is in marked contrast to FSA and APRA's frameworks. In FSA's framework, there is no structured mapping of risk score to a particular supervisory response. However, firms are put into different categories based on their impact assessments, and to a degree their risk assessments. Only those ranked above low impact (Category D) will receive individual risk assessments. This means that over 80 per cent of regulated institutions do not receive individual risk assessments, and there is a considerable difference in the supervisory relationship between firms in different categories. Category D firms receive very little interaction from the FSA. They will not be visited except as part of a 'themed' visit (when the FSA will inspect a certain line of business). There are no routine, or even random, visits. Calls from those firms are directed to a call centre, and monitoring is based on sampling of regulatory returns. In contrast, Category A firms (high impact firms) are monitored on a 'close and continuous' basis. There are dedicated teams working with those institutions, they are individually assessed, and receive close and constant monitoring. Finally, in APRA's framework, risk assessments are performed for all firms. In order to correct for the tendency by supervisors to underestimate risk, there is a non-linear relationship between the assessment and the score. The risk and impact scores together determine the supervisory response. There is no room for supervisory judgement at this stage. Once the impact score and the risk score have been arrived at, they are mapped directly onto a supervisory response category of normal, oversight, mandated improvement or restructure, and this can only be overridden by senior management.

Table 8.1 briefly outlines and compares the main elements of each framework. In each case, the introduction of the risk-based frameworks has replaced far more discretionary supervisory processes. Whilst each framework relies heavily on the judgement of individual supervisors, that judgement is structured to a far higher degree than previously, and moreover there is far greater transparency within the organization as to how those supervisory assessments are being made, and a much higher degree of senior management oversight. Moreover, the risk-based frameworks require supervisors to change the way that they look at a regulated institution, and what they look for. Indeed the degree of change is such that the success, in very general terms, of the frameworks, and indeed the degree to which they mark any change in supervisory practices at all, is highly dependent on reskilling individual officials within the regulatory agency. Whilst the frameworks aim to change the ways in which

Table 8.1 Comparison of the risk-based frameworks

Organization: framework titles Element	FSA: Arrow (Advanced Regulatory Risk Operating Framework)	OSFI: Supervisory Framework and Guides to Intervention	APRA: PAIRS (Probability and Impact System) and SOARS (Supervisory Oversight and Response System)
Outline of Risk Assessment Framework	Impact of risk × probability of risk occurring = risk	Inherent risk minus quality of risk management = net risk Net risk considered against capital support = composite risk rating	Inherent risk minus management and control = net risk Net risk minus capital support = overall risk of failure
Who is assessed?	Firms above 'low impact' category; over 80% of firms are 'low impact'	All regulated institutions	All deposit-taking and insurance institutions; streamlined system for superannuation funds
Which risks are identified and assessed?	Consumer and industry-wide risks – five separate risks Firm specific risks: business risks – 5 further disaggregated into 15 risk elements Control risks – 5 further disaggregated into 20 risk elements	No particular CIW risk categories specified Firm specific risks: inherent risks – 7 Management and control risks – 6	No CIW categories specified Firm specific risks: inherent risks – 9 Management and control risks – 6

163

Table 8.1 continued

Organization: framework titles Element	FSA: Arrow (Advanced Regulatory Risk Operating Framework)	OSFI: Supervisory Framework and Guides to Intervention	APRA: PAIRS (Probability and Impact System) and SOARS (Supervisory Oversight and Response System)
Risk assessment against regulatory objectives	Each risk assessed against each of 7 'risks to objectives' (RTOs)	Assessed against single objective	Assessed against single objective
Risk weighting and risk scoring	Qualitative assessment and 5 descriptive categories	Qualitative assessment and 3 descriptive categories	Qualitative assessment and 4 numerical scores
	Risks not weighted	Risks informally weighted	Risk weighting unstructured for inherent risks; more structured for management and control risks
Method for arriving at final probability assessment (risk ranking)	Aggregation of scores: IT system designed so that score for each risk element automatically becomes the score for the group, subject to supervisory override	Aggregation of inherent and control risks separately based on judgement of supervisor	Aggregation of scores for inherent and control risks performed by IT system, weights towards higher risk assessment
Regulatory response	Development of Risk Mitigation Programme (RMP)	Guides to intervention	SOARS (Supervisory Oversight And Response System):
	Supervisory response not determined by risk assessment	Correlation between intervention and risk assessment	Systematized correlation of risk rating and response

supervisory assessments are made, they are just frameworks – in design they are markedly different from what went before; however for them to be effective and to make a real difference in practice depends on how they are implemented, an issue to which we will return below.

WHY INNOVATE?

In each case, the frameworks used differ radically from the regulatory practices which existed prior to them in the national regulatory regimes. In OSFI's case, its risk-based framework was introduced some years after its initial formation. In FSA's case, it began work almost immediately on developing a risk-based framework, even before it had received its new statutory remit and powers, but it drew to varying degrees on the risk-based frameworks being used by its predecessor regulators, particularly the Bank of England. In APRA's case, it too started to develop risk-based frameworks very soon after its formation, and each of its two main divisions developed their own. However, its practices were heavily criticized after the collapse of the insurance company HIH, which in large part prompted the replacement of the initial models with a new, single integrated risk-based framework.

Developing the frameworks has required a considerable commitment of organizational resources, and in FSA and OSFI's case there has been almost continual organizational restructuring to implement the programmes since their formation. For each agency, the risk-based framework now forms the basis of their supervisory decision-making, and in FSA's case it additionally provides the basis on which it performs all its regulatory functions, including policy-making. Relying on a new, untried set of organizational processes and management system for such fundamental aspects of a regulatory organization's activities clearly involves risks. Why, given those risks, should these regulatory agencies have decided to introduce changes of this nature and on this scale?

In identifying motivations, there inevitability has to be some fluidity in the analysis, for motivations do not tend to come neatly packaged, nor is their influence felt evenly and at the same time. Moreover, because innovation proceeded in stages, trying to pinpoint the 'start' of the innovation process is itself complex. Nonetheless, some rough 'start' dates for the innovation process can be identified, and a similar set of motivations can be identified across the regulators which both prompted the initiation of a search for 'new' approaches, and shaped the form the innovation took.

In each case, the initial motivation to 'do something' came from political and public pressure. Consistently with research on internal organizational change, change is motivated primarily by shock: a significant discrepancy between expectations and performance which goes beyond a certain threshold such that it is brought to the attention of senior management (see e.g. Rogers 2003, p. 422; Parker 2002). In this case, the 'shocks' were financial failures and the consequent public and political outcry at these failures. Those at the top of the regulatory organizations recognized the need to demonstrate to the public and politicians that they could be effective regulators, and to attempt to ensure that similar criticism did not come their way again.

But simply citing public and political pressures to act is not enough of itself to explain why regulators each decided to respond to this very general pressure in this particular way. In fact, each regulator felt that the best defence was, to some extent, attack. Each wanted to try to forestall further demands for increased regulation – to break the cycle of every financial 'scandal' being met with yet more legislation and yet higher expectations of what regulation could achieve. Each therefore had a desire to become more proactive in defining the political agenda. The message they wanted to convey was that regulators could not, and should not be expected to, ensure a 'zero-failure' regime, in which no financial institution failed. However to make this case credibly, the agency needed to be able to demonstrate it had a clear, rational and defensible set of procedures on which it made its decisions as to when and how it should act, and when it should not.

In OSFI's case, the crisis in the mid-1990s led to a number of recommendations for reform, the main thrust of which was that OSFI needed to be more interventionist in dealing with financial institutions. These events coincided with the appointment of a new Superintendent, John Palmer, in September 1994, which provided a window for changes to be introduced in OSFI's practices.

In the FSA's case, the initial motivations stemmed from events which happened prior to, and in part prompted, its formation, notably the collapse of Barings in 1995 and to a lesser extent the pensions misselling scandal of the early 1990s. The Bank of England had been developing RATE (Risk Assessment, Tools and Evaluation), a risk-based framework for banking supervision in 1996–97 as a response to the criticism of its supervisory processes following Barings (Report of the Board of Banking Supervision 1995, paras 13.58–13.68; FSA 1998). A systematic method for determining the allocation of resources and for structuring supervisory processes was seen to be essential if the Bank was to be able to defend its position as banking supervisor, and to define the limits of what it could be expected to achieve.[11] In the view of key senior officials, the problem the Bank faced from the Barings case was not that the Bank made the wrong decision to let Barings go under; it was that it could not give answers for the decisions it had taken in the course of the supervisory process leading up to the collapse. As one senior official commented, 'bureaucracies need tidy processes', and RATE was being developed with that function in mind.[12] The wholesale resiting of the Bank of England's supervisory division, and the move of its deputy governor, Howard Davies, to become chairman of the FSA, ensured these motivations remained very much alive in FSA.

In APRA's case, there had been moves to develop risk-based frameworks in APRA's early days, which had not been particularly prompted by political or public pressure or by scandals. However, these frameworks were relatively rudimentary, and what accelerated their development into the form now adopted was the collapse of HIH, a major general insurance company, and the subsequent political outcry which included the appointment of a Royal Commission of investigation into HIH's collapse. The very scale both of the consequences of the collapse and of the public and political criticism which followed made it clear that APRA had to act, and had to be seen to be acting. Moreover, for it to regain credibility, it was perceived by APRA that its conduct had to be in line with global best supervisory practice. As one APRA official commented, the collapse did not initiate the development of PAIRS (the Probability and Impact Rating System) and SOARS (the Supervisory Oversight and Response System), but it 'put the foot on the accelerator'.[13]

As noted above, however, these pressures were generally to the effect that 'something' must be done. Just what the 'something' should be was shaped by how the regulatory agencies defined the further problems that they wished to address, and their interpretations of their legislative mandates. Despite some differences in these mandates, in fact, each defined their problems in very similar ways, perhaps partly because of their common background. Each was the result of the merger of several other organizations which had now to be cohered into a single one. A new and common organizational culture had to be created if the organization was to function effectively as an integrated unit. The introduction of a new cognitive and procedural framework, which was not associated with any one of the predecessor regulators, and which was common across the organization, was seen as a powerful vehicle for creating organizational cohesion and coherence.

Moreover, despite the fact that they are funded by regulated firms, each was operating under resource constraints and in each case the institution restructuring had been expected to deliver cost savings, though these pressures were felt to differing degrees within and between the regulatory bodies. Each faced, to varying degrees, the familiar problem of 'regulatory overload': too much to do, and not enough resources to do it all, and each had the problem that they remained constantly in 'firefighting' mode – reacting to issues as they came along, rather than anticipating and seeking to prevent them.

These were not new problems, so why address them through 'risk-based' approaches? The answer in part lies in the changes in the organizations' task environments. These changes took two main forms. Each regulator was a new creation, and was facing a task and a remit which was unprecedented nationally, and of which few international examples existed, namely to regulate integrated financial institutions in an integrated way, i.e. one which cut across the traditional institutional divisions of deposit-taking, insurance, pensions, and so on, which had characterized both market and regulatory structures in the past. This required a common way to assess the amount of regulatory resources should be applied to each firm. Further, it was recognized within all three regulators that the regulatory tools which they had been using up were simply not suited to the task that they now faced. Financial institutions and practices had grown more complex, and in particular the large, conglomerate financial institutions were using increasingly sophisticated models of risk assessment and techniques of risk management. It was obvious to regulators that they needed to develop new technologies of supervision in order to regulate these institutions effectively. The old ways, for this complex of reasons, simply would not do.

Further, the organizations were also responding to their broader sectoral environment, and in some respects to the history of regulation in one of those sectors: banking. Prudential banking supervision in the UK had, since the secondary banking crisis in the 1970s, used a risk-weighted system to determine the capital requirements for each bank (Gardener 1986) After initial reluctance by some, the US banking regulators moved to a similar approach in 1986 after the Mexican crisis and the collapse of Continental Illinois, at the time the eighth largest bank in the USA, demonstrated that existing, non-risk sensitive approaches were simply inadequate (Seidman 1986), and drew heavily on the Bank's model in designing their own. In 1987 the USA and UK agreed to harmonize their prudential approaches and requirements, largely on the part of the USA to assuage fears of US banks that they would be subjected to 'unfair' competition from UK banks, and on the part of the UK to provide a counterweight to moves within the EU to agree harmonized capital standards. Ideas and interests thus coincided in forging the alliance. Fearing the dominance of a US–UK axis, the agreement of the rest of the G10 countries in the Basle Committee of Banking Supervision quickly followed, and the Basle Capital Accord was agreed in 1988 (Basle Committee on Banking Supervision 1988; Kapstein 1992). This has been recently revised in Basle II to enhance the 'risk-based' nature of banking supervision (Basle Committee on Banking Supervision 2004).

Risk-based approaches are thus embedded in the standards that regulators administer; they also began filtering into their operations in the course of the 1990s. During that time, risk-based supervision was being further developed in US banking regulation by the Office of the Comptroller of the Currency (OCC) and the Federal Deposit Insurance Corporation (FDIC) in particular. In 1996 the OCC introduced its current risk-based approach to banking supervision, including the targeting of resources on institutions with the highest risk ratings (OCC 1996), and this was in turn influential in shaping the approach of OSFI and FSA. In explaining its supervisory philosophy, the OCC articulates very clearly the reason why risk is the organizing principle: 'Because banking is essentially a business of accepting risk, that [supervisory] philosophy is centred on evaluating risks' (OCC 1996, p. 1). Risk-based regulation is thus in a very direct sense now seen to have a direct affinity with, and be a response to, the nature of the business that the regulated firms are undertaking: if their business is risk, and the regulators' role is to ensure that those risks are 'covered' in some way, a risk-based approach is now seen as the most appropriate, and obvious, approach to take. This fits most clearly with the task of prudential regulation, where the role of the regulator is to ensure the financial institution has sufficient capital to cover its risk exposures. Where the FSA in particular has stretched the risk-based approach is by extending it not just beyond banks, but to other aspects of financial institutions' activities, traditionally seen the preserve of more traditional compliance and enforcement activities, notably conduct of business, financial crime and money laundering.

INNOVATING THE REGULATORY WAY – JUST 'MODELLING THROUGH'?

So how did the organizations 'do innovation'? Within the organizational literature on regulatory innovation, the conventional innovation process consists of a clearly identified sequence of decisions, actions and events (Zaltman et al. 1973; Van den Ven et al. 1989; Van den Vel et al. 1999; Rogers 2003, pp. 417–33). There are five stages: agenda setting, matching, redefining, restructuring, and clarifying and routinizing. The first two are classified as part of the initiation subprocess, that is the process in which information gathering, conceptualizing and planning for the adoption of an innovation occurs, leading up to the decision to adopt; the latter three as part of the implementation subprocess. Agenda setting is when a general organizational problem is defined that creates a perceived need for an innovation. In this case, the problems were defined in the terms set out above – as needing to deal with the problems of political expectations, changes in the task environment, organizational coherence, and regulatory overload. This portrays a process in which the problem precedes the solution, and the development of risk-based approaches in the three regulators does indeed appear to have been an example of problems looking for solutions, rather than solutions looking for problems. The innovation was to an extent 'road tested' within the organization ('matching') to assess its feasibility prior to adoption, and further modifications made ('redefining/restructuring'). Indeed, for OSFI and FSA, who had the most work to do, the analytical work devising the new frameworks took two to three years. All three organizations piloted the approach before it was implemented, and in each case full implementation of the individual firm risk assessments has taken a further two to three years, and this 'clarifying' and 'routinizing' processes are still ongoing.

So who was involved in these processes? The answer is a relatively small number of people, and they came predominantly from within the regulatory organization. Each regulatory organization formed a small unit of between four to eight people charged with the mandate to innovate, known in organizational literature as 'skunkworks' (Rogers 2003, p. 149) and their parameters were set in very broad terms. The backgrounds of those involved varied, but tended to include people with knowledge and experience of each of the financial sectors being regulated. However, personal characteristics were sometimes more important than experience: the initial FSA group, for example, were selected for their ability to think laterally and creatively, rather than for experience alone.

External management consultants were however influential in devising RATE, on which, as noted above, the FSA's framework drew on quite heavily. Consultants were also involved in the development of ARROW, the FSA's current risk-based approach, though they came into the process at a later stage of the latter's development, once the main framework had been set. In particular, the main elements of RATE and subsequently ARROW are familiar to any internal risk management system in profit-making firms. In contrast, in OSFI's and APRA's case the frameworks were developed entirely in-house, though in both cases the leaders of the innovation units were recruited specifically from outside the regulatory body to lead the process. In all three cases, the innovation group was headed, at least initially, by those with backgrounds in banking, which is the area of financial practice in which risk models are the most developed. Indeed one of the main reasons for the dominance of RATE in the development of FSA's risk-based approach was the wholesale transfer of the Bank of England's supervisory department to the FSA, and the move of Howard Davies, the Bank's Deputy Governor, to be chairman of the FSA. Whilst the Bank of England certainly lost power institutionally on the FSA's formation, its institutional influence lived on in significant ways in the FSA's early years.

Who did the innovation groups look to for information and possible models to imitate or build on? They each looked to financial regulators in their own countries, both their predecessor organizations and, in federal systems, any comparable state systems of financial regulation. They also looked to overseas financial regulators, focusing in particular on US regulators and on other integrated financial regulators. It is notable that none of them looked to other national regulators in different domains: these were not perceived to be relevant comparators.

The analogical reasoning broke down quite quickly, however, particularly for the earlier developers, OSFI and FSA, as neither felt that there were any models that they could appropriate and modify. OSFI was the first of the regulators to begin work devising the framework, in 1997, and drew in part on its own system for insurance regulation, in part on the US Federal Deposit Insurance Corporation's framework, and to some extent on the US Office of the Comptroller of the Currency's (OCC) new supervisory framework, which was introduced in 1996. The FSA began its work in 1999. FSA found OSFI's model too limited for its purposes, and indeed it has a much wider set of legislative objectives and a far broader scope of responsibilities than either APRA or OSFI. It also drew on the OCC's 1996 supervisory framework, as the Bank of England had before it in developing RATE, but again that framework was designed and used only in the context of banking regulation and so required modification and adaptation (see further Black 2005a). APRA had the greatest opportunity for modelling, as both OSFI's and FSA's models were fairly well articulated, though not implemented, by the time it started on devising PAIRS and SOARS in late 2001, and APRA consciously used elements of both models in creating its own. In doing so, it drew more heavily on OSFI, which was perceived as a more relevant comparator given the close fit between its remit and mandate and that of APRA (see further Black 2005b).

The organizations differed notably in the extent to which they saw financial institutions themselves as relevant comparators. OSFI was very keen to learn from financial institutions for three reasons. First, OSFI felt that in many cases the institutions, particularly banks, had a better understanding of risk and how it should be managed than OSFI.[14] If it could leverage off that knowledge, it would do so. Second, those institutions were seen as sharing the same basic objectives as OSFI: their financial soundness. Both were oriented to the same end, thus it was appropriate that the analytical tools should be similar.[15] Third, it was felt that it was important for OSFI to have a way of analysing risks which were consistent with the way that institutions were managing their own risks to enable the regulator to have a dialogue with firms. As one senior official commented: 'it would be very difficult to have a dialogue with institutions and to talk about best practices if we weren't all in the same space'.[16] APRA also did not investigate regulated firm's approaches to managing risks, though in this case it was largely because it chose to leverage off the work done by OSFI in developing its model. In contrast, FSA did not see that it shared the same objectives as financial institutions, largely again because of its wider remit, and indeed has had to spend considerable time explaining to firms why its approach to risk management differs from theirs.

OUTCOMES

In their design, the risk-based frameworks are highly rationalizing, systematizing and formalizing; they are intended to render what was previously tacit explicit, what was previously overlooked monitored, and to stimulate and shape organizational responses in very particular ways. In their implementation, as their designers admit, the reality is inevitably more complex. The roll out of the frameworks is only just complete, and so assessing outcomes is difficult and in many ways premature. Nonetheless, some initial observations can be made.

In OSFI and FSA there has been extensive and continuous organizational restructuring to try and implement the framework. In APRA and FSA there has been a clear shift in the deployment of resources away from low impact firms towards higher impact firms, and, in the case of FSA, between different areas of its responsibilities (away from banking to insurance, away from prudential regulation to conduct of business regulation). Modes of interaction with firms have changed in all organizations, and the FSA in particular has changed the basis on which its enforcement decisions are made.

Implementation has been in part through the introduction of detailed guidance and procedures which supervisors are required to follow, and the frameworks have become, or at least are intended to become, part of the routine operational processes of the organizations. However, the innovations are attempting to introduce a new paradigm for carrying out some of the core regulatory functions, and as such are requiring officials to change the way they view and assess firms, and to change the ways in which they interact with them. The frameworks will only be as good, and as 'innovative' as the individuals implementing them allow them to be.

And the fact remains that implementation remains patchy within the organizations. This is largely because the frameworks require officials to operate 'outside their comfort zones': they require officials to commit to assessments, to look at areas of the business they are unfamiliar with, to have face-to-face, detailed meetings with the boards and chief executives of firms, and in many cases to be more interventionist than they might otherwise want to be. Because of their novelty, in using the frameworks, individual supervisors run the risk of making mistakes. The extent to which these are perceived as tolerated within the organization is widely recognized as affecting the framework's implementation. Supervisors need new skills, which were described as not necessarily technical skills, but cultural ones: changes in attitude and approach. This combination of novelty, re-skilling and risk-taking mitigate against change in practices, and all frameworks can be manipulated: it is perfectly possible, in other words, for supervisors to continue to do their assessments on the bases with which they are comfortable, and then just to re-cast them into the new assessment forms.

Moreover, outcomes are difficult to assess: each organization has made attempts to measure their performance, and the performance of the frameworks in particular, but none has yet devised a clear and conclusive measurement, and in any case full implementation has either only recently or not yet fully occurred, as noted above. However, assessed against the initial aims and motivations for devising the frameworks, in particular the need for a defence against charges of incompetence, and a need to devise a way of allocating resources and forging a common organizational culture, the frameworks are assessed by senior officials within the organization as having been successful. The frameworks at least provide a shield to wave at attackers, even if the political reality is that blame cannot be so easily diverted. There is a framework for allocating resources, even if that allocation cannot always be changed as easily and as seamlessly as the risk assessments would demand. The organizations are functioning more cohesively than they were before the frameworks became the main operating procedures, even though differences in the implementation of the frameworks within the agencies remain.

ANALYSING INNOVATION AND DIFFUSION

Why Innovate? Innovation as a Strategy of Proactive Defence

As we have seen, the motivations for innovation were in part to respond to criticism and to provide a defence should future financial failures recur. In particular, they were intended, particularly in the case of FSA, to provide a basis on which to forestall the knee-jerk, or perhaps rather 'Pavlovian' demands (see Hood and Lodge, Chapter 7 in this volume) for further regulation that accompany financial failures. The regulatory agencies 'juridified' their own procedures to prevent further 'juridification' being imposed upon them.

In each case, the innovation process was kick-started by a crisis of legitimacy brought on by the collapse of financial institutions under the supervision of the innovating regulator, or in the case of FSA, by one of its predecessors. Whilst the financial implications of those collapses varied significantly, in each case they prompted serious questions to be asked about the regulator's competence. Each thus had a need to change their practices in a clear and visible way to regain legitimacy and trust as financial supervisors. Each was also motivated by a need to take control of the regulatory agenda. In other words, to move from a stance where it reacted both to regulatees and to demands from political overseers to one in which it was proactive in determining how it would use its resources and what it could be expected to achieve. It therefore chose to move away from the extensive reliance on the discretion of individual supervisors which characterized the pre-innovation regulatory regimes to a situation where that discretion, though by no means removed, is now far more highly structured, the way that judgements are made is more transparent within the organization, and the level of management oversight is far greater. Internal regulatory processes have thus become 'juridified'.

One of the key motivations for this juridification was to present a credible defence to criticism. However, it also had a more proactive dimension, which was to attempt to redefine the expectations politicians and the public should have of what financial regulation could and should achieve. In prioritizing their regulatory activities, the regulators inevitably make a judgement about which areas of their regulatory remit are less important to achieve than others. What the frameworks are in effect saying is that, if something happens in a 'low priority' zone, for example a small pension fund fails to honour its beneficiaries, or a small bank fails, or an individual financial adviser missells a product, that is regrettable, but you cannot expect us to prevent everything, and so these failures have to be accepted as part of the normal risks that a person runs when dealing with a financial institution. However, the association between risk and blame has long been noted (Douglas 1992; Douglas and Wildavsky 1983). Denoting a risk as 'normal' means no blame should attach to anyone when the risk materializes. Not to be blamed is not to be held responsible. Through their risk-based frameworks regulators are attempting to redefine political and public expectations of what they should achieve, what they should be held responsible for, and what they should not (see also FSA 2003b).

Risk-based Regulation and 'Worlds' of Innovation

Given this interpretation of the frameworks, the innovation process is striking in its insularity and in the autonomy exhibited by the regulatory agencies from external political influences. As Heclo famously observed, governments 'puzzle' as well as 'power' (Heclo 1974), and the development of risk-based frameworks is an example of that 'puzzling': the attempt to deal as rationally as it was able to with a set of problems which it had identified. The innovation process has been remarkably 'politics-lite'. The process has not been marked by significant conflicts between different sets of interests, and there have been no clear advocacy coalitions. After the initial public demands that the regulator should 'do something', public, media or political attention has not really been concerned with what that 'something' is, and thus has not been significant in shaping the innovations. This is perhaps to be expected. Risk-based frameworks look like matters of internal regulatory management: they are technical, dry, matters of organizational process, and have been presented as such. The changes in regulatory practices have not involved any legislative act, nor have they involved the imposition of any new regulatory requirements on regulated firms.

Both in their character and their presentation they do not seem to lead to any winners or losers; their biggest claim is that the firm's day-to-day relationship with the regulator might change. They are changes which can thus be expected to have low media and political salience, and this has been exactly the case.

As a result, the regulators have been able to innovate on their own terms and in accordance with their own dynamics, and the innovation process has been far more akin to the process of innovation within the 'organizational' world than a 'state' world marked by the interplay of key political forces. In this process, there has been a clear attempt to 'model through': to reason analogically so far as possible, although 'modelling through' was constrained primarily because the opportunities to do so were limited: there was not much to model.

The choice of models is perhaps more interesting than the fact of modelling itself. Each chose to look to regulators in the same domain in other countries, rather than within their own countries but in different domains, confirming Rose's observation that bureaucracies learn cross-nationally but not cross-domain (Rose 1993). Moreover, only OSFI sought to model from the risk management practices of financial institutions, though, as noted, APRA did so indirectly by choosing to leverage off this aspect of OSFI's work.

Furthermore, these cases of regulatory innovation show that the extent to which modelling occurs depends on the openness of the modeller to other models. As regards organizational openness and modelling, in the FSA's case, and particularly in the Bank of England before it, modelling was inhibited by the organization's own closure: neither the FSA nor the Bank were interested in using others' models; they were intent on devising their own. The FSA has maintained that its position is so unique that it cannot learn from anyone, and there has been resistance to doing so. As one senior official commented, 'never underestimate the arrogance of the Bank and the FSA . . . you had to grow your own, with your own names and your own jargon . . .'.[17] In contrast, APRA has clearly been a modeller. In part this is because of the timing of the innovation processes: by that time it started devising a single risk-based framework, in late 2001, both OSFI's and FSA's models were quite developed and so APRA could profitably reason by analogy. However, APRA had an additional motivation to model: the search for legitimacy. For APRA, uniquely of the three, the motivation of emulation and identity were central to the initiation of the innovation process. Given its public humiliation in the aftermath of HIH, ensuring that its operations were to the standard of global best practice was, and is, critical in the effort to restore its credibility and legitimacy. Nonetheless, APRA has been a model modernizer, not a model miser, modifying and adjusting the model to suit its purposes.

The 'state' world thus has little purchase on understanding these cases of regulatory innovation, whereas in contrast the relevance of the 'organizational' world is clear. There was, to a surprising degree, a relatively boundedly ratio-nal decision process in which organizational environment plays a significant role in shaping organizational behaviour, though in which the organization still manages to maintain its autonomy – an example of normative closure, but cognitive openness (Luhmann 1995; Teubner 1993).

Two further 'worlds' in particular are worthy of note: the global polity world and the world of the innovation. In the diffusion of the innovation, formal transnational networks of communication have been important, but only indirectly. OSFI and the FSA have membership of at least four interna-tional regulatory organizations in common (the Basle Committee on Banking Supervision, the International Association of Insurance Supervisors (IAIS), the Financial Stability Forum and the Financial Action Task Force), although APRA is a member of only one of those (IAIS). However none of these orga-nizations has been a direct conduit of information on, or pressure to adopt, risk-based approaches. None of them focus on regulatory practices, as opposed to the types of principles of conduct that each should have in place to govern financial institutions, and certainly none of these organizations has been advocating 'risk-based approaches' along the lines considered here. Nonetheless, common membership of these networks is attributed by some with helping to raise general awareness of each other's practices and means each is used to dealing with the other.

The forum which has acted as a more direct channel of diffusion is the annual conference of integrated regulators first hosted by APRA in 2000, and by OSFI in 2001. At these conferences, as one participant put it, 'there is a lot of show and tell'.[18] More specifically, and stemming in part from participation in the conferences, APRA had a direct link to OSFI and its systems through John Palmer, who was Superintendent of OSFI from 1995–2001 and wrote the report on APRA's role in HIH which it submitted to the Royal Commission. Further, senior officials interviewed within each organization certainly show a working knowledge of the systems that each is using, although this knowledge may be a year or so out of date in some cases. Each organization has also published details of its approach at its various stages of development on their websites, further facilitating dissemination.

Nevertheless, the process examined here differs from the explanations of the 'global polity' world, and indeed of the 'individual' world, in a number of ways. First, of the 'usual suspects' of policy diffusion, most have been rela-tively quiet. There has been no agitating or pushing by NGOs, inter-govern-mental bodies or corporations. Transnational networks have operated only at an informal level, beneath the level of the global regulatory institutions. Moreover, epistemic communities or other vehicles of a 'world culture' of regulatory technology have not yet emerged in any developed way to play a major role in their development; rather each policy has been to a large extent 'home grown' within the jurisdiction, and to varying degrees within the regulatory body itself. Nor has a single individual yet emerged on the global stage who is promoting the model. There are not yet model mercenaries or model mongers who are out there plying their wares on the world stage, though that may come. Moreover, although within each jurisdiction there have been certain individuals whose role has been significant, there has been in no case a clear champion of the innovation, although in each case those at the top of the organization have actively demanded it. Rather, the innovation process has been a collective one. Whilst the 'innovation teams' have had strong leaders with clear ideas, and there are some identifiable 'names' within the organization who are associated, to varying degrees, with their initiation and design, the innovations are in practice multi-authored, and as such can better be described as an example of 'organizational entrepreneurship' (Barzelay and Campbell 2003) rather than a triumph of individualism.

Perhaps more significantly, and resonating with the 'innovation' world, the formation and adoption by these bodies of global principles of supervision has emphasized the homogeneity of financial regulators: individual differences have been abstracted in the formation of generalized principles. That process of standardization, albeit at a very high level of abstraction, has constructed regulators as similar in the tasks they have to perform, and as recognizing and accepting that there are standard and accepted ways of accomplishing them. In other words, financial regulators are accustomed to seeing themselves as similar to other regulators and thus to seeing the practices of other regulators as being potentially relevant to them. That each is sufficiently similar that they can learn from the other is an accepted social fact in international financial regulation.[19] This notion of relevance is clearly critical in the modelling process: understanding the choice of who to model is critical to understanding modelling itself.

Finally, the innovation is potentially supported by institutional structures, the future effect of which cannot be discounted. The homogenizing influences of global principles, and the processes of their formation, are buttressed by the systems of peer review which exist within the international system of financial regulation, notably the World Bank's Reports on the Observation of Standards and Codes, and the IMF's Financial Sector Stability Assessment Process, which includes an assessment of the regulatory system's compliance with international standards and codes. These standards do not at present require regulators to have 'risk-based' frameworks of supervision; however OSFI, APRA and the FSA have all been assessed under the process, and those who have been assessed subsequently state that the assessors show clear familiarity with the frameworks of those three regulators.[20]

CONCLUSIONS

Risk-based approaches to regulation, as interpreted and practised by financial services regulators in these three countries, are thus innovative both in the sense that they are new to the regulators adopting them, and in the sense that they are new, in the form they have taken, to financial regulation in most major countries. In developing those models, the mix of motivations was remarkably similar, though different ones had different weight for different participants and at different times. These were bureaucratic defensiveness, the perceived need for a procedural and cognitive framework in which to organize practices, to address the particular functional challenges faced by the regulator, and to link practices with statutory objectives and political expectations. Further, for APRA and the FSA (both of which were new organizations), the creation of a common risk-based approach provided a useful and necessary vehicle for the creation of a common organizational culture.

The organizational worlds and the worlds of the innovation play a far greater role in explaining regulatory innovation in these instances than the world of the state, or to an extent the global polity. The processes of regulatory innovation were marked by an absence of the normal play of regulatory politics: regulated firms, consumer bodies, trade associations and politicians are all notable by their absence. Moreover, whilst transnational activity place a limited role, the 'usual suspects' of global polity diffusion were also absent. Regulatory innovation in these cases provides an example of regulators 'puzzling not powering' in relative autonomy, where organizational pressures and the innovation itself are key to understanding the innovation process, and to the extent it has occurred, its diffusion. In each case their development was an incremental process, in which some decision-makers were actively seeking to 'model through', but who found a paucity of models which they could appropriate. Instead they built on and adapted those used by their own predecessors or by other financial regulators. In looking for models to adopt, their reference group was not defined geographically, and other financial regulators were far more influential than other national regulators in other domains. However, others, notably the FSA, were reluctant to adopt policies used by overseas regulators; the determination was that the policy should be 'home grown'. There were few individual 'entrepreneurs', and the adoption of the policies was deliberately cast within the organizations as neutral strategies, as a way of ensuring there were no 'winners' or 'losers' in the organizational restructuring. Moreover, the development of risk-based frameworks also implicitly recognized the 'Pavlovian' world of regulatory innovation in that one of the motivations for their development, certainly in the UK, was to forestall exactly that response when the next 'scandal' came along, as it surely will.

The world of the innovation is also significant as the innovation itself is, and will most likely continue to be, important in analysing the development of risk-based regulation. As discussed above, the frameworks in question are highly rationalizing, synthesizing and homogenizing in their orientation: each seeks to provide certainty, to simplify the complexities of the regulatory task, and to provide cognitive devices and organizational procedures to structure the decision-making of regulatory officials in the pursuit of particular modes of governance (interventionist, proactive, consistent, explicit) and the regulator's particular objectives. The frameworks provide a technology of regulation: a set of understandings of the world and of regulatory practices which abstracts from the complexities of individual organizations and provides a framework for rational action which accords with actors' need to believe that the task of governing and controlling is one which they can achieve. To that extent, as discussed, they follow a 'modernist' trajectory. However, their design, and in particular their entwinement with strategies of 'meta-regulation' (regulation of firms' own internal self-regulation) means they would find sympathy with those who advocate the need for 'decentred' regulatory strategies. But whilst the individual authors of the frameworks resist their reification and admit to their limitations, these qualifications and hesitancies are lost in the confident exposition of risk identification, assessment and validation; in the apparently neat and more or less elegant solutions to complex and often intractable problems. Risk-based frameworks hold out the promise that the challenges and complexities of financial supervision can be rationalized, ordered, managed, controlled. Faced with that temptation, what regulator could resist?

NOTES

1. The empirical research is based on documentary sources and interviews with ten senior officials in the three regulators studied, including the ex-chairmen of two of those organizations. The title of this chapter borrows the phrase 'modelling through' from Braithwaite and Drahos (2000), p. 590.
2. Office of the Superintendent of Financial Institutions Act 1987 (OSFI Act).
3. Bank Act; Trust and Loans Companies Act; Cooperative Credit Associations Act; Insurance Companies Act and Pension Benefits Standards Act 1985.
4. OSFI Act ss. 3–4.
5. OSFI Act ss. 4 (2)(b) and 4(2.1)(b).
6. OSFI Act ss. 4(4) and 4(5).
7. OSFI Annual Report.
8. FSMA s. 2.
9. FSA's five categories (labelled 'business risks') are: financial soundness; market; insurance underwriting and credit risk; strategy; nature of customers/products; these are further disaggregated into twenty separate risk elements. APRA's six categories of inherent risks are: asset quality and counterparty risk; balance sheet and market risk; insurance risk; operational risk; liquidity risk; legal and regulatory risk; strategic risk; contagion; related party risk. OSFI's six categories are: asset quality and counterparty risk; balance sheet and market risk; insurance risk; operational risk; liquidity risk; legal and regulatory risk; strategic risk; contagion; and related party risk.

10. FSA's five categories of control risks are: treatment of customers; organization; internal controls; board management and staff; and business and compliance culture. These are further disaggregated into 20 risk elements. APRA's six categories of management and control risk are: board of directors/trustees; operational management; management information systems/financial control; risk management; compliance; and specialist control functions. OSFI's six categories are: operational management; financial analysis; compliance; internal audit; risk management; senior management; and board oversight.
11. Interview, FSA 17204.
12. Interview FSA 251103.
13. Interview, APRA, 21203.
14. Interview, OSFI, 30304 and OSFI 310304.
15. Interview, OSFI 31304.
16. Interview, OSFI 30304.
17. Interview FSA 102041.
18. Interview, OSFI 30304.
19. Interview, OSFI 30304.
20. Interview, OSFI 30304.

9. Conclusions

Julia Black and Martin Lodge

INTRODUCTION

At the outset we noted that the term 'regulatory innovation' is likely to attract either unbridled enthusiasm or barely mitigated scepticism. It is seen on the one hand as the solution to regulatory and wider economic failings, and on the other as the source of policy fiascos. Its very existence is doubted by sceptics, who argue it is simply a fashionable label in which to dress up changes in policy or modes of implementation, or indeed academic studies of such changes. In seeking to explore these claims, we sought to answer three specific questions: what is regulatory innovation; how can we explain or account for it, and are we living in an age of hyper-innovation, or simply one in which there is a lot of hype about innovation? The case studies have been deliberately diverse, ranging from the 'high tech' to the 'low tech', and from the fashionable to the unfashionable. Innovation in each area in the UK has been compared cross-nationally against at least one other country, in order to explore whether and how regulators in each domain in different countries produced 'innovative' responses to similar policy issues. This conclusion outlines the discoveries that we made during this exploratory study of regulatory innovation, looking at each question in turn, and also asking what this study has to contribute to the debates on 'how to do' regulatory innovation.

WHAT IS INNOVATIVE ABOUT REGULATORY INNOVATION?

Innovation is for many inherently associated with assumptions of 'newism' and 'success', and as such forms an important part of the regulatory reform agenda. In contrast, the 'hyper-innovation' of the last 20 to 30 years is regarded by others as a fiasco. At least both sides of that argument agree that 'innovation' exists; in contrast more sceptical observers argue that innovation is not distinguishable from change, and indeed that the very exercise of studying 'innovation' is to take the hype about innovation too seriously. On this

181

view, 'innovation' need not amount to the introduction of anything that is particularly 'new', even if that 'newness' could be measured in some way.

It was noted at the outset that 'innovation studies' tend to avoid the problem of assessing 'newness' either by adopting a subjective interpretation of innovation ('innovation is that which is perceived to be new to those adopting it') or a narrow objective definition, in which 'newness' was assessed in relative, not absolute terms: an innovation is something that is 'new' to the regulatory regime or state in which it was adopted, but not necessarily to anyone else. The subjective definition gives an insight into participants' reactions and responses, but in itself does not distinguish 'leaders' from 'laggards'; the objective definition facilitates assessments of 'innovativeness' but requires innovation to be distinguished from mere change. In the light of the preceding chapters, is there, on the one hand, any value in uncritically taking subjective perceptions of 'newness' as definitive, and on the other hand, is there something that may be objectively regarded as a 'regulatory innovation' that is distinguishable from a mere change? We offer two affirmative answers to these questions.

First, our chapters revealed that some actors certainly regarded certain changes to the regulatory regime as innovative and that these perceptions are critical for interpretive studies of why and how innovation occurred in those regimes. For example, those owning an American pit bull terrier or American Staffordshire bull terrier would certainly regard a change in regulatory approach from one that presumed that all dogs were equal before the law to one that presumed some breeds and types to be inherently more aggressive than others to be 'innovative', and moreover highly significant. It mattered indeed so much that dog owners succeeded in jamming the British central government switchboards twice in the early 1990s with their protest phone calls. Similarly, changes in gaming regulation in the UK that moved from a prohibitive approach that saw gaming as a vice to be tightly controlled to a liberalized approach which saw gaming as an entertainment to be regulated (and allowed for the generation of income through a 'tax on hope'), are certainly innovative in the eyes of those that regard gambling as a social and moral issue and for whom, moreover, liberalization is an anathema, albeit that the regulatory approach introduced is in fact unremarkable when compared with regulatory structures and approaches in other domains.

Second, our chapters also revealed that in objective terms, regulatory innovation could certainly be regarded as different from just change if defined as *ad minimum* second-order change. The first chapter suggested that regulatory innovation is the use of new solutions to address old problems, or new solutions to address 'new' (or newly constructed) problems, but not old solutions to address old problems. More specifically, in objective terms, regulatory innovations are second- or third-order changes in the performance of regulatory functions, institutional structures and organizational processes which have an impact on the regulatory regime, although the impacts and outcomes of innovation may be unintended, and innovations are not always successful. Moreover, second-order changes may serve to entrench prevailing paradigms further, for example the innovation in enforcement techniques to counter Internet gaming in the USA, and may thus be a force for stability rather than fundamental change.

The individual chapters encountered examples of both second- and third-order changes. Second-order changes are perhaps more numerous: for example the introduction of risk-based frameworks in financial regulation, the use of private parties as bottlenecks in the Internet gaming domain, the (initial) move towards the disclosure of legislators' interests and 'pay for ethics', or the use of auctions or franchising for the allocation of telecommunications licences or the award of passenger services respectively. However, there are instances of third-order changes in which there have been normative and/or cognitive shifts in policy assumptions, notably the shift in the conception of gaming from vice to entertainment, the move from a 'one free bite' to a 'breed type and, risk-based' regulation of dogs, or the shift in the regulation of legislatures towards a greater emphasis on transparency in the late 1980s and early 1990s.

Therefore, in both its subjective and objective guises, we did find changes which could be characterized as regulatory 'innovations'. At the same time, the studies suggest that any difference between 'more' or 'less' innovation should be avoided, especially when comparing examples of second- and third-order changes. Certain second-order changes may cause far more public anxiety than third-order changes and therefore also excitement (for those affected, for politicians, and for students of regulation). Moreover, despite an initial scepticism, we discovered that there is more 'innovation' about than even current proponents of innovation, or indeed observers of 'hyper-innovation', might suspect. In particular, it is certainly not the case that regulatory innovation is the sole preserve of those markets that are characterized by the destruction of established market boundaries through internationalization or technological change, nor is innovation confined to domains such as professions (e.g. politicians), which are affected by wider societal changes and an increase in the distrust of 'club government'. Rather innovation is also evident in less obvious and high-profile areas such as loss-making industries (railways) or what may be regarded as trivial domains by those interested in the presumed 'global transformation' of the economy and politics: dangerous dogs. Further, in contrast to the predominant focus of the 'regulatory state' literature, innovation is not confined to the political institutional structures of regulatory regimes; in other words the creation or redesign of regulatory agencies; rather innovation occurs in all aspects of the regulatory regime, which a focus on purely institutional design overlooks.

WHAT ACCOUNTS FOR REGULATORY INNOVATION?

At the core of our study of regulatory innovation are the five 'worlds' of regulatory innovation that were introduced in Chapter 2. These worlds are sites of analysis, each focusing on different actors, mechanisms, levels of analysis and methodologies, combining to produce somewhat differing answers to the questions of how and why innovations are introduced. As such, they offer partly rival and partly overlapping explanations and perspectives. In seeking to explore the extent to which the 'worlds' of innovation provided insights for understanding regulatory innovation in any of the specific case studies, we shared a broadly similar inductive methodological approach, but given the explorative nature of this study, we did not seek to undertake a positivist 'test' of the explanatory value of the different worlds of regulatory innovation.

Nonetheless, both the identification and the further exploration of the different worlds of regulatory innovation contributes to our understanding of regulatory innovation in at least three ways. First, in identifying the different worlds, it makes explicit what is often left implicit or is even ignored in other studies of regulatory innovation: that innovation studies are prey to falling foul of their disciplinary boundaries, and, particularly in the case of the self-styled 'innovation and diffusion studies' in political science, of cutting themselves off from the rest of their own discipline. The identification and exposition of the worlds thus should raise awareness of the range of differing and often competing accounts of innovation, many of which are often overlooked by writers in different disciplines.

Second, juxtaposing the worlds highlights the different methodologies each entails, and the different ways in which attention is directed in each. Like the drunk who looks for his wallet under the street light because that's the only place he can see, rather than the place where he may have lost it, the worlds focus on different aspects of innovation processes: the role of individuals, political institutions, organizations, global polity networks and the innovation itself. Looking at only one world is like looking under only one street light; whilst one might find a few coins, it may be that richer accounts may be found elsewhere.

Third, the case studies do call into question the extent to which different worlds are significant in explaining regulatory innovation in particular instances. Table 9.1 offers an overview of the worlds, including that of Pavlov, and the way in which they related to the various chapters in this volume.

When looking across the different chapters, it is noticeable how little the world of the individual seemed to have mattered in the accounts given. This is both striking and curious. It stands in contrast to the considerable emphasis that is often placed on the role of 'leaders' in achieving, or failing to achieve organizational transformations or policy innovations (see the examples in

Table 9.1 *The worlds of regulatory innovation*

Site	Individual	Organizational	State	Global polity	Innovation	'Pavlovian'
Site	The individual	Within organizations/ non-state	State and state structures	Transnational networks	The innovation itself	Conditioned response to media-driven political crisis in which politicians and bureaucrats rationally economize on rationality
Analysis of innovation/ innovation because of/	Policy entrepreneurs and 'innovation champions'	Organizational structures and culture Sectoral/ organizational logics of appropriateness System – environment effects	Innovation and diffusion across jurisdictions Learning and policy transfer Historical and political institutionalism	Epistemic communities and global communicative networks World instrumental cultures	Type of innovation links to its own diffusion Ideas play an independent role in policy formation	
Railways	Various individual policy entrepreneurs fade away over time	Importance of competing templates, offering rival logics of appropriateness	Importance of national political– administrative interaction mechanisms in selecting policy template		Supposed paradigms with substantial diversity in regulatory arrangements	

Table 9.1 continued

	Individual	Organizational	State	Global polity	Innovation	'Pavlovian'
Legislatures	Personalisation of the innovations, but not a defining role in their development	Importance of logic of appropriateness in filtering proposals	State structures or supposed 'styles' do not matter, but state as site of regulatory innovation	Asymmetric and negative learning across global networks	Idea of openness matters, but requires fit with organizational logic of appropriateness	
3G mobile phone licensing	Individuals at best 'filled out' existing policy decisions		Neither political institutions nor traditional conceptions of political economy seemed to matter in the choice of policy instrument		The outcome of the innovation in the UK (large revenue) was easily learnt and transmitted, but more complex aspects of the innovation were not	
Internet gaming	Importance of policy entrepeneurship in New York: Attorney-General Spitzer	Policy processed by government bureaucracies to reach workable	Limited policy learning	Limited role which is rarely decisive in policy-making, despite international gaming industry		

Risk-based regulation	No explicit policy entrepreneurs	Importance of self-referential logic of appropriateness	Absence of public salience allows for discretionary process within regulatory organizations	Epistemic community, but no evidence of 'deep learning' across global policy network	Innovation 'fits' with modernist paradigm of risk management and control	Innovation prompted in part to forestall 'Pavlovian' responses to financial failures
		solutions to policy problems, with some recognition of the limits of the state's regulatory capacities				
Dangerous dogs	Individuals did not matter to the outcomes	Organizational structures and environment immaterial	Same responses not accounted for by diffusion or policy learning Institutions did not matter	No global communicative networks or epistemic communities		Conditioned response by politicians and bureaucrats, rationally economizing on rationality

Moore 1995; Heifetz 1993; Barzelay and Campbell 2003, p. 21; see also Wildavsky 1989, Lynn 1996, pp. 109–42). It is the case that we have not undertaken an explicit, positivist 'testing' of the different worlds in the light of our case studies. It may also be that our accounts are coloured by our own individual observer biases. However, conscious of the dominance often given to individuals in accounts of policy innovations, each author did seek out individuals in their case studies, and in some cases, found them. However, with the exception of New York Attonery-General Spitzer in the case of Internet gaming, we found that where policy entrepreneurs mattered, it was only when it came to 'alternative specification' (in the language of Kingdon (1995)) after the policy agenda had been set (as Mark Thatcher argues with respect to the British 3G story). Moreover, more broadly, their role was only significant when looking at individual cases in isolation, and even here only in a limited sense. When the particular examples of regulatory innovation in a domain are looked at in a cross-country comparative perspective, the contribution of individuals seems to have been less prominent and dependent on institutional resources and access as well as wider political support. So whilst particular individuals may have mattered to an extent in one country in one domain, other countries in that domain engaged in similar innovations in the absence of such individuals. Thus, for example, when comparing UK and German responses to dangerous dogs, individual ministers did not matter: each country had the same response. In the case of the railways, the role of individuals at different levels and at different times was mostly a consequence of institutional resource rather than individual character. The British story of parliamentary ethics also reveals a surprising lack of policy entrepreneurship, despite the personalization of particular initiatives in the late 1990s ('Nolan'). Such a diminutive role for individuals in these accounts prompts two obvious questions: on the one hand, despite our searches, have we nonetheless missed something (or someone), but on the other, does the frequent emphasis on the role of individuals in innovation simply overlook the accounts that other 'worlds' of innovation may give, in particular when other countries are seen to innovate in similar ways?

There was also limited evidence in our cases for the importance attributed to the 'world of the global polity'. Whilst we note the importance of international networks in a number of cases, for example financial regulation, 3G auctions and legislatures, they mattered only to a limited extent. In Julia Black's account of financial regulation international networks emerge as fora of information exchange, but hardly as a diffuser of particular professional norms. Robert Kaye's account of the development of ethics regulation in legislatures highlights that 'global networks', or at least in this case awareness of international comparisons, can be asymmetric, for example the adoption of the UK ethics approach by Australia at a time when the British

parliamentarians seem to have rejected the need for any international comparisons in their own reforms. Moreover, it illustrates that global networks can
serve to promote 'negative learning': a response of 'whatever we want, it's
not what they've got'. Furthermore, we did not find global networks to be
prominent even where one might expect them to be. Thus in Colin Scott's
account of Internet gaming, while the providers and the medium are global,
there is a remarkable absence of a transnational policy-making network,
rather the regulation of Internet gaming in the three jurisdictions explored is
characterized by each seeking to address the issue in strategic competition.
Similarly, in Mark Thatcher's account of 3G mobile phone licence auctions,
whilst this could in theory be partly a story of the involvement of transnational companies, international consultants and technocratic epistemic
communities in the development and implementation of an innovation, it
seems rather to be a story of national states responding largely in isolation
from one another, in which the outcome of the UK auction (significant
revenue) was communicated but little else.

The 'world of the innovation' also played a variable, but on the whole
limited, role in explanations of regulatory innovation. The form of the innovation itself is regarded as significant in Julia Black's account of the development of risk-based regulation in financial services, in particular the
emphasis on risk-based regulation on measurement, assessment and management, and the confident message it therefore sends of rationalization and
controllability, and its ability to serve as a prophylactic against 'Pavlovian
innovation'. The idea of the innovation itself also plays a role in Martin
Lodge's account of rail regulation and in Robert Kaye's account of ethics in
legislatures, but again only to the extent that they fit with existing cognitive
and normative understandings in that regulatory regime – even in conditions
where the persistence of normative frameworks should be most unlikely, such
as wartime defeat. Finally, Mark Thatcher's account of 3G auctions illustrates
that only the headline outcome of the innovation may be important for its
diffusion, in this case the very high revenue gained by the UK government. It
was that which set the auction bandwagon rolling, with other states interested
only in the revenue rather than mechanisms of the auction, ignoring the
depletion effect that was arguably inevitable.

Most accounts of regulatory innovation thus fall within the state and organizational worlds. This is in part not surprising, given the breadth and internal complexities of those worlds. The cases highlight, however, the variable
extent to which the inner life of the organizations within the regulatory
regime themselves can operate in the isolation of the wider political pressures
and institutional structures, and thus the extent to which understandings of
innovation can be rooted in the organizational world. Allowing again for
observer bias, in which an account of innovation could differ depending on

the extent to which the researcher chooses to focus on the internal workings of the bureaucratic organizations in which the innovation is devised and implemented or chooses instead to look at the wider political context, the organizational world appears, unsurprisingly, more important in those innovations which are of low political and media salience, such as risk-based approaches to financial regulation, than it does in innovations which are politically more visible, such as 3G mobile phones or dogs, where the state world dominates. Moreover, whilst it might be assumed that innovations in certain parts of the regulatory regime, for example changes in the political-institutional structures of the regime, such as the creation of a new regulatory body for gaming in the UK, will inevitably engage the state world, it is not necessarily the case that innovations in 'lower level' processes or regulatory technologies can be considered in isolation from the political dynamics of the state world. This runs contrary to the organizational focus which dominates the public management literature, in which it is often assumed that 'innovations' can be designed in such a way that precludes these broader political dynamics.

As noted above, the worlds themselves offer competing accounts of innovation for any given site of analysis, and with reference to the state world, in particular its institutionalist 'continent', the comparative perspective of our case studies also throws up questions both for those who argue that 'institutions matter' and for those that argue that they do not. Our cases revealed in some cases important similarities across states regardless of political-institutional differences, such as in the 3G mobile phone licensing or the dangerous dogs case, while in others, such as railways, particular institutional mechanisms within executive government were decisive for the selection of policy templates. In many ways, therefore, our analysis has highlighted the importance of moving beyond broad stereotypes of 'institutions matter' towards a close study of what type of mechanisms and processes are underlying regulatory innovation and how different elements of regulatory regimes interact.

Finally, apart from reassessing worlds of regulatory innovation, our study has also discovered a 'new world', namely that of Pavlovian regulatory innovation. In the 'Pavlovian' world, 'innovation' is a conditioned response by politicians and officials to headline-grabbing news stories which turn into major political crises and elevate what are normally issues of low politics high onto the political agenda. Contrary to the state world, Pavlovian innovation is a form of innovation in which little or no horizontal learning and diffusion (Berry and Berry 1999) takes place, and in which state tradition or institutional milieu (other than the general characteristics of wealthy liberal democracies) do not seem to be very important to outcomes. Contrary to the world of the innovation, it is a world in which proper names or individual leadership qualities do not play a significant role. Contrary to the organizational world, organizational structures or environments are immaterial; in contrast to the global polity world there are no significant global polity networks, and finally, contrary to the world of the innovation, the 'idea' itself seemed not to matter.

Hood and Lodge argue, however, that the Pavlovian world is not simply to be dismissed as an example of how not to 'do' innovation. Rather, they argue that the Pavlovian world of innovation exhibits its own rationality: that it is rational to economize on rationality'.

> Just as for Pavlov's dogs, salivating to the sound of the bell is a response that economizes on intelligence and broadly makes sense (in that it is eventually abandoned when the food no longer appears after the bell), simple conditioned responses to media firestorms may have similar properties for politicians and bureaucrats. (Hood and Lodge, this volume, p.152)

It involves low information gathering costs which, although contrary to the usual prescriptions for elaborate decision-advice procedures as a key to good governance, make sense for issues where such official information as exists is highly unreliable and the cost of supplementing it, in the short term at least, very high. In such circumstances, they argue, a Pavlovian response meets immediate political needs for a quick popular response that passes most of the processing and transactional costs onto other agents in the implementation process. Further, the approach is as capable of being effective as any feasible alternative, if success is assessed in terms of the primary political and bureaucratic interest in assuaging demands for further action and diverting media attention. Whilst they created unanticipated side-effects, as they argue, it is hardly the case that other innovations do not.

The world of Pavolvian innovation was 'discovered' and explored in the example of dangerous dogs regulation, but there were some Pavlovian traces also in the area of risk-based approaches in financial regulation, at least in the sense that these approaches were in part adopted with the view to forestalling such type of innovation. Further probing would be required to establish more firmly that 'Planet Pavlov' is 'out there', and its relationship to the state and organizational worlds which it seems to cut across. Nevertheless, the world of Pavlovian regulatory innovation stresses a particular observable phenomenon, namely the importance of a conditioning process, while also rejecting many of the assumptions that underline the other worlds. Finally, in pointing to potential dominant political and administrative motives when it comes to the incident of a 'Pavlovian response', this world offers arguably a counterpoint to the assumptions of 'benevolence' and inherent 'rationality' of innovation 'cycles' often pronounced in the regulatory reform debate.

HOW TO 'DO' INNOVATION: THE WORLDS OF INNOVATION AND THE REGULATORY REFORM DEBATE

But what about those interested in the practice of 'regulatory innovation'? One of the standard complaints against academic work is that there is a dearth of high-quality research on innovation (especially of the 'how was it done' kind) in the public sector, reiterated in a recent UK Cabinet Office document (Cabinet Office 2003, para 3.6). Whilst that report overlooks the extensive academic attention given to explaining innovation, and more generally policy change, since the 1960s, it is true that most of this work is more concerned with the 'how and why' of innovation, rather than the 'how to'. Such charges of misguided or inapplicable (if not incomprehensible) academic studies chiefly interested in communicating in ivory towers are widespread, and, at first sight at least, neither the 'worlds' of innovation nor our case studies seem to lend themselves well to the universe of practising regulatory innovation. There are at least three responses to this charge.[1]

First, in contrast to the 'how to do' innovation literature, we deliberately employ a definition of regulatory innovation that does not imply success. In so doing, we immediately widen the set of cases from which 'how to' guides can learn, and iterate the message that innovation requires an acceptance of failure. We argue that innovations that have failed against some criteria, which include at a bare minimum that they have not had the impact intended, are as worthy of analysis as those that have succeeded. In contrast, the common definition of innovation employed in studies of public sector innovation is that the change has to have been successful to be worthy to bear the name 'innovation'. Frequently, case studies on innovation are selected because they have been successful, and moreover have won awards for their success (e.g. Borins 2001; Sparrow 2000). Studying only successes, however, means that one does not learn from failures. A vital set of experiences is thus screened out, literally by definition, and as a result the lessons of failure are simply not learned. Moreover, a message to the public sector that innovations necessarily imply success ignores innovation's 'dirty little secret': that innovation requires failure (Altshuler and Behn 1997, p. 15). Unless organizations tolerate and support failure, they are unlikely to get much innovation.

Second, we provide a framework in which it is possible both to ask and to answer the question: what form of innovation is wanted, and what form of innovation is attainable. We argue that innovations cannot easily, and indeed should not, be measured in terms of their 'significance' or degree, but rather should be distinguished on the basis of whether or not they involve paradigm shifts. Thus we distinguish between second-order and third-order innovations: those that occur within existing normative and cognitive paradigms, and those that involve changes in those paradigms. Highlighting this distinction emphasizes the point made above that some innovations, i.e. second-order innovations, may only serve to entrench those paradigms more firmly, and thus preclude third-order changes: innovations may thus be a force for stability, rather than change. Nonetheless, the 'how to do' innovation guides tend to assume that innovations will be second-order innovations, and often, moreover, that they will occur at the level of policy implementation rather than policy formation (Altshuler and Behn 1997). This leaves the third-order changes unexplained; moreover in assuming that the policy even in second-order changes will be left intact ignores the political context to over-optimistic accounts of how structures or processes of innovation can be designed. In addition, given that certain innovations may be a force for stability rather than change 'how to' guides need to develop reflexive systems for indicating when more substantial changes need to occur in the normative and cognitive paradigms of the regulatory regime.

Third, our analyses offer an essential intellectual pluralism. Such intellectual pluralism, the open acknowledgement of different worldviews, is usually missing from accounts of regulatory innovation in particular and innovation more generally. In identifying and delineating the different worlds of regulatory innovation we highlight the limits of taking only one single approach towards the study (or the advocacy) of regulatory innovation. For the different worlds offer distinct and contrasting messages as to 'how to do' regulatory innovation. In particular, the world of Pavlovian regulatory innovation suggests a recipe for innovation that flies in the face of all those accounts that advocate extensive learning and analysis, or those proclaiming the importance of managing 'states of arousal' and the achievement of 'small wins' (Weick 2001). There is not just one 'how to' guide, therefore, but several, each linked to a particular world of innovation, as summarized in Table 9.2.

Moreover, the case studies show that only one or two of these worlds, and thus by implication, their 'how to' guides, may be relevant to regulatory innovation in any one context. Following an 'individual world of regulatory innovation'-type

Table 9.2 The worlds of regulatory innovation and the regulatory reform debate

World of regulatory innovation	'How to do' regulatory innovation
Individual	'Be a leader'
Organization	'Understand organizational structures and cultures'
State	'Utilize political infrastructures'
Global	'Connect to global epistemic communities'
Innovation	'Pick the idea whose time has come'
Pavlov	'Economize on rationality'

'leadership' guide on 'how to do' regulatory innovation, for example, will thus founder if it fails to understand the relatively small role played by individual entrepreneurs in many regulatory innovations, and the reasons why that is the case. Thus the identification and exposition of the different worlds brings to the fore the underlying assumptions and premises of different advocacy claims, and as such can only raise the understanding of their inherent constraints. Whilst it might be complained that the message being given is overly complex (there is no quick fix), it is countered that being aware of the different claims in one central setting is a better way to approach the task of 'doing' regulatory innovation than a reliance on a single approach that fails to acknowledge overlapping and competing views.

Nonetheless, it may be claimed that the 'world of the individual', and in some respects the structural and procedural aspects of the organizational world at least provide clear actors and identifiable tools for them to use. In contrast, it is hard to translate the abstract nouns of the other worlds, such as 'organizational environment' or 'institutional structures' into tools for action. It also means that, given the variability in these environments or structures, there is no single guide that will suit all circumstances (thus reducing its resale value). It is undoubtedly the case that the task is harder, but it is not unachievable. However, what also needs to be done is a clearer linking of the guides that each 'world' may produce with the outcome that results. Is 'Pavlovian' innovation always less successful than that led by an 'innovation champion', for example?

Finally, our accounts of how innovations formed and were introduced into a wide range of regulatory domains emphasize the contingency that characterizes many of the accounts of regulatory innovations. Our comparative perspective (cross-sectoral, cross-national and across time) allows for a better understanding of the nature of regulatory innovation: the underlying processes that can be involved, and the similarities and differences that may arise. If there is a single message that this comparative analysis of regulatory innovation highlights, it is that neither the occurrence nor the outcomes of innovation can be controlled and predicted. One cannot 'design' bureaucracies or legislatures to produce innovations, nor can one predict the results. Innovation simply cannot be engineered.

AN AGE OF 'HYPER-INNOVATION' OR HYPE ABOUT INNOVATION?

As we discussed at the outset, one of the most important recent contributions on UK regulation has been Michael Moran's hyper-innovation thesis (Moran 2003). As noted in Chapter 1, Moran focuses on innovation in institutional design, that is, on the formation of new institutions responsible for regulation both inside and outside government, and the reshaping and replacement of old ones. More particularly he argues that the old institutions of 'club government' have been replaced by new institutional actors, and by a corresponding change in the style of governance, from the informality and secrecy of 'club government' to the drive to 'synoptic legibility' of high modernism, through increased formality, systematization, transparency and measurability.

The third question that we sought to answer, in part prompted by Moran, was whether we are living in an age of hyper-innovation, or one in which there was simply a lot of hype about innovation. This study has not attempted to explicitly 'test' Moran's assumptions concerning an age of 'high modernism' in British government, facilitated by and facilitating the decline of 'club government' and arising from the crises of the 1970s. However, the different studies in this volume, all comparing Britain with different sets of states, have something to add to any debate concerning the supposed 'hyper-innovative' nature of the British regulatory state in the past two decades, in particular concerning the extent of 'hyper-innovation' in a comparative and historical perspective.

Moran stresses the significance of the transformation of regulatory relationships away from informality towards formality, in particular in the areas of professional (or self-) regulation. Moran's definition of regulatory (hyper-) innovation is concerned with scale and degree of extent (or 'radicalness') of innovation in the last two to three decades, a period that he diagnoses to be unique in British history since at least the First World War. The claim that the contemporary period has been characterized by hyper-innovation after a prolonged period of stagnation has certainly resonance with other observers (see Dunleavy 1995; Hayward 1976; Thatcher 2003), but requires further studies of regulatory innovation within one domain across time in order to subject the common claim to much closer scrutiny. For example, the historical study of regulation in railways in this volume has suggested that previous periods of regulatory innovation were similarly proclaimed to have brought about 'grandiose schemes' (William Robson's term for British railway nationalization in 1947). The railway case was part of the wider socialization policy of the post-1945 Labour government, itself a period of intense innovation in a number of domains. Furthermore, the inter-war period was similarly characterized by substantial regulatory innovation, for example the defeat of regulatory ideas concerning the railways in the early 1920s that eventually led to the creation (or 'innovation') of the four 'great' (regional) railways, or, the regulatory innovation of the public corporation as applied to the British Broadcasting Corporation (BBC) or London Transport prior to World War II.

When looking at the British cases covered in this volume in isolation, there are some instances where innovations may be characterized as being in further

pursuit of the modernism, for example Julia Black's discussion of the introduction of risk-based regulation in financial services, but overall there is not
an impression of substantial 'hyper-innovation' across all the different
domains as Moran describes it. In fact, the case of parliamentary ethics regulation seems more an example of incrementalism, and the privatized railways
regulatory regime in the 1990s looked certainly radical, but was built on the
cumulated experiences of utility regulation during the previous decade.

In addition, this volume has stressed the importance of a comparative
perspective across states. Moran's argument is mainly concerned with assessing innovation within British regulatory regimes rather than across states. Our
perspective was explicitly comparative in assessing to what extent regulatory
innovation in Britain could be contrasted with experiences of regulatory innovation elsewhere. We did find cases where British regulatory innovation was
different in either extent (the case of railway privatization with its degree of
industry fragmentation) or in terms of being first in timing (the example of 3G
auctions, dangerous dogs). However, against the widespread stereotype of the
British reform 'hare', our studies did not reveal an extraordinary extent of
regulatory innovation in Britain *vis-à-vis* other states.

Finally, we argue that innovation studies need to pay far more attention to
the outcomes of the innovation than is currently the case. Not only is this a
reiteration of the common cry for attention to be paid to the unintended and
unforeseen effects of regulatory actions, it is a re-emphasis of the competing
criteria against which 'success' or 'failure' is assessed. Technocratic assessments of 'effectiveness', for example, ignore the fact that innovations within
a regulatory regime may be enacted for reasons which are not to do with the
attempt to solve collective social or economic problems, but simply to move
an issue off the political agenda, as the example of dangerous dogs illustrates.
Liberalization of gaming may be seen as a 'success' for increasing tax
revenues, but as a failure for increasing problem gambling. Railway reforms
were seen as a 'success' until the paradigm shifted, and what was once a
'success' was over time assessed to be a failure. Thus, as the case studies have
shown, not only are innovations not necessarily either successes or failures,
who judges what is 'good', when in the innovation's life that assessment is
made, and against what criteria, are inevitably contested.

THE ROAD AHEAD FOR REGULATORY INNOVATION

This study has been explicitly of an explorative nature. Our discoveries
suggest that beyond all the hype there is something about 'regulatory innovation' that merits further study. To move towards a better understanding of regulatory innovation, four particular strategies may be pursued further.

First, in order to advance our understanding of the different worlds of regulatory innovation (including the Pavlovian world), different observers need to explore our (and different) cases. Only if different observers with different biases come to similar conclusions with regard to the persuasive power of particular worlds of regulatory innovation will we be able to stress their relative importance (or non-importance). For example, our discussions have noted the (surprising) absence of the 'world of the individual' in accounting for regulatory innovation, but it would require further studies to advance our understanding regarding that literature's intellectual strength.

Second, in line with the explorative character of this study, we have selected a diverse set of cases to explore regulatory innovation. Future studies would require a more systematic approach towards case selection – drawing both on 'usual suspects' in areas of high technology and 'unusual suspects' in areas of low technological change, such as our studies about parliament and dangerous dogs.

Third, innovation should be considered in a comparative and historical perspective. Such an approach is essential to control against inflated claims of 'newness' and 'uniqueness' in any particular domain, country or historical epoch. A comparative and historical approach also provides additional information on cross-sectoral and cross-national trends which lifts the analysis beyond the level of ungrounded anecdote, and highlights the substantial variety in innovation that is noticeable in regulatory regimes across time, sectors and states.

Finally, far more attention needs to be given to the question of the 'success' or 'failure' of innovation. Only when studies of regulatory innovation make it far clearer what the criteria of 'success' or 'failure' might be, how innovations may be assessed against those criteria and at what point in time that assessment should be made, can we say whether innovation is a cure for the ailing state, or the iatrogenic production of the disease.

NOTE

1. We ignore here the importance of 'unmentionable' motivations for regulatory innovation that may dominate any 'public interest' orientations. Technology, for example, is often seen as a great innovator in allowing for participation and accessibility in government, while it may very well be seen as an opportunity to assert the capability of existing coercive arrangements while taking the appearance of seeking to enhance legitimacy.

Bibliography

Abrahamson, E. (1991), 'Managerial fads and fashions: the diffusion and rejection of innovations', *Academy of Management Review*, **16** (3), 586–612.

Abrams, P. (1963), 'The failure of social reform', *Past and Present*, **24**, 43–64.

Abt, V. (1996), 'The role of the state in the expansion and growth of commercial gambling in the USA', in J. McMillen (ed.), *Gambling Cultures*, London: Routledge, pp. 179–98.

Airo-Farulla, G. (2003), 'Internet content, mandated self-regulation and institutionalizing values', in I. Holland and J. Fleming (eds), *Government Reformed: Values and New Political Institutions*, Aldershot: Ashgate, pp. 205–21.

Aldcroft, D. (1968), *British Railways in Transition: The Economic Problems of Britain's Railways since 1914*, London: Macmillan.

Allen, L. et al. (1991), *Political Scandals and Causes Celebres Since 1945*, Harlow: Longman Current Affairs.

Altshuler, A.A. and R.D. Behn (eds) (1997), *Innovation in American Government*, Washington DC: Brookings Institution Press.

Altshuler, A.A. and M.D. Zegans (1997), 'Bureaucratic innovation: notes from the state house and city hall', in A.A. Altshuler and R.D. Behn (eds), *Innovation in American Government: Challenges, Opportunities and Dilemmas*, Washington DC: Brookings Institution Press, pp. 38–67.

APRA (2002) *How PAIRS Ratings are Determined*, www.apra.gov.au.

APRA (undated a), *PAIRS Explained*, www.apra.gov.au.

APRA (undated b), *Applying PAIRS*, www.apra.gov.au.

Atkinson, M.M. and M. Mancuso (1991), 'Conflict of interest in Britain and the United States – an institutional argument', *Legislative Studies Quarterly*, **16** (4), 471–94.

Australian Senate Select Committee on Information Technologies (2000), *Netbets: A Review of Online Gambling in Australia*, Canberra: Parliament of Australia.

Ayres, I. and J. Braithwaite (1992), *Responsive Regulation: Transcending the Deregulation Debate*, Oxford: Oxford University Press.

Baggot, R. (1989), 'Regulatory reform in Britain: the changing face of self-regulation', *Public Administration*, **67** (4), 435–54.

Balestra, M. and A. Cabot (2003), *Internet Gambling Report*, 6th edn, St. Charles, MO: River City Group.

Bardach, E. (1998), *Getting Agencies to Work Together: The Practice and Theory of Managerial Craftsmanship*, Washington DC: Brookings Institution Press.

Bartlett, C. and P. Dibben (2002), 'Public sector entrepreneurship: case studies in local government', *Local Government Studies*, **28** (6), 107–21.

Barzelay, M. and C. Campbell (2003), *Preparing for the Future: Strategic Planning in the US Air Force*, Washington, DC: Brookings Institution Press.

Basle Committee on Banking Supervision (1988), *International Convergence of Capital Measures and Capital Standards*, Basle: Bank for International Settlements.

Basle Committee on Banking Supervision (2004), *International Convergence of Capital Measures and Capital Standards: A Revised Framework*, Basle: Bank for International Settlements.

Baumgartner, F. and B. Jones (1993), *Agendas and Instability in American Politics*, Chicago: Chicago University Press.

Beck, U. (1992), *Risk Society: Towards a New Modernity*, London: Sage.

Becker, G. (1983), 'A theory of competition among pressure groups for political influence', *Quarterly Journal of Economics*, **98**, 371–400.

Bennett, C.J. (1991), 'Review article: what is policy convergence and what causes it?', *British Journal of Political Science*, **21**, 215–33.

Bennett, C.J. (1997), 'Understanding ripple effects: the cross national adoption of policy instruments for bureaucratic accountability', *Governance*, **10** (3), 213–33.

Bennett, C.J. and M. Howlett (1992), 'The lessons of learning: reconciling theories of policy learning and policy change', *Policy Sciences*, **25**, 274–94.

Bernstein, R. (1992), 'The sleeper wakes: the history and legacy of the twenty-seventh amendment', *Fordham Law Review*, **61** (497), 539–40.

Berry, F.S. (1994), 'Sizing up state policy innovation research', *Policy Studies Journal*, **22**, 442–56.

Berry, F.S. and W.D. Berry (1990), 'State lottery adoptions as policy innovations: an event history analysis', *American Political Science Review*, **84**, 395–415.

Berry, F.S and W.D Berry (1992), 'Tax innovation in the states: capitalizing on political opportunity', *American Journal of Political Science*, **36**, 715–42.

Berry, F.S. and W.D. Berry (1994), 'The politics of tax increases in the States', *American Journal of Political Science*, **38**, 855–9.

Berry, F.S. and W.D. Berry (1999), 'Innovation and diffusion models in policy research', in P.A. Sabatier (ed.), *Theories of the Policy Process*, Boulder, CO. Westview Press, pp. 169–200.

Binmore, K. and P. Klemperer (2002), 'The biggest auction ever: the sale of the British 3G telecom licences', *Economic Journal*, **112**, c74–c96.

Black, J. (1997), 'The new institutionalism and naturalism in socio-legal analysis: institutional approaches to regulatory decision making', *Law & Policy*, **19** (1), 51–93.

Black, J. (2002), 'Critical reflections on regulation', *Australian Journal of Legal Philosophy*, **27**, 1–37 and CARR Discussion Paper no. 4, London School of Economics, January 2002 (available at www.lse.ac.uk/collections/carr/publications.htm).

Black, J. (2005a), 'The emergence of risk based regulation and the new public risk management in the UK', *Public Law* (Autumn) 512–48.

Black, J. (2005b), 'Regulating the "risk based" way: the case of the Australian Prudential Regulatory Authority', *Law and Policy* (forthcoming).

Blau, P.M. (1972), 'A formal theory of differentiation in organizations', *American Sociological Review*, **35**, 201–18.

Bleich, E. (1998), 'From international ideas to domestic politics: educational multiculturalism in England and France', *Comparative Politics*, **31** (1), 81–100.

Blyth, M. (1997), 'Any more bright ideas? The ideational turn of comparative political economy', *Comparative Politics*, **29** (2), 229–50.

Bogdanor, V. (1997) 'The Downey Report: out with club government', *The Guardian*, 4 July 1997.

Boli, J. and G.M. Thomas (1997), 'World culture in the world polity: a century of international non-governmental organization', *American Sociological Review*, **62** (2), 171–90.

Börgers, T. and C. Dustmann (2002), 'Rationalizing the UMTS spectrum bids: the case of the UK auction', *Ifo Studien*, **48** (1), 77–109.

Borins, S. (2000), 'Loose cannons and rule breakers, or enterprising leaders? Some evidence about innovative public managers', *Public Administration Review*, **60**, 498–507.

Borins S. (2001), 'Public management innovation in economically advanced and developing countries', *International Review of Administrative Sciences*, **67**, 715–31.

Bovens, M. and P. t'Hart (1996), *Understanding Policy Fiascos*, New Brunswick, NJ: Transaction Publishers.

Braithwaite, J. and P. Drahos (2000), *Global Business Regulation*, Oxford: Oxford University Press.

Breyer, S. (1991), *Breaking the Vicious Circle*, Cambridge/MA: Harvard University Press.

BT (British Telecommunications) (1997), *BT Response to Government Consultative Document 'Multimedia on the Move'*, London: Department for Trade and Industry.

Cabinet Office (2000), *Successful IT: Modernising Government in Action*, London: HMSO.

Cabinet Office (2003), *Innovation in the Public Sector*, London: HMSO.

Cain, D. M., G. Loewenstein, and D.A. Moore (2005), 'The dirt on coming clean: the perverse effects of disclosing conflicts of interest', *Journal of Legal Studies*, **34** (1), 1–25.

Campbell, J.L. (1998), 'Institutional analysis and the role of ideas in political economy', *Theory and Society*, **27**, 377–409.

Cartelier, L. (2003), 'Auctions versus beauty contests: the allocation of UMTS licences in Europe', *Annals of Public and Corporate Economics*, **74** (1), 63–85.

Cassese, S. (2000), *La nuova costituzione economica*, Rome: Laterza.

Chamoux, J-P. 2000, 'Pour de véritables enchères', *Les Echos*, 18 May 2000.

Chandler, A.D. (1962), *Strategy and Structure: Chapters in the History of the American Industrial Enterprise*, Cambridge, MA: MIT Press.

Chester, N. (1974), *The Nationalisation of British Industry 1945–1951*, London: HMSO.

Christensen, C. (2001), *The Innovator's Dilemma: The Revolutionary Work That Will Change the Way You Do Business*, New York: HarperCollins.

Christensen, C. and M. Raynor (2003), *The Innovator's Solution*, New York: Harper Collins.

Christensen, C., M. Overdorf, M. Ian, R. McGrath and S. Thomke (eds) (2001), *Harvard Business Review on Innovation*, Cambridge, MA: Harvard Business Review Press.

Clarke, R. and G. Dempsey (2001), 'The feasibility of regulating gambling on the Internet', *Managerial and Decision Economics*, **22**, 125–32.

Clegg, S. (1998), 'Foucault, power and organisations' in A. McKinlay and K. Starkey (eds), *Foucault, Management and Organization Theory: From Panopticon to Technologies of Self*, London: Sage, pp. 29–48.

Coase, R.H. (1959), 'The Federal Communications Commission', *Journal of Law and Economics*, **2**, 1–40.

Coen, D., A. Héritier and D. Böllhoff (2002), *Regulating the Utilities: Business and Regulator Perspectives in the UK and Germany*, Berlin: Anglo-German Foundation.

Cohen, E. and M. Bauer (1985), *Les Grandes manoevres industrielles*, Paris: Belfond.

Cohen, M.D., J.G. March, and J.P. Olsen (1972), 'A garbage can model of organizational choice', *Administrative Science Quarterly*, **17** (1), 1–25.

Collins, P. (2003), *Gambling and the Public Interest*, Westport, CT: Praeger.

Coombes, R., P. Narandren and A. Richards (1996), 'A literature based innovation output indicator', *Research Policy*, **25**, 403–13.

Cortell, A.P. and S. Peterson (1999), 'Altered states: explaining domestic institutional change', *British Journal of Political Science*, **29**, 177 203.

Curien, N. (2002), 'UMTS en France et en Europe: quelles procédures pour l'attribution des licences?', *Annals of Public and Cooperative Economics* **73** (2), 149–79.

Cyert, R. and J. March (1963), *A Behavioral Theory of the Firm*, Englewood Cliffs, NJ: Prentice-Hall.

D'Aunno, T., R.I. Sutton and R.H. Price (1991), 'Isomorphism and external support in conflicting institutional environments: a study of drug abuse treatment units', *Academy of Management Journal*, **34** (3), 636–61.

Day, D. (1994), 'Raising radicals: different processes for championing innovative corporate ventures', *Organization Science*, **6**, 111–19.

DCITA (Department of Communications, Information Technology and the Arts) (2004), *Report of the Review of the Interactive Gambling Act 2001*, Canberra: DCITA.

DCMS (2001), *Gambling Review Report*, London: DCMS.

DCMS (Department for Culture, Media and Sport) (2003a), *The Future Regulation of Remote Gambling: A DCMS Position Paper*, London: DCMS.

DCMS (2003b), *Draft Gambling Bill: The Policy*, London: DCMS.

DCMS (2003c), *The Future Regulation of Remote Gambling: A DCMS Position Paper*, London: DCMS.

DiMaggio, P.J. and W.W. Powell (1983), 'The iron cage revisited: institutional isomorphism and collective rationality in organizational fields', *American Sociological Review*, 48, 147–60.

DiMaggio, P.J. and W.W. Powell (1991), 'Introduction', in W.W. Powell and P.J. DiMaggio (eds), *The New Institutionalism in Organizational Analysis*, Chicago: Chicago University Press, pp. 1–38.

Dixon, D. (1996), 'Illegal betting in Britain and Australia: contrasts in control strategies and cultures', in J. McMillen (ed.), *Gambling Cultures*, London: Routledge, pp. 86–100.

Dobbin, F. (1994), *Forging Industrial Policy. The United States, Britain, and France in the Railway Age*, Cambridge: Cambridge University Press.

Doig, A. (1979), 'Self-discipline and the House of Commons: the Poulson affair in a parliamentary perspective', *Parliamentary Affairs*, **32** (2), 248–67.

Doig, A. and C. Skelcher (2001), 'New standards? Conduct, misconduct and the ethical framework', University of Birmingham, School of Public Policy occasional paper 36.

Doig, J.W. (1997), 'Leadership and innovation in the administrative state', *International Journal of Public Administration*, **20** (4 and 5), 861–79.

Dolowitz, D. and D. Marsh (1996), 'Who learns what from whom? A review of the policy transfer literature', *Political Studies*, **44**, 343–57.

Dolowitz, D. and D. Marsh (2000), 'Learning from abroad: the role of policy transfer in contemporary policy-making', *Governance*, **13**, 5–24.

Donaldson, L. (1995), *American Anti-Management Theories of Organization: A Critique of Paradigm Proliferation*, Cambridge: Cambridge University Press.

Douglas, M. (1992), *Risk and Blame*, London, Routledge.

Douglas, M. and A. Wildavsky (1983), *Risk and Culture*, Berkeley, CA: University of California Press.

Drewry, G. (1985), *The New Select Committees*, Oxford: Clarendon Press.

Drucker, P. (1985), *Innovation and Entrepreneurship*, New York: HarperCollins.

DTI (Department for Trade and Industry) (1996), *Spectrum Management into the 21st Century*, London: HMSO.

DTI (1997), *Multimedia Communications on the Move. A Consultative Document from the Department of Trade and Industry*, London: DTI.

DTI (1998), *Mobile Multimedia Communications*, London: DTI Press Notice.

Dunleavy, P.J. (1995), 'Policy disasters: explaining the UK's record', *Public Policy & Administration*, **10** (2), 52–70.

Dusenberry, J. (1960), 'Comment on "An Economic Analysis of Fertility" ' in National Bureau for Economic Research (ed.), *Demographic and Economic Change in Developed Countries, a Conference of the Universities*, Princeton, NJ: Princeton University, pp. 231–4.

Dyson, K. (1980), *The State Tradition in Western Europe*, Oxford, Oxford University Press.

European Commission (2002), *Innovation Policy and the Regulatory Framework*, Brussels: European Commission.

Finnemore, M. (1993), 'International organizations as teachers of norms: UNESCO and science policy', *International Organization*, **47**, 565–97.

Foster, C. (1992), *Privatisation, Public Ownership, and the Regulation of Natural Monopoly*, Oxford: Blackwell.

Freeman, C. (1982), *Economics of Industrial Innovation*, London: Pinter.

Freeman, C. (1987), *Technology Policy and Economic Performance: Lessons from Japan*, London: Pinter.

Fromm, G. (1994), 'Juristische Probleme der Reform der Eisenbahnen: Verfassungsrecht, Eisenbahnrecht, Wettbewerbsrecht', *Internationales Verkehrswesen*, **45**, 97–102.

FSA (Financial Services Authority) (1998), *Risk Based Approach to the Supervision of Banks*, London: FSA.

FSA (2000a), *A New Regulator for a New Millenium*, London: FSA.

FSA (2000b), *Building the New Regulator: Progress Report 1*, London: FSA.

FSA (2002a), *Building the New Regulator: Progress Report 2*, London: FSA.

FSA (2002b), *The Future Regulation of Insurance: A Progress Report*, London: FSA.

FSA (2003a), *The Firm Risk Assessment Framework*, London: FSA.

FSA (2003b), *Reasonable Expectations: Regulation in a Non Zero-Failure World*, London: FSA.

Gardener, P.M. (1986), *UK Banking Supervision*, London: Allen & Unwin.

Giddens, A. (1984), *The Constitution of Society: Outline of the Theory of Structuration*, Cambridge: Polity Press.

Glick, H. and S. Hays (1991), 'Innovation and reinvention in state policymaking: theory and the evolution of living will laws', *Journal of Politics*, **53**, 835–50.

Goldstein, J. (1993), *Ideas, Interests, and American Trade Policy*, Ithaca, NY: Cornell University Press.

Goldstein, J. and R.O. Keohane (1995a), *Ideas and Foreign Policy: Beliefs, Institutions and Political Change*, Ithaca, NY: Cornwell University Press.

Goldstein, J. and R.O. Keohane (1995b), 'Ideas and foreign policy: an analytical framework', in J. Goldstein and R.O. Keohane (eds), *Ideas and Foreign Policy: Beliefs, Institutions and Political Change*, Ithaca, NY: Cornell University Press, pp. 3–30.

Gourvish, T. (1990), 'British Rail's "business-led" organization 1977–1990: Government-industry relations in Britain's public sector', *Business History Review*, **64** (1), 109–49.

Grabosky, P.N. (1995), 'Counterproductive regulation', *International Journal of the Sociology of Law*, **23**, 347–69.

Granovetter, M. (1985), 'Economic action and social structure: the problem of embeddedness', *American Journal of Sociology*, **91**, 481–510.

Gray, P. (1996), 'Disastrous explanations – or explanations of disaster? A reply to Patrick Dunleavy', *Public Policy & Administration*, **11** (1), 74–82.

Gray, V. (1973), 'Innovation in the States: a diffusion study', *American Political Science Review*, **67** (4), 1174–85.

Gray, V. (1994), 'Competition, emulation, and policy innovation', in L.C. Dodd and C. Jillson (eds), *New Perspectives on American Politics*, Washington, DC: CQ Press, pp. 230–48.

Gregory, R. (1997), 'The Ombudsman – a burnt out star?', *The Ombudsman: Newsletter of the British and Irish Ombudsman Association*, issue no 6, July.

Gregory, R. and P. Giddings (1997), 'New challenges for a successful institution: the ombudsman and the new managerialism', in *Australasian Political Studies: Proceedings of the Australian Political Studies Association*, vol. I, Department of Politics, Flinders University of South Australia, Adelaide, pp. 295–312.

Grimm, V., F. Riedel and E. Wolfstetter (2002), 'The third generation (UMTS) spectrum auction in Germany', *Ifo Studien*, **48** (1), 123–43.

Grinols, E.L., D.B. Mustard and C.J. Hunt Dilley (2000), 'Casinos, crime and community costs', http://ssrn.com/abstract=233792 and http://papers.ssrn.

com/sol3/papers.cfm?abstract_id=233792#Paper Download (accessed 8 September 2004).

Gunningham, N and P. Grabovsky (1998), *Smart Regulation: Designing Environmental Policy*, Oxford: Oxford University Press.

Haas, P (1992a), 'Introduction: epistemic communities and international policy co-ordination', *International Organization*, **46** (1), 1–35.

Haas, P. (1992b), 'Obtaining international environmental protection through epistemic consensus', in I. Rowlands and M. Greene (eds), *Global Environmental Change and International Relations*, Basingstoke: Macmillan, pp. 38–59.

Haas, P. (1993), 'Epistemic communities and the dynamics of international co-operation', in V. Rittberger and P. Mayer (eds), *Regime Theory and International Relations*, Oxford: Clarendon Press, pp. 168–201.

Hall, P.A. (1983), 'Policy innovation and the structure of the state: the politics-administrative nexus in France and Britain', *Annals of the AAPSS*, **466** (3), 43–55.

Hall, P.A. (1986), *Governing the Economy: The Politics of State Intervention in Britain and France*, New York: Oxford University Press.

Hall, P.A. (ed.) (1989), *The Political Power of Economic Ideas: Keynesianism Across Nations*, Princeton, NJ: Princeton University Press.

Hall, P.A. (1993), 'Policy paradigms, social learning, and the state: the case of economic policymaking in Britain', *Comparative Politics*, **25** (3), 275–96.

Hall, P. and D. Soskice (2001), 'An introduction to varieties of capitalism', in P. Hall and D. Soskice (eds) (2001), *Varieties of Capitalism: The Institutional Foundations of Comparative Advantage*, Oxford: Oxford University Press, pp. 1–68.

Hall, P. and R. Taylor (1996), 'Political science and the three new institution-alisms', *Political Studies*, **44** (4), 936–57.

Hannan, M.T. and J.H. Freeman (1977), 'The population ecology of organiza-tions', *American Journal of Sociology*, **82**, 929–64.

Hannan, M.T. and J.H. Freeman (1984), 'Structural inertia and organizational change', *American Sociological Review*, **49**, 149–64.

Hansen, R. and D. King (2001), 'Eugenic ideas, political interests and policy variance: immigration and sterilization policy in Britain and the US', *World Politics*, **53**, 237–63.

Hardy, C. and S.R. Clegg (1999), 'Some dare call it power', in S. Clegg and C. Hardy (eds), *Studying Organisations*, London: Sage, pp. 622–41.

Hawkins, K. (2002), *Law as a Last Resort: Prosecution Decision Making in a Regulatory Agency*, Oxford: Oxford University Press.

Hayward, J.E.S. (1976), 'Institutional Inertia and Political Impetus in France and Britain', *European Journal of Political Research*, **4**, 341–59.

Hayward, J.E.S. (ed.) (1995), *Industrial Enterprise and European Integration*, Oxford: Oxford University Press.

Heclo, H. (1974), *Modern Social Politics in Britain and Sweden*, New Haven, CT: Yale University Press.

Heiber, H. (1981), *Die Republik von Weimar*, Munich: Deutscher Taschenbuch Verlag.

Heifetz, R. (1993), *Leadership without Easy Answers*, Cambridge, MA: Harvard University Press.

Hennessy, P. (1996), *The Hidden Wiring*, 2nd edn, London: Indigo.

Hirschman, A.O. (1982), *Shifting Involvements*, Oxford: Oxford University Press.

Hollingsworth, J. and R. Boyer (eds) (1997), *Contemporary Capitalism: The Embeddedness of Institutions*, Cambridge: Cambridge University Press.

Hood, C. (1986), *Administrative Analysis: An Introduction to Rules, Enforcement and Organizations*, Brighton: Wheatsheaf.

Hood, C. (1995), 'The politics of fasting and feasting', in F.F. Ridley and A. Doig (eds), *Sleaze: Politicians, Private Interest and Public Reaction*, Oxford: Oxford University Press, pp. 190–201.

Hood, C. (1996), 'United Kingdom: from second chance to near-miss learning', in J.P. Olsen and B.G. Peters (eds), *Lessons from Experience*, Oslo: Scandinavian University Press, pp. 36–70.

Hood, C. and B.G. Peters (2004), 'The middle aging of new public management: into the age of paradox?', *Journal of Public Administration Research and Theory*, **14** (3), 267–82.

Hood, C. and H. Rothstein (2001), 'Risk regulation under pressure: problem solving or blame shifting', *Administration and Society*, **33** (1), 21–53.

Hood, C., R. Baldwin and H. Rothstein (2000), 'Assessing the Dangerous Dogs Act: when does a regulatory law fail?', *Public Law*, Summer, pp. 282–305.

Hood, C., H. Rothstein and R. Baldwin (2001), *The Government of Risk: Understanding Risk Regulation Regimes*, Oxford: Oxford University Press.

Horn, M. (1995), *The Political Economy of Public Administration*, Cambridge: Cambridge University Press.

Ikenberry, G. (1988), 'Conclusion: an institutional approach to foreign economic policy', in G. Ikenberry, D.A. Lake and M. Mastanduno (eds), *The State and American Foreign Economic Policy*, Ithaca, NY: Cornell University Press, pp. 219–43.

Immergut, E.M. (1992), 'The rules of the game: the logic of health policy-making in France, Switzerland and Sweden', in S. Steinmo, K. Thelen and F, Longstreth (eds.), *Structuring Politics: Historical Institutionalism in Comparative Politics*, Cambridge: Cambridge University Press, pp. 57–89.

Immergut, E.M. (1998), 'The theoretical core of the New Institutionalism', *Politics and Society*, **25** (1), 5–34.

Internet Industry Association (2001), *Interactive Gambling Industry Code – A Code for Industry Co-Regulation in the Area of Internet Gambling Content Pursuant to the Requirements of the Interactive Gambling Act 2001*, Canberra: IIA.

Jackson, B.S. (1978), 'Liability for animals in Roman law: an historical sketch', *Cambridge Law Journal*, **37** (1), 122–43.

Jacobsen, J.K. (1995), 'Much ado about ideas: the cognitive factor in economic policy', *World Politics*, **47**, 283–310.

James, O. and Lodge, M. (2003), 'The limitations of "policy transfer" and "lesson drawing" for public policy research', *Political Studies Review*, **1** (2), 179–93.

Jensen, J. (2003), 'Policy diffusion through institutional legitimation: state lotteries', *Journal of Public Administration Research and Theory*, **13** (4), 521–41.

Jepperson, R.L. (1991), 'Institutions, institutional effects and institutionalism', in W.W. Powell and P.J. DiMaggio (eds), *The New Institutionalism in Organizational Analysis*, Chicago: University of Chicago Press, pp. 143–63.

Joint Parliamentary Committee on the Draft Gambling Bill (2004), *Draft Gambling Bill Volume 1*, HC Paper 139-I, HL Paper 63-I, London: HMSO.

Jordan, A., R. Wurzel, A. Zito and L. Bruckner (2003), ' "Policy innovation" or "muddling through"? "New" environmental policy instruments in the United Kingdom', *Environmental Politics*, **12** (1), 179–98.

Kagan, R. (2000), 'Introduction: comparing national styles of regulation in Japan and the United States', *Law and Policy*, **22**, 225–44.

Kapstein, E. (1992), 'Between power and purpose: central bankers and the politics of regulatory convergence', *International Organization*, **46** (1), 265–87.

Kaye, R. (2002), 'Regulating Parliament: the House of Commons Select Committees on members' interests and standards and privileges', unpublished D.Phil. thesis, Department of Politics and International Relations, University of Oxford.

Kaye, R. (2003), 'Regulating Westminster: the regulatory state within Parliament', Centre for Analysis of Risk and Regulation discussion paper, London: CARR.

Kingdon, J.W. (1984), *Agendas, Alternatives, and Public Policies*, Boston: Little Brown.

Kingdon, J.W. (1995), *Agendas, Alternatives, and Public Policies*, 2nd edn, New York: HarperCollins.

Kitschelt, H. (1991), 'Industrial governance, innovation strategies, and the case of Japan: sectoral or cross-national analysis?', *International Organization*, **45** (4), 453–93.

Kitschelt, H. (1994), 'Technologiepolitik als Lernprozeß', in D. Grimm (ed.), *Staatsaufgaben*, Frankfurt an Main, Germany: Suhrkamp, pp. 391–425.

Klemperer, P. (2002), 'How (not) to run auctions: the European 3G telecom auctions', *European Economic Review*, **46** (4–5), 829–45.

Klemperer, P. (2004), *Auctions: Theory and Practice*, Princeton, NJ and Oxford: Princeton University Press.

Knill, C. (1999), 'Explaining cross-national variation in administrative reform: autonomous versus instrumental bureaucracies', *Journal of Public Policy*, **19** (2), 113–39.

Knill, C. (2001), *The Europeanisation of National Administrations*, Cambridge: Cambridge University Press.

Kolb, E. (1999), 'Die Reichsbahn vom Dawes-Plan bis zum Ende der Weimarer Republik', in L. Gall and M. Pohl (eds), *Die Eisenbahn in Deutschland von den Anfängen bis zur Gegenwart*, Munich, Germany: Beck, pp. 109–63.

Kolko, G. (1965), *Railroads and Regulation 1877–1916*, Cambridge, MA: Harvard University Press.

Kraemer, K., V. Gubuxani and J. King (1992), 'Economic development, government policy and the diffusion of computing in Asia-Pacific countries', *Public Administration Review*, **52**, 146–56.

Kuhn, T. (1962), *The Structure of Scientific Revolutions*, Chicago: Chicago University Press.

Lehmbruch, G. (2000), 'The institutional framework: federalism and decentralisation in Germany', in H. Wollmann and E. Schröter (eds), *Comparing Public Sector Reform in Britain and Germany*, Aldershot: Ashgate, pp. 85–106.

Leigh, D. and E. Vulliamy (1997), *Sleaze: The Corruption of Parliament*, London: Fourth Estate.

Levy, B. and P. Spiller (1994), 'The institutional foundations of regulatory commitment: a comparative analysis of telecommunications regulation', *Journal of Law, Economics and Organisation*, **10**, 201–46.

Levy, B. and P. Spiller (1996), 'A framework for resolving the regulatory problem', in B. Levy and P. Spiller (eds), *Regulation, Institutions and Commitment*, Cambridge: Cambridge University Press, pp. 1–35.

Levy, J.S. (1994), 'Learning and foreign policy: sweeping a conceptual minefield', *International Organization*, **48**, 279–312.

Light, P. (1998), *Sustaining Innovation*, San Francisco: Jossey-Bass.

Lindblom, C. (1965), *The Intelligence of Democracy: Decision-Making through Mutual Adjustment*, New York: Free Press.

Locke, R. (1995), *Remaking the Italian Economy*, Ithaca, NY: Cornell University Press.

Lodge, M. (2002), *On Different Tracks: Designing Railway Regulation in Britain and Germany*, Westport, CT: Praeger.

Lodge, M. (2003), 'Institutional choice and policy transfer: reforming British and German railway regulation', *Governance*, **16** (2), 159–78.

Lodge, M. and C. Hood (2002), 'Pavlovian policy responses to media feeding frenzies? Dangerous dogs regulation in comparative perspective', *Journal of Contingencies and Crisis Management*, **10** (1), 1–13.

Lowe, R. (1978), 'The erosion of state intervention in Britain 1917–24', *Economic History Review*, **31**, 270–86.

Luhmann, N. (1995), *Social Systems*, Stanford, CA: Stanford University Press.

Lynn, L. (1996), *Public Management as Art, Science, and Profession*, Chatham, NJ: Chatham House.

Mackenzie, C.G with M. Hafken (2002), *Scandal Proof: Do Ethics Laws Make Governments Ethical*, Washington DC: Brookings Institution Press.

Maddock, S. (2002), 'Making modernisation work. New narratives, change strategies and people management in the public sector', *International Journal of Public Sector Management*, **15** (1), 13–43.

Mahler, A. and E.M. Rogers (1999), 'The diffusion of interactive communications and the critical mass: the adoption of telecommunications services by German banks', *Telecommunications Policy*, **23**, 719–40.

Majone, G. (1994), 'The emergence of the regulatory state in Europe', *West European Politics*, **17**, 77–101.

Majone, G. (1996), 'Regulation and its modes', in G. Majone (ed.), *Regulating Europe*, London: Routledge, pp. 9–27.

Majone, G. (1997), 'From positive to the regulatory state', *Journal of Public Policy*, **17** (2), 139–67.

March, J. and J. Olsen (1984), 'The New Institutionalism: organizational factors in political life', *American Political Science Review*, **78**, 734–49.

Marmer, L. (1984), 'The new breed of municipal dog control laws: are they constitutional?', *University of Cincinatti Law Review*, **53**, 1067–81.

Marquand, D. (1988), *The Unprincipled Society: New Demands and Old Politics*, London: Jonathan Cape.

McCubbins, M. and T. Schwartz (1984), 'Police patrols vs. fire alarms', *American Journal of Political Science*, **28**, 165–79.

McKinley, W. and M.A. Mone (1988), 'The re-construction of organization studies: wrestling with incommensurability', *Organization*, **5**, 169–89.

McKinley, W. and M.A. Mone (2003), 'Micro and macro perspectives in organization theory: a tale of incommensurability', in H. Tsoukas and C. Knudsen (eds), *The Oxford Handbook of Organization Theory: Meta-Theoretical Perspectives*, Oxford: Oxford University Press, pp. 345–72.

McLean, I. and C. Foster (1992), 'The political economy of regulation: interests, ideology, voters and the UK Regulation of Railways Act 1844', *Public Administration*, **70**, 313–22.

McMillen, J. (2003), 'Online gambling', in J. Forder and P. Quirk (eds), *E-Commerce and the Law*, Sydney: Wiley Jacaranda, pp. 331–66.

McMillen, J. and P. Grabosky (1998), '*Internet gambling*', Australian Institute of Criminology, Trends and Issues in Criminal Justice paper, no 88, June 1998.

Meyer, J.W. (1980), 'The world polity and the authority of the nation state', in A. Bergesen (ed.), *Studies of the Modern World System*, New York: Academic Press, pp. 109–37.

Meyer, J.W. (2000), 'Globalization: sources and effects on national states and societies', *International Sociology*, **15** (2), 233–48.

Meyer, J.W. and R.L. Jepperson (2000), 'The "Actors" of modern society: the cultural construction of social agency', *Sociological Theory*, **18** (1), 100–20.

Meyer, J.W. and B. Rowan (1977), 'Institutionalized organizations: formal structure as myth and ceremony', *American Journal of Sociology*, **83**, 340–63.

Meyer, J.W. and W.R. Scott (eds) (1992), *Organizational Environments: Ritual and Rationality*, Beverley Hills, CA: Sage.

Meyer, J.W., J. Boli and G.M. Thomas (1994), 'Ontology and rationalization in the western cultural account', in W.R. Scott, J.W. Meyer and Associates (eds), *Institutional Environments and Organizations: Structural Complexity and Individualism*, Thousand Oaks, CA: Sage.

Miers, D. (2004), *Regulating Commercial Gambling*, Oxford: Oxford University Press.

Mierzejewski, A.C. (1999), *The Most Valuable Asset of the Reich: A History of the German National Railway*, vol I: 1920–1932, Chapel Hill: University of North Carolina Press.

Mintrom, M. (1997), 'Policy entrepreneurs and the diffusion of innovation', *American Journal of Political Science*, **42**, 738–70.

Mintrom, M. and S. Vergari (1996), 'Advocacy coalitions, policy entrepreneurs and policy change', *Policy Studies Journal*, **24**, 420–34.

Mohr, L. (1969), 'Determinants of innovation in organizations', *American Political Science Review*, **75**, 111–26.

Moon, M.J. (1999), 'The pursuit of managerial entrepreneurship: does organization matter?', *Public Administration Review*, **59** (1), 31–43.

Mooney, C. and M-H. Lee (1995), 'Legislating morality in the American states: the case of pre-*Roe* abortion regulation reform', *American Journal of Political Science*, **39**, 599–627.

Moore, M.H. (1995), *Creating Public Value*, Cambridge, MA: Harvard University Press.

Moran, M. (2003), *The British Regulatory State: High Modernism and Hyper-Innovation*, Oxford: Oxford University Press.

Morris, M.H. and F.F. Jones (1999), 'Entrepreneurship in established organizations: the case of the public sector', *Entrepreneurship Theory and Practice*, **24** (1), 71–83.

Morrison, H. (1933), *Socialisation and Transport*, London: Constable & Co.

NAO (National Audit Office) (2001), *The Auction of Radio Spectrum for the Third Generation of Mobile Telephones*, London: Stationary Office.

Nelson, R. (1993), *National Innovation Systems*, New York: Oxford University Press.

Netto, W.J. and D.J.U. Planta (1997), 'Behavioural testing for aggression in the domestic dog', *Applied Animal Behaviour Science*, **52** (3–4), 243–63.

New Shorter Oxford English Dictionary, Oxford: Oxford University Press.

New Zealand Institute for Economic Research (2002), *New Zealand Public Service Innovation: Practical Prospects Based on Experience – A Report to the Treasury*, accessed at www.treasury.govt.nz/innovation.

Nicholls, A.J. (1999), 'Zusammenbruch und Wiederaufbau: Die Reichsbahn während der Besatzungszeit', in L. Gall and M. Pohl (eds), *Die Eisenbahn in Deutschland von den Anfängen bis zur Gegenwart*, Munich, Germany: Beck, pp. 245–79.

Nolan, Baron M. (1995-I) *Standards in Public Life – First Report of the Committee on Standards in Public Life, Volume 1: Report*, Cm 2850-I, London: HMSO.

North, D. (1990), *Institutions, Institutional Change and Economic Performance*, New York: Cambridge University Press.

OCC (Office of the Comptroller of the Currency) (1996), *Supervisory Handbook*, Washington, DC: OCC.

OECD (Organisation for Economic Co-operation and Development) (1995), *Regulatory Reform and Innovation*, Paris: OECD.

OECD (2003a), *The Forty Recommendations*, Paris: OECD Financial Action Task Force on Money Laundering.

OECD (2003b), *OECD Guidelines for Protecting Consumers from Fraudulent and Deceptive Commercial Practices Across Borders*, Paris: OECD.

Oliver, D. (1997), 'The Nolan Committee', in F.F. Ridley and A. Doig (eds), *Sleaze: Politicians, Private Interest and Public Reaction*, Oxford: Oxford University Press, pp. 42–53.

Osborne, D. and T. Gaebler (1993), *Reinventing Government*, New York: Plume.

Osborne, S.P. (1998a), *Voluntary Organizations and Innovation in Public Services*, London: Routledge.

Osborne, S.P. (1998b), 'The innovative capacity of voluntary organisations: managerial challenges for local government', *Local Government Studies*, **24** (1), 19–40.

Osborne S.P. and N. Flynn (1997), 'Managing the innovative capacity of

voluntary and non-profit organisations in the provision of public services',
Public Money & Management, **17** (4), 31–39.

OSFI (Office of the Superintendent of Financial Institutions) (1999),
Supervisory Framework 1999 and Beyond, Ottawa: OSFI.

OSFI (2002), *Supervisory Framework Ratings Assessment Criteria*, Ottawa:
OSFI.

OSFI (2003), *Annual Report*, Ottawa: OSFI.

Palmer, J. (2002), *Review of the Role Played by the Australian Prudential
Regulatory Authority and the Insurance and Superannuation Commission
in the Collapse of HIH Insurance Group of Companies*, Sydney: Corrs
Chambers Westgarth.

Parker, C. (2002), *The Open Corporation*, Cambridge: Cambridge University
Press.

Peltzman, S. (1976), 'Towards a more general theory of regulation', *Journal
of Law and Economics*, **19**, 211–40.

Peltzman, S. (1989), 'The economic theory of regulation after a decade of deregulation', *Brookings Papers on Economic Activity* (Microeconomics), 1–41.

Penard, T. (2002), 'Competition and strategy on the mobile telephony market',
Communications & Strategies, **45**, 49–79.

Perez, Rita (2002), *Telecomunicazione e Concorrenza*, Milan: Guiffrè.

Peters, T.J. and R.H. Waterman (1982), *In Search of Excellence: Lessons from
America's Best Run Companies*, New York: Harper and Row.

Polsby, N. (1984), *Political Innovation in America: The Politics of Policy
Initiation*, New Haven, CT: Yale University Press.

Power, M. (2004), *The Risk Management of Everything: Rethinking the
Politics of Uncertainty*, London: Demos.

Radiocommunications Agency (2004), *The Future Management of Radio
Spectrum: A Consultative Document*, London: Department of Trade and
Industry.

*Regulation and Consumer Protection in the Federally Regulated Financial
Services Industry: Striking a Balance*, 22 November 1994, chair Hon
Michael Kirby.

Report of the Board of Banking Supervision (1995), *Inquiry Report of the
Board of Banking Supervision Inquiry in to the Circumstances of the
Collapse of Barings*, HC Papers 1994–5 673, London: HMSO.

Rhodes, R.A.W. (1997), *Understanding Governance: Policy Networks,
Governance, Reflexivity and Accountability*, Buckingham: Open University
Press.

Richardson, J. (ed.) (1982), *Policy Styles in Western Europe*, London: Allen &
Unwin.

Robson, W. (1962), *Nationalized Industry and Public Ownership*, 2nd edn,
London: Allen & Unwin.

Rogers, E.M. (2003), *Diffusion of Innovations*, 5th edn, New York: Free Press.

Rose, R. (1993), *Lesson Drawing in Public Policy*, Chatham, NJ: Chatham House.

Royal Commission (2003), *A Report on the Failure of HIH Insurance*, by Ld Justice Owen, Camberra: Attorney General's Department.

Ryan, B. and Gross, N. (1943), 'The diffusion of hybrid seed corn in two Iowa communities', *Rural Sociology*, **8**, 15–24.

Salmon Commission (1976), *Report of the Salmon Commission on Standards in Public Life*, Cm 6524, London: HMSO.

Schall E. (1997), 'Public sector succession: a strategic approach to sustaining innovation', *Public Administration Review*, **57** (1), 4–10.

Scheurle, K-D. (2002), 'Spectrum auctions and regulation in telecommunications', *Ifo Studien*, **48** (1), 73–5.

Schlager, E. (1999), 'A comparison of frameworks, theories and models of policy processes', in P.A. Sabatier (ed.), *Theories of the Policy Process*, Boulder, CO: Westview Press, pp. 233–60.

Schmidt, V. (2002), *The Futures of European Capitalism*, Oxford: Oxford University Press.

Schofer, E. (1999), 'Science associations in the international sphere, 1875–1990', in J. Boli and G. Thomas (eds), *Constructing World Culture*, Stanford, CA: Stanford University Press, pp. 249–66.

Schumpeter, J. (1976), *Capitalism, Socialism and Democracy*, London: Allen & Unwin.

Scott, C. (2004), 'Regulatory innovation and the online consumer', *Law and Policy*, **26**, 453–82.

Scott, W.R. (1995), *Institutions and Organizations*, Thousand Oaks, CA: Sage.

Scott, W.R. and J.W. Meyer (1983), 'The organization of societal sectors', in J.W. Meyer and W.R. Scott (eds), *Organizational Environments: Ritual and Rationality*, Beverley Hills, CA: Sage, pp. 129–53.

Seidman, W. (1986), 'Bank supervision in the United States', in R. Dale (ed.), *Financial Deregulation*, Cambridge: Woodhead-Faulkner.

Seldon, A. (1997), *Major: a Political Life*, London: Phoenix.

Sikkink, K. (1991), *Ideas and Institutions: Developmentalism in Argentina and Brazil*, Ithaca, NY: Cornell University Press.

Simon, H. (1947), *Administrative Behavior*, New York: Free Press.

Skocpol, T. (1985), 'Bringing the state back in', in P. Evans, P. Rueschmeyer and T. Skocpol (eds), *Bringing the State Back In*, Cambridge: Cambridge University Press, pp. 3–37.

Smith, D. and R.C. Alexander (1988), *Fumbling the Future: How Xerox Invented, and Then Ignored, the First Personal Computer*, New York: Morrow.

Soskice, D (1999), 'Divergent production regimes: coordinated and uncoordinated market economies in the 1980s and 1990s', in H. Kitschelt, P. Lange, G. Marks and J. Stephens (eds), *Continuity and Change in Contemporary Capitalism*, Cambridge: Cambridge University Press, pp. 101–34.

Sparer, M.S. (1997), 'Laboratories and the health care marketplace: the limits of state workforce policy', *Journal of Health Politics, Policy and Law*, **22** (3), 789–814.

Sparrow, J. (1998), *Management by Perception: Methods for Capturing Knowledge in Organizations*, London: Sage.

Sparrow, M.K. (2000), *The Regulatory Craft: Controlling Risks, Solving Problems and Managing Compliance*, Washington, DC: Brookings Press.

Ständige Konferenz der Innenminister und –senatoren der Länder (2000), *Bericht über die Vorschläge zur Verbesserung des Schutzes der Bevölkerung vor gefährlichen Hunden – in der Öffentlichkeit oft "Kampfhunde" genannt – der von dem Arbeitskreis 1 der Konferenz der Innenminister und – senatoren eingerichteten länderoffenen Arbeitsgruppe*, Bonn: Geschäftsstelle der Ständigen Konferenz.

Stark, A. (2001), 'Conflict of interest in American public life', *Annals of the American Academy of Political and Social Science*, **578**, 193–4.

Steil, B.V., D.G. Victor and R.R. Nelson, (eds) (2002), *Technological Innovation and Economic Performance*, Princeton, NJ: Princeton University Press.

Stigler, G.J. (1971), 'The theory of economic regulation', *Bell Journal of Economics and Management Science*, **2** (1), 3–21.

Strang, D. and J. Meyer (1993), 'Institutional conditions for diffusion', *Theory and Society*, **22**, 487–511.

Strategy Unit (2002), *Risk: Improving Government's Capability to Handle Risk and Uncertainty*, London: Cabinet Office.

Terry, F. (2001), 'The nemesis of privatization: railway policy in retrospect', *Public Money & Management*, **21** (1), 4–6.

Teubner, G. (1986), 'After legal instrumentalism: strategic models of post-regulatory law', in G. Teubner (ed.), *Dilemmas of Law in the Welfare State*, Berlin: de Gruyter, pp. 3–48.

Teubner, G. (1987), 'Juridification – concepts, aspects, limits, solutions', in G. Teubner (ed.), *Juridification of the Social Spheres*, Berlin: de Gruyter.

Teubner, G. (1993), *Law as an Autopoietic System*, Oxford: Blackwell Publishers.

Thatcher, M. (1999), *The Politics of Telecommunications*, Oxford: Oxford University Press.

Thatcher, M. (2002), 'Regulation after delegation: independent regulatory agencies in Europe', *Journal of European Public Policy*, **9** (6), 954–72.

Thatcher, M. (2003), 'From industrial policy to a regulatory state: contrasting institutional change in Britain and France', in J. Hayward and A. Menon (eds), *Governing Europe*, Oxford: Oxford University Press, pp. 313–29.

Thelen, K. (1999), 'Historical institutionalism in comparative perspective', *Annual Review of Political Science*, **2**, 369–404.

Thelen, K. (2003), 'How institutions evolve: insights from comparative historical analysis', in J. Mahoney and D. Rueschemeyer (eds), *Comparative Historical Analysis in the Social Sciences*, Cambridge: Cambridge University Press, pp. 208–40.

Thelen, K. and S. Steinmo (1992), 'Historical institutionalism in comparative politics', in S. Steinmo, K. Thelen and F. Longstreth (eds), *Structuring Politics. Historical Institutionalism in Comparative Analysis*, Cambridge: Cambridge University Press, pp. 1–32.

Thompson, D. (1987), *Political Ethics and Public Office*, Cambridge, MA: Harvard University Press.

Thomson, D. and M. Abbott (2000), 'Australian financial prudential supervision: an historical view', *Australian Journal of Public Administration*, **59** (2), 75–88.

Tivey, L. (1973), *Nationalisation in British Industry*, London: Jonathan Cape.

Tivey, L. (1982), 'Nationalised industries as organised interests', *Public Administration*, **60**, 42–55.

True, J. and M. Mintrom (2001), 'Transnational networks and policy diffusion: the case of gender mainstreaming', *International Studies Quarterly*, **45**, 27–57.

Tsebelis, G. (2003), *Veto Players*, Princeton, NJ: Princeton University Press.

Van den Ven, A., D.E. Polley, R. Garud and S. Venkataramam (1999), *The Innovation Journey*, New York: Oxford University Press.

Van den Ven, A., H. Angle and M. Scott Poole (eds) (1989), *Research on the Management of Innovation: The Minnesota Studies*, New York: Ballinger/ Harper-Row.

Vogel, D. (1986), *National Styles of Regulation: Environmental Policy in Great Britain and the United States*, Ithaca, NY: Cornell University Press.

Volden, C. (2003), 'States as policy laboratories: experimenting with the children's health insurance program', paper presented at the annual meeting of the American Political Science Association, Philadelphia, August.

Walker, J.L. (1969), 'The diffusion of innovations among the American states', *American Political Science Review*, **63**, 880–99.

Walker, J.L. (1973), 'Comment: problems in research on the diffusion of policy innovations', *American Political Science Review*, **67** (4), 1186–91.

Walker R.M. and E. Jeanes (2001), 'Innovation in a regulated service – the case of English Housing Association', *Public Management Review*, **4** (1), 525–50.

Walker, R.M., E. Jeanes and R. Rowland (2002), 'Measuring innovation:

applying the literature based innovation output indicator to public services',
    Public Administration, **80** (1), 201–14.
Wallis Report (1997), *Financial System Inquiry Final Report*, Canberra: AGPS.
Watson, A. (1992), *The Evolution of Historical Society: A Comparative
    Historical Analysis*, London: Routledge.
Weick, K (2001), *Making Sense of the Organization*, Oxford: Blackwell.
Weir, M. and T. Skocpol (1985), 'State structures and the possibilities for
    "Keynesian" responses to the Great Depression in Sweden, Britain and the
    United States', in P. Evans, D. Rueschemeyer, T. Skocpol (eds), *Bringing
    the State Back In*, New York: Cambridge University Press, pp. 107–63.
Werle, R. (1999), 'Liberalisation of telecommunications in Germany', in K.
    Eliassen and M. Sjøvaag (eds), *European Telecommunications
    Liberalisation*, London: Routledge, pp. 110–27.
Werle, R. (2003), '*Institutionalistische Technikanalyse: Stand und
    Perspektiven*', MPIfG discussion paper 03/08, Cologne: Max Planck
    Institute for the Study of Societies.
Wildavsky, A. (1964), *The Politics of the Budgetary Process*, Boston, MA:
    Little Brown.
Wildavsky, A (1989), 'A cultural theory of leadership', in B.D. Jones (ed.),
    Leadership and Politics: New Perspectives in Political Science, Lawrance,
    KS: University of Kansas Press, pp. 87–113.
Williams, S. (1985), *Conflict of Interest: The Ethical Dilemma in Politics*,
    Aldershot: Gower.
Williamson, O.E. (1975), *Markets and Hierarchies*, New York: Free Press.
Williamson, O.E. (1985), *The Economic Institutions of Capitalism: Firms,
    Markets and Relational Contracting*, New York: Free Press.
Williamson, O.E. (1996), *Mechanisms of Governance*, New York: Oxford
    University Press.
Witte, B. (1932), *Eisenbahn und Staat: Ein Vergleich der europäischen und
    nordamerikanischen Eisenbahnorganisationen in ihrem Verhältnis zum
    Staat*, Jena: Verlag von Gustav Fischer.
Wolman, H. (1992), 'Understanding cross national policy transfers: the case of
    Britain and the US', *Governance*, **5**, 27–45.
Wood, S. (2001), 'Business, government, and patterns of labour market policy
    in Britain and the Federal Republic of Germany' in P. Hall and D. Soskice
    (eds), *Varieties of Capitalism: The Institutional Foundations of
    Comparative Advantage*, Oxford: Oxford University Press, pp. 247–74.
Woodhouse, D. (1998), 'The Parliamentary Commissioner for Standards:
    lessons from the "Cash for Questions" Inquiry', *Parliamentary Affairs*, **51**
    (1), 51–61.
Wyatt, B. J. (2002), 'The origins of state public financing of elections', unpub-
    lished B.A. thesis, Wesleyan University, Middletown, CT.

Yee, A.S. (1996), 'The causal effects of ideas on policies', *International Organisation*, **50** (1), 69–108.

Young, R.C. (1988), 'Is population ecology a useful paradigm for the study of organizations?', *American Journal of Sociology*, **94**, 1–24.

Zaltman, G., R. Duncan and J. Holbek (1973), *Innovations and Organizations*, New York: John Wiley and Sons.

Zucker, L.G. (1989), 'Combining institutional theory and population ecology: no legitimacy, no history', *American Sociological Review*, **54**, 542–5.

Index